C0-GAJ-482

Human Well-Being Research and Policy Making

Series Editor

M. Joseph Sirgy, Department of Marketing
Virginia Polytechnic Institute & State University
Blacksburg, USA

This series includes policy-focused books on the role of the public and private sectors in advancing quality of life and well-being. It creates a dialogue between well-being scholars and public policy makers. Well-being theory, research and practice are essentially interdisciplinary in nature and embrace contributions from all disciplines within the social sciences. With the exception of leading economists, the policy relevant contributions of social scientists are widely scattered and lack the coherence and integration needed to more effectively inform the actions of policy makers. Contributions in the series focus on one more of the following four aspects of well-being and public policy:

- Discussions of the public policy and well-being focused on particular nations and worldwide regions.
- Discussions of the public policy and well-being in specialized sectors of policy making such as health, education, work, social welfare, housing, transportation, use of leisure time.
- Discussions of public policy and well-being associated with particular population groups such as women, children and youth, the aged, persons with disabilities and vulnerable populations.
- Special topics in well-being and public policy such as technology and well-being, terrorism and well-being, infrastructure and well-being.

This series was initiated, in part, through funds provided by the Halloran Philanthropies of West Conshohocken, Pennsylvania, USA. The commitment of the Halloran Philanthropies is to "inspire, innovate and accelerate sustainable social interventions that promote human well-being." The series editors and Springer acknowledge Harry Halloran, Tony Carr and Audrey Selian for their contributions in helping to make the series a reality.

Louise Dalingwater • Arnaud Page
Liana B. Winett
Editors

Structural and Systemic Perspectives on Health and Well-being

Springer

Editors
Louise Dalingwater
Faculty of Arts and Humanities
Sorbonne University
Paris, France

Arnaud Page
Faculty of Arts and Humanities
Sorbonne University
Paris, France

Liana B. Winett
Faculty of School of Public Health
Oregon Health & Science
University-Portland State University
Portland, OR, USA

ISSN 2522-5367 ISSN 2522-5375 (electronic)
Human Well-Being Research and Policy Making
ISBN 978-3-031-99923-9 ISBN 978-3-031-99924-6 (eBook)
https://doi.org/10.1007/978-3-031-99924-6

© The Editor(s) (if applicable) and The Author(s), under exclusive license to Springer Nature Switzerland AG 2025

This work is subject to copyright. All rights are solely and exclusively licensed by the Publisher, whether the whole or part of the material is concerned, specifically the rights of translation, reprinting, reuse of illustrations, recitation, broadcasting, reproduction on microfilms or in any other physical way, and transmission or information storage and retrieval, electronic adaptation, computer software, or by similar or dissimilar methodology now known or hereafter developed.
The use of general descriptive names, registered names, trademarks, service marks, etc. in this publication does not imply, even in the absence of a specific statement, that such names are exempt from the relevant protective laws and regulations and therefore free for general use.
The publisher, the authors and the editors are safe to assume that the advice and information in this book are believed to be true and accurate at the date of publication. Neither the publisher nor the authors or the editors give a warranty, expressed or implied, with respect to the material contained herein or for any errors or omissions that may have been made. The publisher remains neutral with regard to jurisdictional claims in published maps and institutional affiliations.

This Springer imprint is published by the registered company Springer Nature Switzerland AG.
The registered company address is: Gewerbestrasse 11, 6330 Cham, Switzerland

If disposing of this product, please recycle the paper.

Acknowledgments

Many thanks to the Springer publishers for their support and guidance. Thank you family and friends. Thank you also to all the authors for their kind understanding, responsiveness, and excellent contributions.

Contents

About the Editors

Louise Dalingwater is full professor of British politics and health policy at Sorbonne Université. Her current research focuses on health policy, healthcare delivery and well-being in the United Kingdom, with comparative research on European health systems and global health policy research. Recent publications include a book on the UK service economy, a monograph on the NHS and several book chapters and articles on well-being and health. She has also co-edited several publications on well-being in Europe (*The Unequal Costs of Covid-19 on Well-being in Europe*, Springer International Publishing AG (2022) and Well-being in an Educational Setting, *International Journal of Health, Wellness and Society* (2024)). She is Principal Investigator (PI) for the *Digital Health Systems* IITD Delhi-Sorbonne Multi-Institutional Faculty Interdisciplinary Research Project, a member of the steering group for the 4EU+ global outreach project Meta-UN and Chair of the Health Wellness and Society research network based in Illinois, United States.

Arnaud Page is Associate Professor of British History at Sorbonne University. His work lies at the crossroads of environmental history, food history, and the history of medicine. Recent publications include work on the history of flour bleaching in the United Kingdom (*Technology and Culture*, 2023) and on the history of nutrition science in Great Britain and the British Empire (*Journal of British Studies*, 2025). His research primarily explores the history of nutrition—plant, animal, and human—with a particular emphasis on quantification and indicators. He is currently completing a monograph that traces the contested emergence of quantitative approaches to nutrition, with a particular focus on the history of nitrogen in Britain and its Empire between 1840 and 1914.

Liana B. Winett is Associate Professor in the Oregon Health & Science University-Portland State University School of Public Health. She researches how communities and societies discuss potential solutions to the complex and controversial problems that affect the public's health and well-being, and how framing of these problems can support broad participation in these important debates. She has explored discourse surrounding US federal school foods policy; child healthy food access; early childhood care and education; gun violence prevention; the developmental origins of health and disease (DOHaD); breast, cervical, and prostate cancers; the US public health response to bioterrorism; state responses to COVID-19; and policy related to menopause and menstruation. In 2022–2023, she was an invited researcher at le Centre d'Études Politiques et Sociales (CEPEL), Faculté de Droit et de Sciences Politiques, l'Université de Montpellier.

Chapter 1
Introduction

Louise Dalingwater, Arnaud Page, and Liana B. Winett

Abstract The link between health and well-being has been well established for decades and is clear from the WHO's definition of health as "a state of complete physical, mental and social well-being and not merely the absence of disease or infirmity" (WHO, *Preamble to the Constitution of the World Health Organization as adopted by the International Health Conference,* 1948). In 2015, well-being was added to the Sustainable Development Goals (SDGs) of the United Nations. It is in fact in the health domain that well-being discourse is most common. Very few health institutions or promoters can afford to exclude the notion of well-being when formulating health policies. But it is equally true in education in low, medium, and high income countries with, for example, the Education for Well-being Program in the UK, France's Well-being and Education of Students, the Psychosocial Support Programs for Learner and Teacher Well-being in South Africa, and the School Health and Wellness Program in India. These all place clear emphasis on mental health in their well-being frameworks. Similar initiatives have also been taken across higher education establishments. Further, well-being at work has been the focus of many micro and macro initiatives, taking into consideration stress and quality of life factors affecting employees.

The link between health and well-being has been well established for decades and is clear from the WHO's definition of health as "a state of complete physical, mental and social well-being and not merely the absence of disease or infirmity" (WHO, 1948). In 2015, well-being was added to the Sustainable Development Goals

L. Dalingwater (✉) · A. Page
Faculty of Arts and Humanities, Sorbonne University, Paris, France
e-mail: louise.dalingwater@sorbonne-universite.fr; arnaud.page@sorbonne-universite.fr

L. B. Winett
Faculty of School of Public Health, Oregon Health & Science University-Portland State University, Portland, OR, USA
e-mail: lwinett@pdx.edu

© The Author(s), under exclusive license to Springer Nature Switzerland AG 2025

L. Dalingwater et al. (eds.), *Structural and Systemic Perspectives on Health and Well-being*, Human Well-Being Research and Policy Making,
https://doi.org/10.1007/978-3-031-99924-6_1

(SDGs) of the United Nations. It is in fact in the health domain that well-being discourse is most common. Very few health institutions or promoters can afford to exclude the notion of well-being when formulating health policies. But it is equally true in education in low, medium, and high income countries with, for example, the Education for Well-being Program in the UK, France's Well-being and Education of Students, the Psychosocial Support Programs for Learner and Teacher Well-being in South Africa, and the School Health and Wellness Program in India. These all place clear emphasis on mental health in their well-being frameworks. Similar initiatives have also been taken across higher education establishments. Further, well-being at work has been the focus of many micro and macro initiatives, taking into consideration stress and quality of life factors affecting employees.

However, the definition of well-being is fraught with difficulties. While the notion can be traced back to Aristotle (Barnes, 1984), in recent times it has become almost a buzzword following the Stiglitz report of 2009 (Stiglitz et al., 2009) and the development of measures by international institutions such as the OECD and national statistical bodies. Recent analyses and statistical studies have tended to separate well-being into that which is subjective (i.e., how life is experienced and perceived by individuals, and involving affective measures) and that which is material or objective (i.e., income and wealth, life expectancy, educational attainment, community safety and security, and using societal measures) (Scott, 2012; OECD, 2020).

Despite attempts to more precisely identify the different strands, well-being-related policy remains complex and inconclusive, especially when reflecting on subjective well-being or happiness. Some commentators have even pointed to a "well-being pandemic" or "well-being washing," whereby the term is used in order to exploit specific policy planning or implementation at the expense of advancing welfare or tackling inequalities (Dalingwater et al., 2019; Jackson et al., 2022). The fact that well-being at work rhetoric has been taken up by some of the biggest multinationals, such as McKinsey, who have published extensively on well-being and wellness (McKinsey, n.d.), is testimony to this. And beyond the question of definition, the practical implications for, and policies implemented to promote, well-being in specific social contexts remain even more elusive.

1.1 Focus of the Book

The focus of this special issue is thus to analyze structural and systemic factors and interventions that can support population and individual health and well-being. The selection of papers in this special issue aims to illustrate a number of salient aspects on these topics. While there are a vast number of domains in which we might consider health and well-being, after opening with a chapter on the global impact of inequality on health and well-being, this volume focuses on two specific and important areas in which enhancing health and well-being is essential for societal cohesion: education and the workplace.

First, we explore how the post-pandemic world would seem to be at a tipping point in terms of worsening outcomes for the social determinants of health and well-being due to widening inequalities (*Schrecker*). Then, the authors examine how approaches to enhancing health and well-being in educational sectors can promote reform and enhance student flourishing (*Sikawar; Gibbs; Nkala-Dlamini Ntshongwana & Pillay; Di Marco & Sadoux*). Finally, the workplace is also at focus, with chapters illustrating opportunities to enhance the health and well-being of employees through workplace policy, programs, and outreach (*Wiltshire & Prescott; Dalingwater, Winett & Peru-Pirotte; Guillaumond & Boullet*).

1.2 Health, Well-being, and Inequality

There are several ways in which inequality can have an adverse impact on well-being. Despite the contention of Professor Richard Easterlin, known as the "Easterlin Paradox," indicating that increased income does not necessarily result in greater happiness, higher levels of financial inequality within societies have been found to result in lower levels of well-being or happiness for all (Easterlin, 1974). Buttrick et al. (2017) posit that both material or objective inequalities and subjective perceptions can have an impact on levels of well-being. People with relatively lower incomes tend to have poorer health outcomes, are more likely to suffer from ill health, and have shorter life spans. It has been predicted that each incremental increase of $15,000 in household income decreases health risks. Pickett and Wilkinson (2009, 2018) emphasize the extent to which income inequality can have a significant impact on health, well-being, capital formation, and social cohesion. Inequality is associated with not only reduced life expectancy, but also high levels of infant mortality, lowered educational attainment, and significant mental health strains.

According to Ted Schrecker (this volume; also see 2022), worldwide inequality has reached a crisis stage. While global Gross Domestic Product (GDP) has risen for several decades, wealth is not evenly distributed within or among counties. The wealth of nations is in the hands of the richest 1%, who hold 45% of total wealth, globally. South Africa is now at the top of the Gini Index as the most unequal nation across the globe. But developed countries in Europe, as well as the US, have also seen inequality rising (Pew Research Center, 2020). To remedy this, Schrecker and others argue, would require reversing trends in many developed and developing countries by raising taxes, namely income taxes and wealth taxes, to ensure more even wealth distribution (Schrecker, 2022 and his contribution in this volume; also see Evans, 2012; Piketty, 2014). However, the likelihood of this happening is very low, as Schrecker's contribution effectively shows. Indeed, in his chapter, *Ted Schrecker* illustrates how the global experience of COVID-19—including both disease spread and the efforts to contain it—represented a "tipping point" in which already significant inequalities were pushed to their limits and population-level gaps in health and well-being were set to further rise in future. He demonstrates significant inequalities across all areas of labor markets and social policies, including in education and the workplace.

1.3 Health and Well-being in Education

Increased attention has been given in recent years to enhancing student well-being, especially at secondary and higher educational levels, although the very broad nature of the commitment may sometimes be hindering implementation.

Khatri et al. (2024) argue that while well-being and wellness have become buzzwords in the educational domain, policies and policy recommendations to enhance the well-being of students at higher education levels should be distinct from those applied to secondary education to avoid over generalizations and limited effectiveness.

Explorations of well-being in higher education have focused on the factors which can lead to diminished well-being, with particular focus on reduced student mental health. Attention to the signs of low well-being such as stress, anxiety, and burnout, as well as suicidal thoughts, attempts, and deaths by suicide, has been significant in recent years, both in academic literature and government reports and policy proposals (Flinchbaugh et al., 2012; Mahatmya et al., 2018; Ministère Éducation, 2020). A number of factors contributing to diminished student well-being have been identified, including pressure to succeed, burnout related to the need for concurrent employment, and other financial considerations. The drivers of enhanced student health and well-being in higher education have also been the focus of research and are stratified along four dimensions: psychological, social, emotional, and physical (Flinchbaugh et al., 2012; Mahatmya et al., 2018 Plakhotnik et al., 2021). For example, a body of research which focuses on students' subjective well-being highlighted the importance of satisfaction with life, balancing positive and negative emotions and effectively navigating the university environment and study course (Pluut et al., 2015; Khatri et al., 2024). As for emotional well-being more specifically, the literature points to the importance of positive emotions such as hope, optimism, and happiness (Lin & Shek, 2019; Maybury, 2013; Smith et al., 2021; Khatri et al., 2024). Social capital and peer support were also noted as instrumental in improving student mental health and well-being (Bye et al., 2019).

So how can this be differentiated from the focus on student well-being at secondary school? The factors of concern are indeed somewhat different. While the stress caused by a need to succeed is also pervasive among secondary school pupils and can lead to diminished mental health and well-being, other factors are unique to secondary education. These notably include the significant rise in bullying, especially cyber-bullying, and harassment in recent years at the secondary school level, which can have a breadth of adverse impacts on victims. Socio-economic inequalities can also reinforce differences in student attainment and academic well-being. In her piece, *Rachna Sikarwar* traces the gradual broadening of the concept of health to include well-being in Indian educational policies at the secondary level. She highlights how, despite its increased prominence in official documents, the implementation of measures to promote the well-being of students remains a challenging task. She argues that in order for the heightened preoccupation with well-being to become more effective, it needs to be accompanied by efforts at conceptual clarification, as well as the introduction of more precise indicators and evaluation frameworks. Translating well-being principles into more tangible outcomes, she notes, also requires acknowledging the deeply rooted inequalities in Indian society.

What seems to be common across all policy approaches at national and sector-specific levels, however, is the emphasis on the importance of promoting healthy behaviors, including attention to diet, exercise, and sleep quality (Guan et al., 2020; Khatri et al., 2024). Support from administration staff, teaching staff, and all others involved in delivering education and ensuring well-being is essential (Plakhotnik et al., 2021). Student self-regulation and autonomy are also important for enhanced well-being (Rodriguez et al., 2022), as is access to resources (academic resources, information, curricular and co-curricular activities (Flinchbaugh et al., 2012, Mokgele and Rothman, 2014, Yazici et al., 2016, Plakhotnik et al., 2021). While these strategies will be quite different whether applied to secondary schools or higher education, ensuring access to resources and necessary support remains fundamental, as is meeting students' essential nutritional needs, as promoted in the educational systems of many countries. However, to achieve optimal success in supporting student health and well-being, sometimes it is also necessary to change the very approach and/or paradigm on which education establishments are based. To this point, two contributions in this volume analyze the concept of "care" and how approaches grounded in this value and practice can ensure student flourishing in very different educational settings.

Paul Gibbs' contribution offers a philosophically grounded case for cultivating an ethic of care within the university, notably one that would promote altruism and greater social connectedness. He makes the case for a broad, ontological, understanding of care that goes beyond simple functional caring practices. The vision he develops in this chapter calls for a significant shift in the role of universities, from institutions focused primarily on the provision of skills and knowledge for economic benefits, to those that foreground care as a core principle. Articulating his ideas around the concept of "transdisciplinary care," Gibbs argues in favor of an ethic that not only accepts vulnerability, but also recognizes the richness and creativity made possible by a plurality of worldviews and ways of being.

Likewise, *Busisiwe Nkala-Dlamini, Zintle Ntshongwana, and Roshini Pillay*'s chapter illustrates how applying the ethics of care approach enabled university social work lecturers in South Africa to identify issues which might compromise students' well-being and undermine academic success, especially during periods of heightened challenges such as the first years of the COVID-19 pandemic. The authors show how tailored support structures designed around a caring philosophy, which take into consideration students' unique circumstances, can help overcome these challenges and enhance student learning and flourishing.

Stéphane Di Marco and Cecilia Sadoux's chapter explores how higher education may play a crucial role in fostering awareness of health and well-being as essential components of students' future professional lives. They present an innovative pilot program aimed at integrating health-related issues into the Master's of Architecture curriculum at the Grenoble School of Architecture. The authors discuss various strategies used to raise students' awareness of how urban and architectural design impact health and well-being. Overall, their study illustrates the importance of combining diverse disciplinary approaches, fostering student creativity, and incorporating immersive, hands-on experiences to deepen students' understanding of the complex implications of architectural and urban design on population health and well-being.

1.4 Health and Well-being at Work

There has been an abundance of literature on health and well-being at work in recent years. The UK Health and Safety Executive's research to understand how work can impact mental health, for example, shows that workplace conditions can adversely affect employees' health and well-being. In particular, they point to several key drivers which can diminish workers' well-being: high demands resulting in increased workload, other adverse work patterns or work environments, low levels of employee autonomy to manage workloads, lack of support at work, the presence of negative work relationships or perceived lack of respect for roles or responsibilities, and organizational change all can have adverse impacts on workers (Health and Safety Executive, n.d.). Work conditions can also exacerbate chronic diseases and cause or amplify injuries, due to the nature of many activities and tasks in the workplace. Technology can impact health and well-being both positively (e.g., through better work facilities, greater access to information and knowledge) and negatively (e.g., cognitive load, potential for injury, and increased monitoring of employees' work). The health and well-being of workers also depends upon the extent of physical and mental strain, working hours, and efficacy of overall staffing levels and rotations.

Healthcare professionals tend to report significantly high levels of stress, distress, sickness, absenteeism, and burnout (Brand et al., 2017). Indeed, *Kim Wiltshire and Dawn Prescott*'s contribution illustrates the specific significant stress and anxiety that frontline healthcare workers experienced during and immediately following the COVID-19 pandemic. Through an innovative program that embedded participatory arts into UK National Health Service (NHS) settings, program sponsors found that health providers were able to better manage the challenges to their general well-being and mental health that the pandemic posed. The findings reported in this chapter show that embedding arts into such work environments can be an effective way of enhancing employee health and well-being.

Governments, enterprise, and labor groups also can design and enact legislation, policies, and programs to support worker health and well-being. Workplace regulations provide for minimum standards and ensure that employers have established mechanisms to prevent risks, manage health and safety, and actively promote worker well-being. These can include, for example, limiting working hours, providing for paid sick and family leave, and ensuring flexibility in work conditions to meet employee needs. In some countries, tax credits and subsidies are provided to encourage the promotion of health and well-being in the workplace. Working with trade unions, employer associations, and occupational health specialists also can help ensure the design and effective implementation of measures to improve physical and mental health and well-being.

During the first years of the COVID-19 pandemic, collaboration at both macro and micro levels was necessary to ensure implementation of sanitary measures, teleworking, and other sector-specific protective strategies (OECD, 2022). Industry standards and voluntary certification also help employers ensure that employee needs are met at the workplace. At the same time, company-level environmental, social, and governance investments can also promote policies intended to improve employee health and well-being (OECD, 2022), although these usually lack the force of law to help ensure that all workers benefit from the same protections. Indeed, *Louise Dalingwater, Liana Winett, and Laurence Peru-Pirotte*'s contribution illustrates this through the example of workplace design to support employees in menopause. The chapter underlines that workplaces often fail to anticipate the challenges faced by employees managing the menopausal transition while at work. The authors draw upon legislative and other discourse from three countries—France, the UK, and the US—and examine workplace legislation, policy, and programs to see where progress has been made and what still needs to be taken into account.

Similarly, insufficient attention has been paid to mobile workers (those who spend the majority of time away from their home or office base) and/or cross-border workers (those who may spend time away from home, or may face specific problems in relation to taxes or administration because of their unique employment status). For example, mobile workers can face musculoskeletal problems, with conditions worsening depending on the length of the journey. At the same time, better mental health has been reported because of higher pay and greater job prospects from traveling to work, despite the role requiring crossing borders and/or significant distances (Crawford et al., 2011). In their chapter in this volume, *Julien Guillaumond and Vanessa Boullet* consider the issue of well-being among cross-border workers on the island of Ireland. While the well-being of workers is an increasingly prominent topic in both Northern Ireland and the Republic of Ireland, it appears that the particular situation of citizens regularly crossing the border is not very prominent in the public sphere. The chapter explores the question of how the well-being of this specific group may be enhanced by pointed information on their particular situation. The chapter concludes with a case study of three informational websites targeted specifically at cross-border workers to assess their achievements and limitations in this regard.

In total, the chapters in this volume analyze systemic and structural questions relating to how to better support population health and well-being across contexts. These feel particularly resonant following the first years of COVID-19, when existing societal frameworks were disrupted worldwide, and disparities in the benefits and challenges experienced across groups were brought into sharp relief. We hope that these chapters support ongoing reflection at all levels regarding future approaches to the protection of population health and well-being around the globe.

References

Barnes, J. (Ed.). (1984). *Metaphysics, in the complete works of Aristotle*. Princeton University Press.

Brand, S. L., Thompson Coon, J., Fleming, L. E., Carroll, L., Bethel, A., & Wyatt, K. (2017). Whole-system approaches to improving the health and wellbeing of healthcare workers: A systematic review. *PLoS One, 12*(12), Article e0188418. https://doi.org/10.1371/journal.pone.0188418

Buttrick, N. R., Heintzelman, S. J., & Oishi, S. (2017). Inequality and well-being. *Current Opinion in Psychology, 18*, 15–20. https://doi.org/10.1016/j.copsyc.2017.07.016

Bye, L.-A., Muller, F., & Oprescu, F. (2019). The impact of social capital on student wellbeing and university life satisfaction: A semester-long repeated measures study. *Higher Education Research & Development, 39*(5), 898–912. https://doi.org/10.1080/07294360.2019.1705253

Crawford, J. O., MacCalman, L., & Jackson, C. A. (2011). The health and well-being of remote and mobile workers. *Occupational Medicine (London), 61*(6), 385–394. https://doi.org/10.1093/occmed/kqr071

Dalingwater, L., Costantini, I., & Champroux, N. (Eds.). (2019). Wellbeing: Political discourse and policy in the anglosphere. *Papers in Political Economy, 62*.

Easterlin. (1974). Does economic growth improve the human lot? some empirical evidence. In P. A. David & M. W. Reder (Eds.), *Nations and households in economic growth: Essays in honor of Moses Abramovitz*. Academic Press, Inc.

Evans, R. G. (2012). A casualty in the class war: Canada's Medicare. *Healthcare Policy, 7*(3), 14–22.

Flinchbaugh, C. L., Moore, E. W. G., Chang, Y. K., & May, D. R. (2012). Student well-being interventions: The effects of stress management techniques and gratitude journaling in the management education classroom. *Journal of Management Education, 36*(2), 191–219. https://doi.org/10.1177/1052562911430062

Guan, S. A., Xie, H., & Boyns, D. (2020). Sleep, stress, or social support? Exploring the mechanisms that explain the relationship between student recreation center use and well-being. *Journal of American College Health, 68*(2), 124–131. https://doi.org/10.1080/07448481.2018.1535493

Health and Safety Executive. (n.d.). *Health and safety statistics*. Retrieved from https://www.hse.gov.uk/statistics/

Jackson, S., Dawson, M., & Sam, M. (2022, February 22). The wellbeing 'pandemic' – How the global drive for wellness might be making us sick, *The Conversation*. Retrieved from https://theconversation.com/the-wellbeing-pandemic-how-the-global-drive-for-wellness-might-be-making-us-sick-198662

Khatri, P., Duggal, H. K., Lim, W. M., Thomas, A., & Shiva, A. (2024). Student well-being in higher education: Scale development and validation with implications for management education. *The International Journal of Management Education, 22*(1). https://doi.org/10.1016/j.ijme.2024.100933

Lin, L., & Shek, D. (2019). Does service leadership education contribute to student well-being? A quasi-experimental study based on Hong Kong university students. *Applied Research in Quality of Life, 14*(5), 1147–1163. https://doi.org/10.1007/s11482-018-9644-x

Mahatmya, D., Thurston, M., & Lynch, M. E. (2018). Developing students' well-being through integrative, experiential learning courses. *Journal of Student Affairs Research and Practice, 55*(3), 295–307. https://doi.org/10.1080/19496591.2018.1474756

Maybury, K. K. (2013). The influence of a positive psychology course on student well-being. *Teaching of Psychology, 40*(1), 62–65. https://doi.org/10.1177/0098628312465868
McKinsey. (n.d.). *Well-being in the workplace*. Retrieved from https://www.mckinsey.com/featured-insights/well-being-in-the-workplace
Ministères éducation, jeunesse, sports, enseignement supérieur, recherche. (2020). *Favoriser le bien-être pour la réussite de chacun*. Retrieved from https://www.enseignementsup-recherche.gouv.fr/sites/default/files/2021-10/rapport-du-m-diateur-de-l-ducation-nationale-et-de-l-enseignement-sup-rieur-2020-14116.pdf
Mokgele, K. R. F., & Rothman, S. (2014). A structural model of student well-being. *South Africa Journal of Psychology, 44*, 514–527. https://doi.org/10.1177/0081246314541589
OECD. (2020). *How's life*. Retrieved from https://www.oecd.org/en/publications/how-s-life/volume-/issue-_9870c393-en/full-report.html
OECD. (2022). *Promoting health and wellbeing at work*. Retrieved from https://www.oecd.org/en/publications/promoting-health-and-well-being-at-work_e179b2a5-en.html
Pew Research Center. (2020, January 9). *Trends in US income and wealth inequality*. Retrieved from https://www.pewresearch.org/social-trends/2020/01/09/trends-in-income-and-wealth-inequality/
Piketty, T. (2014). *Capital in the twenty-first century*. Harvard University Press.
Plakhotnik, M. S., Volkova, N. V., Jiang, C., Yahiaoui, D., Pheiffer, G., McKay, K., Newman, S., & Reißig-Thust, S. (2021). The perceived impact of COVID-19 on student well-being and the mediating role of the university support: Evidence from France, Germany, Russia, and the UK. *Frontiers in Psychology, 12*, 642689. https://doi.org/10.3389/fpsyg.2021.642689
Pluut, H., Curşeu, P. L., & Ilies, R. (2015). Social and study related stressors and resources among university entrants: Effects on well-being and academic performance. *Learning and Individual Differences, 37*, 262–268. https://doi.org/10.1016/j.lindif.2014.11.018
Rodríguez, S., González-Suárez, R., Vieites, T., Piñeiro, I., & Díaz-Freire, F. M. (2022). Self-regulation and students well-being: A systematic review 2010–2020. *Sustainability, 14*(4), 2346. https://doi.org/10.3390/su14042346
Schrecker, T. (2022). Building back worse? The prognosis for health equity in the post-pandemic world. In L. Dalingwater et al. (Eds.), *The unequal costs of Covid-19 on well-being in Europe* (pp. 21–39). Springer International Publishing.
Scott, K. (2012). *Measuring wellbeing: Towards sustainability?* Routledge.
Smith, B. W., Ford, C. G., Erickson, K., & Guzman, A. (2021). The effects of a character strength focused positive psychology course on undergraduate happiness and well-being. *Journal of Happiness Studies, 22*(1), 343–362. https://doi.org/10.1007/s10902-020-00233-9
Stiglitz, J., Sen, A., & Fitoussi, J. P. (2009). *Rapport de la commission sur la measure des performances économiques et du progrès social*. Retrieved from http://www.stiglitz-sen-fitoussi.fr
Wilkinson, R., & Pickett, K. (2009). *The spirit level: Why more equal societies almost always do better*. Allen Lane.
Wilkinson, R., & Pickett, K. (2018). *The inner level: How more equal societies reduce stress, restore sanity and improve everyone's well-being?* Allen Lane.
World Health Organization (WHO). (1948, April 7). *Preamble to the constitution of the World Health Organization as adopted by the international health conference*. New York. Retrieved from https://www.who.int/about/governance/constitution
Yazici, A. B., Gul, M., Yazici, E., & Gul, G. K. (2016). Tennis enhances well-being in university students. *Mental Illness, 8*(1), 6510. https://doi.org/10.4081/mi.2016.6510

Louise Dalingwater has published 10 edited or co-edited volumes and is currently co-editing two other special issues. She is chief editor of the International Journal of Health, Wellness and Society, a peer-reviewed journal indexed in Scopus. She is the principal investigator on a COST project consisting of a Consortium of 20 international researchers across Europe and Asia. This can guarantee a significant outreach for international contributions on the subject of health and wellbeing.

Arnaud Page is Associate Professor in British History at Sorbonne University. His research sits at the intersection of environmental history, food history and the history of medicine. His work has notably been published in Technology and Culture, Environment and History and History of Science. He is currently finalizing a monograph on the history of plant, animal and human nutrition science in Britain and the British Empire (1840–1914).

Liana B. Winett is Associate Professor at the Oregon Health & Science University-Portland State University School of Public Health (USA). She explores how communities and societies discuss the complex and controversial problems that affect the public's health, and how framing of these problems can help support broad public participation in these important debates. She has explored, among other topics, issue framing of U.S. federal school foods policy; child healthy weight; early childhood care and education; interpersonal violence; the developmental origins of health and disease (DOHaD); cancer; the U.S. public health response to bioterrorism; COVID-19; and most recently policy discourse around menstruation and menopause.

Part I
Health, Well-being, and Social Inequalities

Chapter 2
The COVID-19 Pandemic as Tipping Point: Analysis and Prognosis for *La Longue Durée*

Ted Schrecker

Abstract The central argument of this paper is that by magnifying inequalities that were already growing within national borders, the COVID-19 pandemic represented a tipping point into a future of yet more extreme inequalities in health and well-being. After explaining the tipping point concept with reference to climate change research and a wider multidisciplinary literature, I describe the events and policies, notably in labor markets and social policy, that created the pre-pandemic landscape of inequality. These are inseparable from the global diffusion of neoliberalism, starting with the founding of the Mont Pèlerin Society in 1947. I then describe the ways in which the pandemic and responses to it magnified inequality, in ways that are likely to be extraordinarily difficult to reverse. Early casualties will include the remaining tax-funded (Beveridge-style) systems for financing health care. The concluding section situates my analysis as an example of the historical perspective of *la longue durée* identified with Fernand Braudel and suggests that the road that began at Mont Pèlerin led in 2024 to Mar-a-Lago with the election of Donald Trump and to the political ascent of the far right more broadly.

Keywords Inequality · *La longue durée* · Neoliberalism · Path dependence · Tipping points

T. Schrecker (✉)
Newcastle University, Newcastle upon Tyne, UK
e-mail: theodore.schrecker@newcastle.ac.uk

© The Author(s), under exclusive license to Springer Nature Switzerland AG 2025

L. Dalingwater et al. (eds.), *Structural and Systemic Perspectives on Health and Well-being*, Human Well-Being Research and Policy Making,
https://doi.org/10.1007/978-3-031-99924-6_2

2.1 Introduction

I began my first effort to describe the probable contours of the post-pandemic world[1] (Schrecker, 2022) with the opening sentences of J. G. Ballard's magnificent dystopian novel *High-Rise*:

> Later, as he sat on his balcony eating the dog, Dr. Robert Laing reflected on the unusual events that had taken place within this huge apartment building during the previous three months. Now that everything had returned to normal, he was surprised that there had been no obvious beginning, no point beyond which their lives had moved into a clearly more sinister dimension (Ballard, 1975, p. 7).

The novel describes a ruinous, often homicidal conflict among the affluent residents of a high-rise tower block, with the wealthiest at the top in a pungent allegory of contemporary life. As we follow the narrative, we learn that the "normal" to which life has returned is a nightmare in which bands of surviving residents—and some did not survive—have barricaded themselves into enclaves within the internally demolished building. All essential services have collapsed, and access to basic requisites of life involves such measures as cooking and eating the pets of residents whose survival strategies were less successful. Meanwhile many residents continue their lives and work in the outside world, somehow separating these from the internal chaos of the tower block. My argument was, and is, that the "normal" to which most societies return in the years to come will be nothing like the pre-pandemic world, because the pandemic and responses to it magnified and accelerated the effects of the "inequality machine [that] is reshaping the planet" (Halimi, 2013), as the editor of *Le Monde Diplomatique* wrote in 2013, creating a tipping point into a darker, more unequal (and probably even less democratic) future.

In 2022, this prognosis might have seemed improbable. Social protection policies that directly transferred resources to people who had been deprived of livelihoods by lockdowns had offset the collapse of many economic sectors, in some highly unequal countries like the United States (US) actually reducing officially defined poverty rates to a degree that would never have been tolerated by the political mainstream under less extreme circumstances (Reducing poverty, 2021). Indeed, the US Federal Reserve's annual survey of households in 2021 found the highest levels of several indicators of financial well-being since the survey began in 2013 (Federal Reserve Board, 2022), although this was before the cost-of-living crisis, driven in part by expansionary fiscal policies that responded to pandemic-driven economic contractions, started to bite.

Globally, such policy options were only available to governments of relatively affluent polities with the fiscal capacity and autonomy to undertake them; the effect

[1] The term "post-pandemic" is perhaps problematic, because COVID-19 remains endemic in many places. For convenience, it is used here to refer to the period after the global public health emergency declared by the World Health Organization (WHO) was ended in June 2023. By then, most domestic lockdowns and other extraordinary measures had also been ended, and many economic and social policy supports were also ending.

was to magnify global inequality. International Monetary Fund (IMF) figures published in October 2021 showed the scale of this issue, with advanced economies (as classified by the IMF) having deployed far more extensive spending and investment and forgone far more revenue than the so-called emerging market countries and, in particular, low income developing countries (IMF Fiscal Affairs Department, 2021). This form of fiscal apartheid on a global scale mirrored and compounded differences in vaccine availability (Kavanagh & Singh, 2023; Sirleaf, 2022) that led one historian to describe the interaction of underlying inequalities as a regime of "necrostratification" (Regilme, 2023). As for temporary reductions in inequality associated with pandemic responses in some jurisdictions, their fate was exemplified by a 2023 *New York Times* headline: "The US Built a European-Style Welfare State. It's Largely Over" (Miller & Parlapiano, 2023); poverty had rebounded to pre-pandemic levels as the programs expired (Casselman & DePillis, 2023; Parolin & Filauro, 2023). Meanwhile, in the United Kingdom (UK) the number of people living in destitution, defined as a condition "where people cannot afford to meet their most basic physical needs to stay warm, dry, clean and fed" (Joseph Rowntree Foundation, 2024, p. 9), increased from 2.388 million in 2019, the last pre-pandemic year, to 3.8 million in 2022 (Fitzpatrick et al., 2020, 2023). Although it may be premature to generalize from this limited number of case examples drawn from the Anglosphere, I suggest later in the chapter several reasons to consider them as harbingers of the politics and policy of a more unequal future.

Why should we care about inequality? From a health equity perspective, the most obvious answer is that its extreme material manifestations, like destitution in the UK and the record number of homeless people in the US in 2024 (Bhattarai, 2024; de Sousa & Henry, 2024), are increasingly widespread and directly hazardous to health. At least two further reasons can be identified. First, inequality—more specifically concentration of wealth at the very top of the income distribution and under the control of large corporations—increases the ability of owners of such ultra-wealth to resist the policies of "rights, redistribution and regulation" (Labonté & Schrecker, 2009) that are necessary to reducing health inequalities by way of the social determinants of health. Second, epidemiologists Richard Wilkinson and Kate Pickett (2010; Pickett & Wilkinson, 2015; Pickett et al., 2024) have produced a compelling argument that societies with higher levels of economic inequality also exhibit higher prevalence of a variety of health and social problems including lower life expectancy, higher infant mortality rates, educational underperformance, homicide, and imprisonment. Considerable variation may exist with regard to any individual variable among countries with comparable levels of economic inequality, reflecting differences in national contexts. However, when these researchers combined multiple indicators into a composite index of health and social problems, "the correlation with an index of problems was so high ($r = 0.87$) that any alternative explanations would have to have extraordinarily strong effects" (Pickett & Wilkinson, 2015, p. 320). Intriguingly, in a follow-up study that used more recent data they added a number of environmental problems to the index, and the correlation remained as strong (Pickett et al., 2024, p. 11; Pickett, 2024). Their research is arguably the strongest body of evidence linking inequality with negative outcomes for health and well-being across entire societies. It is also important to note that inequality reduces the political viability of policies that prioritize "social justice" rather than "market justice," the distinction long ago drawn by Beauchamp (1976).

2.2 Tipping Points and the Inequality Machine

The tipping point concept is central to the prognosis sketched out in the preceding section. It is probably most familiar in recent years from research and journalism on the consequences of climate change. According to one leading climate researcher, tipping points "occur when there is strongly self-amplifying (mathematically positive) feedback within a system such that a small perturbation can trigger a large response from the system, sending it into a qualitatively different future state" (Lenton, 2020, p. 20190123). Stated more simply, "sometimes little things can make a big difference," or at least a disproportionate difference, "to the state and/or fate of a system" (Lenton, 2013, p. 2). Anticipated consequences of continued deforestation in the Amazon basin are a case in point. Tropical rainforests generate a substantial proportion of their own rain; in other words, much of the water that falls as rain in a rainforest is the product of evapotranspiration within the forest itself (Smith et al., 2023). Incremental ongoing forest loss could create a tipping point beyond which the rainforest transitions to savannah or steppe (Fig. 2.1).

Beyond such analogies, a multidisciplinary review of literature on tipping points arrived at the following definition: "a tipping point is a threshold at which *small quantitative changes* in the system trigger *a non-linear change process* that is driven by *system-internal feedback mechanisms* and inevitably leads to *a qualitatively different state of the system,* which is *often irreversible*" (Milkoreit et al., 2018, p. 11, italics added to foreground the major analytic points). In the Amazonian example, incremental deforestation is the small quantitative change. Here, I argue that magnification of pre-pandemic trends of increasing inequality was the decisive variable, in combination with several other contextual factors identified later in the chapter.

It is important to emphasize that tipping points involve "small quantitative changes" rather than sharp departures from existing trends, although they may create such departures. In the Amazonian case, current and cumulative levels of deforestation can be traced back at least to the 1970s' decision of the military dictatorship in Brazil, then as now one of the world's most economically unequal countries, to "open up" the Amazon region to settlement, by way of highway construction in the first instance, as "a land without people for people without land" (Søndergaard et al., 2023, p. 3; see generally Hecht & Cockburn, 2010, Chap. 6). (This locution, of course, exhibited typical colonial disregard for existing Indigenous inhabitants.) Especially after the turn of the millennium, corporate agribusiness as well as other forms of extractive industry expanded rapidly (Søndergaard et al., 2023; Watts et al., 2023). The pace of deforestation slowed considerably after 2004 during the Workers' party governments, then accelerated dramatically during the government of Jair Bolsonaro, with strong ties to agribusiness and described by the *Economist*

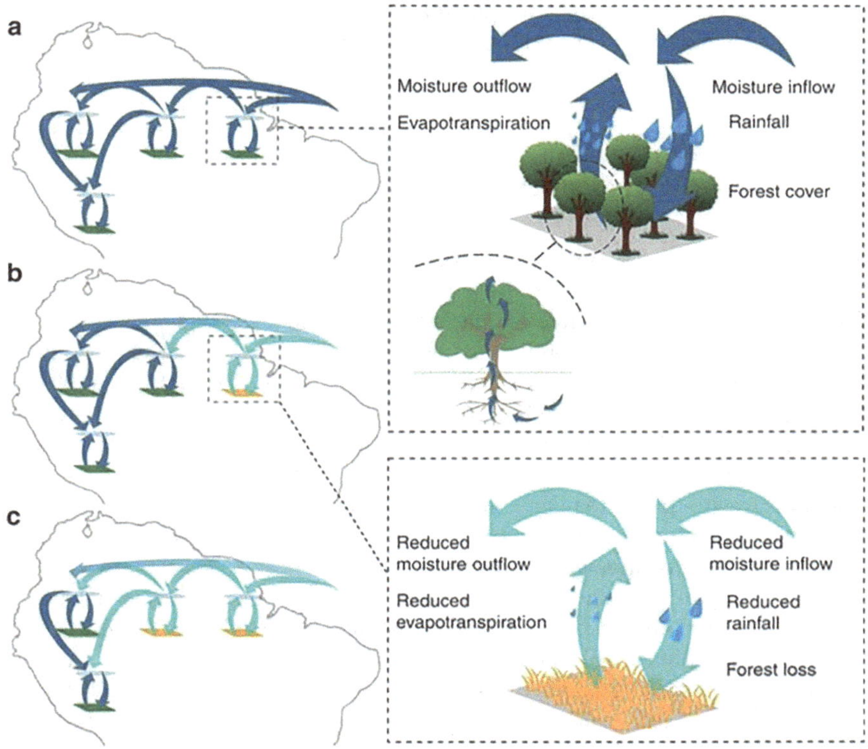

Fig. 2.1 Schematic representation of cascading effects in the vegetation–rainfall system. (**a**) Vegetation–atmosphere system in equilibrium. (**b**) Initial forest loss triggered by decreasing oceanic moisture inflow. This reduces local evapotranspiration and the resulting downwind moisture transport. (**c**) As a result, the rainfall regime is altered in another location, leading to further forest loss and reduced moisture transport. Source: Reproduced from D.C. Zemp et al. (2017), Self-amplified Amazon forest loss due to vegetation-atmosphere feedbacks, *Nature Communications, 8*, 14681 under a Creative Commons Attribution 4.0 International Licence

at the time as "arguably the most environmentally dangerous head of state in the world" (The Amazon, 2019; Deforestation in the Amazon, 2019). In the words of a later article, "[l]and grabbing has become an industry" in itself, as: "Land-grabbers invade public land, deforest it, and sell it to ranchers. When the ranchers move on, they resell it to soya farmers" (Preserving rainforests, 2023, p. 53). Thus, the possibility of an imminent tipping point in the ecology of Amazonia must be understood with reference to half a century of political economy. This capsule history is seriously lacking in detail, but it suffices to indicate the importance of the *longue durée* perspective, identified with the great historian Fernand Braudel. He has characterized it (Braudel, 2009, p. 182–183) as the basis for "distinguish[ing] between long-term movements and momentary pressures" and avoiding "a purely episodic historiography," an error in which "all the social sciences participate." I return to the value of this perspective for understanding the pandemic as tipping point in the concluding section of the chapter, after providing necessary historical detail about inequality trends and their origins over a comparable period.

2.3 A Superficial History of the Inequality Machine

Two Organisation for Economic Co-operation and Development (OECD) studies that appeared shortly before and after the commentary in *Le Monde Diplomatique* (OECD, 2011, 2015) identified increasing income inequalities as measured using the Gini coefficient, a commonly used but imperfect measure (Blesch et al., 2022), starting in the mid-1980s, in most high-income countries, although not in all. This pattern can be attributed in the first instance to the way globalization restructured labor markets: "probably the most profound global reshuffle of people's economic positions since the Industrial Revolution" (Milanovic, 2013, p. 202). Gains from economic growth flowed to people in the bottom third of the global income distribution; literally hundreds of millions of people escaped extreme poverty as production was reorganized globally, with China becoming the world's workshop. At the other end of the income distribution, the most significant gainers were people in the global top 1% (some 60 million people worldwide, including "the richest 12% of Americans (more than 30 million people) and between 3 and 6% of the richest Britons, Japanese, Germans and French" (Milanovic, 2013, p. 203). Many of these fell into the category described as the "working rich" by Duménil and Lévy (2004), whose high incomes also meant enhanced opportunity to accumulate assets. Conversely, the biggest losers were people in the rich countries whose incomes stagnated as jobs disappeared with deindustrialization or labor markets were restructured to increase flexibility (and for those workers affected, insecurity).

Milanovic's data covered the period 1988–2008. The first edition of the indispensable *World Inequality Report*[2] (Alvaredo et al., 2017) expanded the time frame and updated the picture to 2016, finding that "the top 0.1% [of the global income distribution] has captured as much growth as the bottom half of the world adult population since 1980" (Alvaredo et al., 2017, p. 40). Data on the US, among the most unequal of OECD countries, add some texture to this picture. "[F]ully 43% of all private-sector jobs fell below the [Bureau of Labor Statistics] definition of 'low wage' by 2010" (Moody, 2017, p. 21) and "[b]y 2011 28% of all workers earned less than the official poverty-level wage of $11.06 an hour. So stagnant has been the income of the working-class majority that 30% of the workforce … now relies on public assistance to get by" (Moody, 2017, p. 30). RAND Corporation researchers

[2] The report is the flagship publication of the Paris-based World Inequality Lab. Its senior researchers include Thomas Piketty, the author of the surprise bestseller *Capital in the Twenty-First Century*, and Gabriel Zucman, the 2023 winner of the American Economic Association's John Bates Clark medal for "that American economist under the age of 40 who is judged to have made the most significant contribution to economic thought and knowledge" (Saez, 2024).

have concluded that "[f]undamentally, the majority of workers did not share in the benefits of economic growth to any significant degree" between 1975 and 2018 (Price & Edwards, 2020, p. 11) and changes in the distribution of income in the US over that period had the effect of redistributing at least *US$47 trillion* from the bottom 90% of the income distribution to the top 10% (Price & Edwards, 2020, p. 12, 40). As for wealth rather than income, between 1983 and 2019, the last pre-pandemic year, the number of US households with at least US$10 million in assets after adjusting for inflation grew from 66,000 to 693,000 (Turchin, 2023, p. 7), continuing a pattern in which top wealth shares had been increasing since the mid-1980s, "as the accumulation of financial assets by the wealthy [had] led to a rise in capital income concentrations, allowing for more wealth accumulation at the top" (Alvaredo et al., 2017, p. 212). It is perhaps not surprising that, starting circa 1990, a specific segment of the US working class—white non-Hispanic workers—began to exhibit sharply increasing rates of "deaths of despair" from alcohol and drug poisoning, suicide and alcoholic liver disease, as described by economists Anne Case and Angus Deaton (2017). There was almost no increase, however, among people with at least a four-year university degree (Case & Deaton, 2017, p. 416)—highly significant in view of the tripling of the cost of a university education relative to the median US wage between 1976 and 2016 (Turchin, 2023, p. 66) and its predictable effects on economic mobility.

It must be emphasized that such trends are not universal. A major comparative study of low-wage work in several high-income countries found that its prevalence varied considerably among countries and increased over the 1980–2005 period in some countries, like the UK, *but not in others,* even though the six countries in the study "[had] all been exposed … to the same increases in globalization, technology, and competition within national product markets" (Appelbaum et al., 2010, p. 5). On the other hand, welfare state retrenchment appears to have been remarkably consistent, especially under the rubric of austerity (which has been shown consistently to increase inequality; see Ball et al., 2013) after the financial crisis of 2007–2008, including in the historically generous Nordic countries (Baccini & Sattler, 2024, p. 3–4; Sowula et al., 2024; Therborn, 2020).

Where such changes as labor market deregulation and welfare state retrenchment occurred, they were underpinned by the core set of presuppositions both empirical and normative that comprise neoliberalism. Scholar-activist Susan George (2000, p. 27) wrote at the start of the new millennium that: "In 1945 or 1950, if you had seriously proposed any of the ideas and policies in today's standard neoliberal toolkit, you would have been laughed off the stage or sent off to the insane asylum." This may be an exaggeration, but not by much, as illustrated by a statement by former US President Eisenhower quoted by Turchin (2023, p. 155). Certainly, a powerful consensus existed in much of the high-income world around Keynesian economics, labor market regulation, and at least some degree of social provision. The attack on that consensus can be traced back at least to the 1947 establishment of the Mont Pèlerin Society (Harvey, 2005, p. 20–23; Plehwe, 2009) under the leadership of Friedrich Hayek, the author of *The Road to Serfdom* (Hayek, 1944) whose work was later to inspire UK Prime Minister Margaret Thatcher. Historian Daniel

Stedman Jones (2012, p. 134–135; see generally Chap. 4, also Wrenn, 2024) provides a detailed account of how "[a] transatlantic network of sympathetic businessmen and fundraisers, journalists and politicians, policy experts and academics grew and spread neoliberal ideas between the 1940s and the 1970s" by way of a new kind of institution: the think tank. "To a large extent this network was held together by the Mont Pèlerin Society." The elections of Margaret Thatcher's Conservatives in the United Kingdom (1979) and Ronald Reagan as Republican President of the United States (1980) represent milestones, and although the course of neoliberalism or neoliberalization (Ward & England, 2007) has varied considerably among countries, by 1995 a multidisciplinary panel of social scientists examining the prospects for "sustainable democracy" after the collapse of the Soviet Union could describe neoliberalism as "the central ideological force in the Western world" (Przeworski et al., 1995, p. 5).

The international network of think tanks was well funded, as it continues to be to this day, in an illustration of how the instrumental and discursive dimensions of power identified by Fuchs (2005) interact by way of the ability to fund such institutions. Well before the pandemic, personal and corporate owners of wealth had attained remarkable degrees of influence, not only in the direct resourcing of political campaigns and parties but also in the arguably more important processes that define the thinkable (see, e.g., Mayer, 2016, 2017a, 2017b; Geoghegan, 2020; Hacker & Pierson, 2020). In October 1936, US President Franklin Roosevelt's campaign speech in New York City combined a defense of his New Deal programs against intensive criticism from business with a ringing declaration that: "Government by organized money is just as dangerous as Government by organized mob." Few if any serious aspirants to national political office in most of the world would make such a speech today. As political scientist Peter Gourevitch (2013, p. 211) observed in the aftermath of the financial crisis of 2007–2008: "The grip of capital lies in its ability to define the boundaries of acceptable discourse, to cast challenges as extremism." Similarly, UK journalist Peter Geoghegan (2020, p. 124) begins a discussion of how the billionaire Koch brothers in the US built an empire of public policy influence by observing that "if you wanted to change the whole political conversation so that low taxes across the board became the norm" then: "The way to do that isn't to buy the politicians. It's to own the ideas that dominate the political conversation." As just one illustration, another organization built on a family fortune, the Olin Foundation, provided the funding that enabled Charles Murray to write his notorious attack on an already-ungenerous US social protection system, *Losing Ground* (Murray, 1984), which provided some of the impetus for the US Clinton administration's 1996 termination of a decades-old guarantee of minimal financial support for lone mothers (Mayer, 2016, p. 111–112; Lichtenstein & Stein, 2023, Chap. 10).

2.4 The Pandemic and Inequality

The preceding section describes the policy landscape when the pandemic hit. Globally, the second *World Inequality Report*, which includes data on wealth from the early stages of the pandemic, found that between 1995 and 2021 the bottom half of the global wealth distribution captured just 2% of global wealth growth, while the top 1% (average wealth per adult of €2,755,200, adjusted for purchasing power) captured 38%, with gains especially pronounced for the top 0.001% of the distribution (Chancel et al., 2021). "Between 2021 and 2019, the wealth of the top 0.001% grew by 14%, while average global wealth is estimated to have risen by just 1%. At the top of the top, global billionaire wealth increased by more than 50% between 2019 and 2021" (Chancel et al., 2021, p. 46). At a national level, the pandemic and responses to it accelerated the trend of rising economic inequality in at least three ways.

First, workers who were officially considered essential (ranging from front-line care providers to meat-packing plant operatives) continued at their jobs, often with seriously inadequate protection, placing them at high risk of infection and subsequent income loss (see, e.g., Bambra et al., 2021). At the same time, many workers whose jobs were not considered essential by the jurisdiction in question were disproportionately vulnerable to the economic effects of lockdown-related job and income loss. They were also vulnerable to economic losses associated with illness given dramatic variation across the high-income world in statutory entitlement to sickness pay, which was non-existent in some jurisdictions at the start of the pandemic (OECD, 2020, p. 9) and was implemented only on a partial, temporary basis in others. Conversely, high-income earners were disproportionately more likely to be able to work from home and escape risks both of infection and of income loss (Badger et al., 2023).

Second, expansionary asset purchase programs by central banks, like earlier initiatives packaged as quantitative easing (see Green & Lavery, 2015 on the UK situation), inflated the price of financial assets that are disproportionately held by the wealthy (UNDESA, 2022, p. xiii). According to the *Global Wealth Reports*, the number of US dollar millionaires worldwide rose from 46.8 million in mid-2019, the last pre-pandemic year, to 62.5 million in 2021, and the number of ultra-high-net-worth (UHNW) individuals, with net worth of more than US$50 million, rose by 21% in 2021 alone (Shorrocks et al., 2019, 2022). An especially dramatic illustration of the associated effects on inequality was provided by US researchers at the end of the first pandemic year: the controlling shareholders of giant retailers Amazon and Walmart, Jeff Bezos and the Walton family, had seen their wealth increase by US$11.5 million and US$6.2 million respectively, *per hour*, while Amazon and Walmart "associates" had seen their hourly pay increase by only US$0.99 and

US$0.77 (Kinder & Stateler, 2020).[3] Tighter labor markets in many jurisdictions may since have attenuated this effect slightly, but have certainly not eliminated it.

Third, the pandemic and fiscal stimuli that responded to it provided an accelerant to the nearly global pre-pandemic housing affordability crisis (Wetzstein, 2017), driven by the financialization of housing (Deva & Farha, 2019; Farha, 2015). As the effects of expansionary fiscal policies that were intended to counteract the destructive consequences of lockdowns combined with ultra-low interest rates, many countries saw a rapid increase in housing prices (both purchase prices and rents) throughout the pandemic (see, e.g., Flynn, 2022; IMF Blog, 2021). Across the European Union, house prices rose 10% between the fourth quarter of 2020 and the fourth quarter of 2021, with considerably higher increases in some countries (European Commission, 2022). In historically affordable Berlin, rents had more than doubled in the decade before 2023 and were undermining the booming technology industry's recruitment efforts (Cantrill, 2023). In the UK, average sale prices increased by 18.5% between the end of 2019 and the end of 2021 (Office for National Statistics, 2022), along with rising private-sector rents—leading one researcher to warn in 2021 that "the UK [was] sleepwalking into a potential evictions crisis" (Blakeley, 2021, p. 79) that quickly became evident (Goodley, 2023). In Canada, already stratospheric housing prices relative to median household incomes in many of the country's 15 largest cities (Gordon, 2020) metastasized to suburbs and peri-urban areas as far as 80 km from city centers (Morel, 2022).

A further issue related to the entry of major corporate investors, including private equity firms, into housing markets as they took advantage of the price slump that materialized in the wake of the financial crisis (Rolnik, 2020; Ballou, 2023, Chap. 2; Kaysen & Koeze, 2023). In the US, income-seeking investors bought 24% of all single-family homes sold in 2021, driving up rents as a consequence (Henderson, 2022). The flip side of housing unaffordability as of 2024 was not only the rising profitability of rental housing for institutional investors but also an increase of US$12 trillion in households' housing wealth since the start of the pandemic (Federal Reserve Bank of St. Louis, 2024)—comparable as of September 2024 to the value of *all* the outstanding shares of Apple, Microsoft, Nvidia, and Amazon, the four most valuable companies by market capitalization trading on Wall Street. Meanwhile by 2022, "a record-high 22.4 million [US] renter households spent more than 30% of their income on rent and utilities," and 12.1 million spent more than half of their income (Joint Center, 2024, p. 2). A massive, inequality-magnifying intergenerational transfer of housing wealth lies ahead, in the US and elsewhere. As one team of researchers has put it, "sustained inflation of property values … has fundamentally shifted the social class structure, from a logic that was structured around employment towards one that is organized around participation in asset ownership and appreciation" (Adkins et al., 2022, p. 17).

[3] Online sales platform Amazon and discount department store Walmart are the largest retailers in the world, ranked by sales, and also the two largest private sector employers in the US, and in the world (Largest Retailers, 2024; Biggest Employers, 2025).

2.5 Post-pandemic Realpolitik, and Early Casualties

The post-pandemic policy history of proposals for wealth taxation is instructive. As noted in the preceding section, increases in asset values (shares and housing) were a primary mechanism by which inequality was ratcheted up during the pandemic. In a response to the pandemic even before the full extent of its effects on wealth concentration became evident, one United Nations agency argued that "[in] light of the further increase in inequality resulting from this crisis the case for a wealth tax seems irrefutable" (UNCTAD, 2020, p. x). Even the Financial Times Editorial Board (2020) conceded that wealth taxes would "have to be in the [policy] mix." Yet for the most part, subsequent silence on this point has been deafening even in the shrinking number of countries that still have functioning parties on the electoral left. For example, a January 2023 poll found that roughly three-quarters of Britons, with majority support from *both* Conservative and Labour Party voters, would approve of a wealth tax on millionaires (Smith, 2023). Comparable levels of support were evident in Canada (Bubbers, 2021), yet parties of the center-left both there and in the UK emphatically rejected wealth taxes (Cole, 2022; Crerar, 2023). Although it is possible that this rejection is now being cautiously rethought in the UK as the country's fiscal position deteriorates, it is perhaps not surprising given that some of the best pre-pandemic comparative political science research from multiple, mostly high-income democracies finds "remarkably strong and consistent evidence of substantial disparities in responsiveness to the preferences of affluent and poor people. Insofar as policy-makers respond to public preferences, they seem to respond primarily or even entirely to the preferences of affluent people. Indeed … the influence attributed to poor citizens is not just less than that attributed to affluent citizens, but consistently *negative*" (Bartels, 2017, p. 47, emphasis in original).[4] That lack of influence can be attributed to the hypermobility of wealth and corporate investment and the vulnerability of national fiscal capacity to tax competition (Harrington, 2016; Alstadsæter et al., 2023); to the hegemonic ideational influence of neoliberalism; or, perhaps most reliably, to a combination of the two. As Fuchs emphasizes, the material, structural, and discursive dimensions of power do not operate in isolation.[5]

---

[4] As an aside, this is why the findings of Wilkinson and Pickett, as compelling as they may be intellectually, are likely to have seriously limited political salience: increasing concentration of income and ultra-wealth enables those at the very top of the economic distribution to insulate themselves from the situations experienced by the rest of the population. Tellingly, neither Brazil nor South Africa, two of the world's most economically unequal countries, has experienced significant shifts towards support for equality-oriented policies on the part of the ultra-wealthy.

[5] In this context, structural power is exemplified by the "privileged position of business" in any national or sub-national economy that depends heavily on private investment (Lindblom, 1977, p. 170–200); the ability of ultra-wealthy individuals to choose their country of residence and (often) of citizenship based on tax considerations (Harrington, 2016); and the ability of transnational corporations to shift profits to corporate units in jurisdictions where they will be taxed at minimal rates (Toplensky, 2018; Tørsløv et al., 2023).

Responses to the crisis of housing affordability, especially in the US (Golestaneh, 2024; Hubler & Baker, 2024; Hubler, 2024; Knight, 2024) but also elsewhere (Rajagopal & De Schutter, 2024), have focused on criminalizing the growing number of unhoused people rather than addressing underlying distributions of resources. This is just one manifestation of a larger pattern that sociologist Saskia Sassen has described as a basic shift in economic and social policy understandings: "The dynamics that pushed towards the active expanding of a middle class and a prosperous working class in that earlier 'Keynesian' period have been replaced by dynamics that produce their shrinking and impoverishment" (Sassen, 2015, p. 72). Stated more bluntly, such dynamics mean either tacit acceptance of the disposability of some portion of the population or their recasting as a reservoir of value whose remaining wealth can be extracted via mechanisms ranging from rising rents and exploitative mortgages and loans to legal frameworks that are designed to raise revenue from unaffordable traffic and misdemeanor fines (Desmond, 2023, Chap. 4; Page & Soss, 2021; Sassen, 2009; Wamsley, 2019).

Beveridge-style, tax-financed health systems like those in Canada and the UK will probably be among early casualties, if they survive at all, gradually deteriorating into residual services for users (who may be quite numerous, but politically weak) unable to afford private provision. The waiting list for elective procedures in England's National Health Service (NHS), by far the largest of the UK's four "devolved" health services, stood at 3.2 million by mid-2017, and rose to 7.6 million by May 2024 as a consequence of delays related to the COVID-19 pandemic (Fisher & Taylor, 2024). Analysis for the Institute for Fiscal Studies (IFS) suggested in 2024 that waiting lists would shrink only slightly by 2027 (Warner & Zaranko, 2024). Admittedly small-scale surveys have found that more than 25% of general practitioners, knowledgeable health system insiders, and 22% of the general population had private health insurance (Fleck, 2023; Price, 2023). Wait times of more than 12 h for patients requiring hospital admission from A&E (emergency) departments had become routine by early 2025 (Searles, 2025). In 2023, IFS researchers estimated that funding a long-overdue workforce plan designed to address shortages of health personnel would require a substantial real (inflation-adjusted) increase in spending for the NHS: an extra £50 billion (in 2023 currency values) in tax revenues or spending redirected from elsewhere (Warner & Zaranko, 2023); the government has since retreated from commitment to the plan. The situation in Canada, where private health insurance for procedures covered under provincial and territorial health insurance is prohibited outside Québec province, is if anything even more dire. More than one in five Canadians lack access to a regular primary care provider (Kiran et al., 2024), with obvious implications for such objectives as timely diagnosis and management of chronic or multiple conditions. In the most populous province (Ontario), between 2012 and 2017 (so pre-pandemic) a quarter of patients received their cancer diagnosis only after presenting in often-overcrowded emergency departments (Grewal & Varner, 2024).

Against the background described so far, the political plausibility of measures to reverse such trends is doubtful. The explanation was succinctly stated by Robert Evans, the magnificently acerbic dean of Canadian health economists: "[A] well-functioning modern health system requires the transfer, through taxation, of a very significant amount of money from the healthy and wealthy to the care of the unhealthy and unwealthy" (Evans, 2012, p. 17–18). When we hear arguments that such tax-financed systems of health care provision are unsustainable, this is code for saying that the richest members of those societies do not want to pay for the care of those purportedly undeserving others; they will find themselves increasingly able to translate that preference into policy outcomes. Even in some of the world's richest countries, then, the future of the Sustainable Development Goal objective of universal health coverage is precarious.

2.6 Tipping Points and *La Longue Durée*

It is characteristic of tipping points that they can only be identified in retrospect, and even then sometimes not precisely. Journalist David Rieff (1993, p. 22) has captured this characteristic eloquently: "After all, nobody got up one balmy afternoon on the Capitoline Hill sometime in the fifth century and said that the Roman Empire was over and the Dark Ages had begun." Returning to examples from climate science, a climatologist observed about record-high temperatures in 2024: "We don't know whether something else has happened [in addition to El Niño] in the climate system and we may have passed some tipping point" (Carlo Buontempo quoted by Nicholson, 2024). From the vantage point of late 2024, it seems likely that the pandemic will be regarded as a tipping point that accelerated a trend toward qualitatively more extreme inequality, new levels of economic brutalization and a new Gilded Age in much of the world, and made reversing that pattern much more difficult in the absence of some of the cataclysmic social upheavals that historian Walter Scheidel (2017) has identified as antecedents of reduced inequality: wars of mass mobilization; revolutions; state collapse; and epidemics with far more casualties than the COVID-19 pandemic. Scheidel's work is a fine example of the *longue durée* perspective, and forces us to consider the likelihood that the "great compression" of income inequality that occurred during and after the two World Wars of the twentieth century (Scheidel, 2017, p. 115–173) was an historical anomaly. Historian and sociologist of economic development Sandra Halperin has made a similar point with reference to "the post-World War II interregnum" (Halperin, 2013, Chap. 7). This view is entirely congruent with Thomas Piketty's (2014) argument in *Capital in the Twenty-First Century*, although he is elsewhere less deterministic about the path to higher inequality (Piketty & Saez, 2014).

It would be a great relief to be wrong about this assessment. Historical trend is not destiny. Perhaps sub-national initiatives to tame the inequality machine and its consequences will be successful. Perhaps the OECD-led 2021 agreement among 136 countries on a worldwide minimum tax rate of 15% on transnational corporate profits (Clausing, 2023) will reduce the effectiveness of tax avoidance strategies—an important topic that has not been addressed here—although it is difficult to envision enthusiasm about this agreement on the part of a Trump-ruled United States.

Even before the political events of late 2024 implementation was seen as challenging because of the need for domestic legislation in the face of what is likely to be fierce corporate opposition, and (in the case of the European Union) the need for unanimous agreement on implementation measures among member countries. While trying to sustain optimism, we must also be concerned with what happens when either policy failures or governmental indifference lead to cynical fatalism of a kind that already seems to pervade the political process in some quarters (see an eerily prescient paper by Berman, 2021), and arguably manifested itself in the US presidential election victory of Donald Trump in November, 2024.

Since the first version of this analysis was presented at a conference in Montréal, it is appropriate to end by thinking about what the city's poet laureate, Leonard Cohen, wrote and sang about what happens when "Everybody Knows." When enough everybodies know, for instance, that "the poor stay poor and the rich get rich," as political discourse casts progressive responses to rising inequality as simply incredible and the so-called social media ecosystem is dominated, if not directly controlled[6] by the far right, the consequences can be very dangerous indeed for what remains of democracy. In the US, with the Democratic party unwilling to recognize the economic damages to working-class livelihoods associated with their decades-long embrace of the neoliberalizers, much less repudiate that path (Moody, 2017, Chaps. 8, 9; Lichtenstein & Stein, 2023, Chaps. 8–9, 11; Weisman, 2025), the road from Mont Pèlerin led, in November 2024, to Mar-a-Lago. Economic impacts of restrictions on resource-based industries added fuel to the resistance (Vanderklippe, 2025).[7] At this writing few if any mainstream political parties in the OECD have offered credible responses to such threats to working-class livelihoods, much less built a viable electoral coalition in support of them. Using a European legislative election data set that covers the period 1986–2018, Baccini and Sattler (2024, p. 1) conclude that "austerity increases support for populist parties in economically vulnerable regions, but has little effect in less vulnerable regions. .... [T]he success of populist parties hinges on the government's failure to protect the losers of structural economic change." In a similar vein, Schraff and Pontusson (2024) note that the far right appears especially successful in regions where voters perceive themselves as "falling behind" either richer regions of the country (for the longer-standing, higher-income members of the EU) or the richer countries of the Union (for the poorer, more recent members). As policy measures that would reduce the relevant inequalities and vulnerabilities are banished from the political imaginary, it is far from clear that a return journey from destinations like Mar-a-Lago will be possible. Much the

[6]As in the case of X (Twitter) and Meta (Facebook), controlled respectively by Elon Musk and Mark Zuckerberg, two of the world's richest individuals.

[7]This observation invites discussion of class divides between those who can afford to worry about "the end of the world" and those who must concern themselves in the first instance with "the end of the month," in the words of a French *gilet jaune* protester quoted by Martin and Islar (2021), against a background of widespread economic insecurity and increasingly unaffordable necessities like food and housing. This discussion cannot be pursued here, yet is central to the future of almost any progressive political project.

same may well turn out to be the case with regard to the ascendancy of the far right since 2018 in countries including France, Germany, Italy, the Netherlands, and Switzerland (see, e.g., Bernhard, 2024; Biskamp, 2024; Durovic, 2023; Garzia, 2023; van Holsteyn & Galen, 2025). The last word of Albert Camus' famous essay on suicide is "hope," but even before the re-election of US President Trump in 2024, it was difficult to sustain in these times.

Acknowledgments Earlier versions of this argument were presented at the Annual Meeting of the International Studies Association, Montréal and (virtually) to the Histoire et Dynamiques des Espaces Anglophones (HDEA) conference on Exploring the Contours of Wellness and Health, Paris (March 2023); the Thirteenth International Conference on Health, Wellness & Society, Vancouver (September 2023); (virtually) to the University of Oslo conference on The Political Determinants of Health—10 years on, Oslo (January 2024) and to a seminar of the Health and Social Theory Group, Durham University (May 2024). Comments received at those sessions and from two anonymous reviewers substantially improved the analysis.

References

Adkins, L., Cooper, M., & Konings, M. (2022). The asset economy: Conceptualizing new logics of inequality. *Distinktion: Journal of Social Theory, 23*, 15–32. https://doi.org/10.1080/1600910X.2021.1904429

Alstadsæter, A., Godar, S., Nicolaides, P., & Zucman, G. (2023). *Global tax evasion report 2024*. EU Tax Observatory. https://www.taxobservatory.eu/www-site/uploads/2023/10/global_tax_evasion_report_24.pdf

Alvaredo, F., Chancel, L., Piketty, T., Saez, E., & Zucman, G. (2017). *World inequality report 2018*. World Inequality Lab. http://wir2018.wid.world/files/download/wir2018-full-report-english.pdf

Appelbaum, E., Bosch, G., Gautié, J., Mason, G., Mayhew, K., Salverda, W., et al. (2010). Introduction and overview. In J. Gautié & J. Schmitt (Eds.), *Low-wage work in the wealthy world* (pp. 1–32). Russell Sage Foundation.

Baccini, L., & Sattler, T. (2024). Austerity, economic vulnerability, and populism. *American Journal of Political Science, 69*. https://doi.org/10.1111/ajps.12865

Badger, E., Gebeloff, R., & Katz, J. (2023). The places most affected by remote workers' moves around the country. *New York Times*. https://www.nytimes.com/interactive/2023/06/17/upshot/17migration-patterns-movers.html?smid=nytcore-android-share

Ball, L., Furceri, D., Leigh, D., & Loungani, P. (2013). *The distributional effects of fiscal consolidation* (Working Paper No. 13/151). International Monetary Fund. Retrieved from http://www.imf.org/external/pubs/ft/wp/2013/wp13151.pdf

Ballard, J. G. (1975; Panther edition 1977). *High rise*. Jonathan Cape.

Ballou, B. (2023). *Plunder: Private equity's plan to pillage America*. Public Affairs.

Bambra, C., Lynch, J., & Smith, K. E. (2021). *The unequal pandemic: COVID-19 and health inequalities*. Policy Press.

Bartels, L. M. (2017). *Political inequality in affluent democracies: The social welfare deficit* (CSDI Working Paper No. 5-2017. Center for the Study of Democratic Institutions, Vanderbilt University). http://www.vanderbilt.edu/csdi/research/Working_Paper_5_2017.pdf

Beauchamp, D. E. (1976). Public health as social justice. *Inquiry, 13*, 3–14.

Berman, S. (2021). The political conditions necessary for addressing inequality. In O. Blanchard & D. Rodrik (Eds.), *Combating inequality* (pp. 75–84). MIT Press.

Bernhard, L. (2024). The 2023 Swiss federal elections: The radical right did it again. *West European Politics, 47*, 1435–1445. https://doi.org/10.1080/01402382.2024.2303277
Bhattarai, A. (2024, July 28). They have jobs, but no homes. Inside America's unseen homelessness crisis. *Washington Post*. https://www.washingtonpost.com/business/2024/07/28/homeless-lack-of-affordable-housing-economy/
Biskamp, F. (2024). A societal shift to the right or the political mobilisation of a shrinking minority? Explaining rise and radicalisation of the AfD in Germany. *International Journal of Public Policy, 17*, 139–165. https://doi.org/10.1504/IJPP.2024.138373
Blakeley, G. (2021). Financialization, real estate and COVID-19 in the UK. *Community Development Journal, 56*, 79–99. https://doi.org/10.1093/cdj/bsaa056
Blesch, K., Hauser, O. P., & Jachimowicz, J. M. (2022). Measuring inequality beyond the Gini coefficient may clarify conflicting findings. *Nature Human Behaviour, 6*, 1525–1536. https://doi.org/10.1038/s41562-022-01430-7
Braudel, F. (2009). History and the social sciences: The longue durée. *Review (Fernand Braudel Center), 32*, 171–203.
Bubbers, M. (2021, April 22). The federal budget's new tax on luxury cars is just a smokescreen. [Toronto] *Globe and Mail*. https://www.theglobeandmail.com/drive/mobility/article-the-federal-budgets-new-tax-on-luxury-cars-is-just-a-smokescreen/
Cantrill, A. (2023). Berlin's barren housing market is putting its tech boom at risk. *Bloomberg News*. https://www.bloomberg.com/news/articles/2023-02-11/berlin-s-lack-of-housing-poses-a-challenge-for-the-city-s-tech-sector
Case, A., & Deaton, A. (2017). Mortality and morbidity in the 21st century. *Brookings Papers on Economic Activity, 2017*, 397–476. https://doi.org/10.1353/eca.2017.0005
Casselman, B., & DePillis, L (2023, September 13). Poverty rate rose in 2022 as aid ended. *New York Times*. https://www.nytimes.com/2023/09/12/business/economy/income-poverty-health-insurance.html?searchResultPosition=4
Chancel, L., Piketty, T., Saez, E., & Zucman, G. (2021). *World inequality report 2022*. World Inequality Lab. https://wir2022.wid.world/www-site/uploads/2023/03/D_FINAL_WIL_RIM_RAPPORT_2303.pdf
Clausing, K. A. (2023). *The international tax agreement of 2021: Why it's needed, what it does, and what comes next?*, Policy Brief No. 23–4. Peterson Institute for International Economics. https://papers.ssrn.com/sol3/Delivery.cfm/SSRN_ID4431077_code356528.pdf?abstractid=4431077&mirid=1
Cohen, L (1988). "Everybody Knows." I'm Your Man. Columbia Records.
Cole, T. (2022, March). Minister of everything: Chrystia Freeland has taken on some of the Liberal government's toughest portfolios. *Report on Business Magazine*, 8–11.
Crerar, P. (2023, August 27). Rachel Reeves rules out wealth tax if Labour wins next election. *Guardian*. https://www.theguardian.com/politics/2023/aug/27/rachel-reeves-rules-out-wealth-tax-if-labour-wins-next-election
de Sousa, T., & Henry, M. (2024). *The 2024 annual homelessness assessment report (AHAR) to congress*. U.S. Department of Housing and Urban Development. https://www.huduser.gov/portal/sites/default/files/pdf/2024-AHAR-Part-1.pdf
Deforestation in the Amazon may soon begin to feed on itself. (2019). *Economist*. https://www.economist.com/graphic-detail/2019/08/15/deforestation-in-the-amazon-may-soon-begin-to-feed-on-itself
Desmond, M. (2023). *Poverty, by America*. Crown.
Deva, S., & Farha, L. (2019). Letter to Blackstone L.P. United Nations Office of the High Commissioner for Human Rights. https://www.ohchr.org/Documents/Issues/Housing/Financialization/OL_OTH_17_2019.pdf
Duménil, G., & Lévy, D. (2004). Neoliberal income trends: Wealth, class and ownership in the USA. *New Left Review, 30*, 105–133.
Durovic, A. (2023). Rising electoral fragmentation and abstention: The French elections of 2022. *West European Politics, 46*, 614–629. https://doi.org/10.1080/01402382.2022.2123095

European Commission (2022). Housing price statistics - House price index. *Eurostat*. https://ec.europa.eu/eurostat/statistics-explained/index.php?title=Housing_price_statistics_-_house_price_index

Evans, R. G. (2012). A casualty in the class war: Canada's Medicare. *Healthcare Policy, 7*(3), 14–22.

Farha, L. (2015). *Report of the special rapporteur on adequate housing as a component of the right to an adequate standard of living, and on the right to non-discrimination in this context*, A/HRC/31/54. United Nations. http://unhousingrapp.org/user/pages/04.resources/Thematic-Report-5-Homelessness-as-a-Global-Human-Rights-Crisis.pdf

Federal Reserve Board (2022). *Economic Well-Being of U.S. Households in 2021. U.S. Federal Reserve.* https://www.federalreserve.gov/publications/files/2021-report-economic-well-being-us-households-202205.pdf.

Federal Reserve Bank of St. Louis. (2024). *Households; owners' equity in real estate, level*. https://fred.stlouisfed.org/series/OEHRENWBSHNO

FinanceCharts. (2025). *Biggest employers in the world for Jan 2025*. https://www.financecharts.com/screener/biggest-private-employers

Financial Times Editorial Board. (2020, April 4). Virus lays bare the frailty of the social contract. *Financial Times*. https://www.ft.com/content/7eff769a-74dd-11ea-95fe-fcd274e920ca

Fisher, E., & Taylor, B. (2024, October 10). *NHS hospital care: Who is waiting and what are they waiting for?* Nuffield Trust. https://www.nuffieldtrust.org.uk/news-item/nhs-emergency-and-planned-care-who-is-waiting-and-what-waiting-for

Fitzpatrick, S., Bramley, G., Blenkinsopp, J., Wood, J., Sosenko, F., Littlewood, M. et al. (2020). *Destitution in the UK 2020*. Joseph Rowntree Foundation. https://www.jrf.org.uk/file/57076/download?token=d06VOyU6&filetype=full-report

Fitzpatrick, S., Bramley, G., Treanor, M., Blenkinsopp, J., McIntyre, J., Johnsen, S. et al. (2023). *Destitution in the UK 2023*. Joseph Rowntree Foundation. https://www.jrf.org.uk/deep-poverty-and-destitution/destitution-in-the-uk-2023

Fleck, A. (2023). Overburdened NHS pushes more Brits to go private. *Statista*. https://www.statista.com/chart/29261/share-of-uk-paying-for-private-health-insurance/

Flynn, L. B. (2022). The pandemic worsens Europe's housing problems. *Current History, 121*, 83–89. https://doi.org/10.1525/curh.2022.121.833.83

Fuchs, D. (2005). Commanding heights? The strength and fragility of business power in global politics. *Millennium, 33*, 771–801. https://doi.org/10.1177/03058298050330030501

Garzia, D. (2023). The Italian parliamentary election of 2022: The populist radical right takes charge. *West European Politics, 46*, 1038–1048. https://doi.org/10.1080/01402382.2022.2148603

Geoghegan, P. (2020). *Democracy for sale: Dark money and dirty politics*. Head of Zeus.

George, S. (2000). A short history of neoliberalism: Twenty years of élite economics and emerging opportunities for structural change. In W. Bello, N. Bullard, & K. Malhotra (Eds.), *Global finance: New thinking on regulating speculative capital markets* (pp. 27–35). Zed Books.

Golestaneh, S. (2024). Pushed into the shadows: The criminalization of homelessness and its health consequences. *Houston Journal of Health Law and Policy, 23*, 1–42.

Goodley, S. (2023, March 3). 'It makes me want to cry': Inside crumbling courts as judges wrestle with rise in rent eviction cases. *Guardian*. https://www.theguardian.com/business/2023/mar/03/eviction-cases-mount-in-northern-england-and-wales

Gordon, J. C. (2020). Reconnecting the housing market to the labour market: Foreign ownership and housing affordability in urban Canada. *Canadian Public Policy, 46*, 1–22. https://doi.org/10.3138/cpp.2019-009

Gourevitch, P. (2013). Choice and constraint in the Great recession of 2008. In M. Finnemore & J. Goldstein (Eds.), *Back to basics: State power in a contemporary world* (pp. 196–215). Oxford University Press.

Green, J., & Lavery, S. (2015). The regressive recovery: Distribution, inequality and state power in Britain's post-crisis political economy. *New Political Economy, 20*, 894–923. https://doi.org/10.1080/13563467.2015.1041478

Grewal, K., & Varner, C. (2024). The emergency department is no place to be told you have cancer. *Canadian Medical Association Journal, 196,* Article E626. https://doi.org/10.1503/cmaj.240612

Hacker, J. S., & Pierson, P. (2020). *Let them eat tweets: How the right rules in an age of extreme inequality*. Liveright/W.W. Norton.

Halimi, S. (2013, May). *Tyranny of the one per cent*. Le Monde Diplomatique (English edition).

Halperin, S. (2013). *Re-envisioning global development: A horizontal perspective*. Routledge.

Harrington, B. (2016). *Capital without borders: Wealth managers and the one percent*. Harvard University Press.

Harvey, D. (2005). *A brief history of neoliberalism*. Oxford University Press.

Hayek, F. A. (1944). *The road to serfdom*. University of Chicago Press.

Hecht, S., & Cockburn, A. (2010). *The fate of the forest: Developers, destroyers, and defenders of the Amazon* (updated, original edition 1990 ed.). University of Chicago Press.

Henderson, T. (2022). *Investors bought a quarter of homes sold last year, driving up rents*. Pew Stateline. https://www.pewtrusts.org/en/research-and-analysis/blogs/stateline/2022/07/22/investors-bought-a-quarter-of-homes-sold-last-year-driving-up-rents

Hubler, S. (2024, July 25). Newsom will order California officials to remove homeless encampments. *New York Times*. https://www.nytimes.com/2024/07/25/us/newsom-homeless-california.html

Hubler, S., & Baker, M. (2024, July 14). In the West, cities cautiously exercise homeless enforcement. *New York Times*. https://www.nytimes.com/2024/07/13/us/homeless-camps-supreme-court-ruling.html

IMF Blog. (2021). *Housing prices continue to soar in many countries around the world*. International Monetary Fund. https://blogs.imf.org/2021/10/18/housing-prices-continue-to-soar-in-many-countries-around-the-world/

IMF Fiscal Affairs Department. (2021). *Fiscal monitor database of country fiscal measures in response to the COVID-19 pandemic*. International Monetary Fund. https://www.imf.org/en/Topics/imf-and-covid19/Fiscal-Policies-Database-in-Response-to-COVID-19

Joint Center for Housing Studies of Harvard University. (2024). *America's rental housing 2024*. Harvard University. https://www.jchs.harvard.edu/sites/default/files/reports/files/Harvard_JCHS_Americas_Rental_Housing_2024.pdf

Joseph Rowntree Foundation. (2024). *UK poverty 2024: The essential guide to understanding poverty in the UK*. JRF. https://www.jrf.org.uk/pdf/15211

Kavanagh, M. M., & Singh, R. (2023). Vaccine politics: Law and inequality in the pandemic response to COVID-19. *Global Policy, 14*, 229–246. https://doi.org/10.1111/1758-5899.13203

Kaysen, R., & Koeze, E. (2023). What happens when Wall Street buys most of the homes on your block? *New York Times*. https://www.nytimes.com/interactive/2023/09/16/realestate/home-sales-north-carolina-wall-street.html

Kinder, M., & Stateler, L. (2020). *Amazon and Walmart have raked in billions in additional profits during the pandemic, and shared almost none of it with their workers*. Brookings Institution. https://www.brookings.edu/blog/the-avenue/2020/12/22/amazon-and-walmart-have-raked-in-billions-in-additional-profits-during-the-pandemic-and-shared-almost-none-of-it-with-their-workers/

Kiran, T., Daneshvarfard, M., Wang, R., Beyer, A., Kay, J., Breton, M. et al. (2024). Public experiences and perspectives of primary care in Canada: Results from a cross-sectional survey. *Canadian Medical Association Journal, 196,* Article e646. https://doi.org/10.1503/cmaj.231372

Knight, H. (2024, August 4). Defying its reputation, San Francisco toughens stance on homeless camps. *New York Times*. https://www.nytimes.com/2024/08/03/us/san-francisco-homeless-london-breed.html

Labonté, R., & Schrecker, T. (2009). Rights, redistribution, and regulation. In I. R. Labonté et al. (Eds.), *Globalization and health: Pathways, evidence and policy* (pp. 317–333). Routledge.

Largest Retailers. (2024). *CapitalOne Shopping*. https://capitaloneshopping.com/research/largest-retailers

Lenton, T. M. (2013). Environmental tipping points. *Annual Review of Environment and Resources, 38*, 1–29. https://doi.org/10.1146/annurev-environ-102511-084654
Lenton, T. M. (2020). Tipping positive change. *Philosophical Transactions of the Royal Society B: Biological Sciences, 375*, 20190123. https://doi.org/10.1098/rstb.2019.0123
Lichtenstein, N., & Stein, J. (2023). *A fabulous failure: The Clinton presidency and the transformation of American capitalism*. Princeton University Press.
Lindblom, C. (1977). *Politics and markets: The world's political economic systems*. Basic Books.
Martin, M., & Islar, M. (2021). The "end of the world" vs. the "end of the month": Understanding social resistance to sustainability transition agendas, a lesson from the Yellow Vests in France. *Sustainability Science, 16*, 601–614. https://doi.org/10.1007/s11625-020-00877-9
Mayer, J. (2016). *Dark money: The hidden history of the billionaires behind the rise of the radical right*. Doubleday.
Mayer, J. (2017a, June 5). In the withdrawal from the Paris Climate Agreement, the Koch Brothers' campaign becomes overt. *New Yorker*.
Mayer, J. (2017b, March 27). The reclusive hedge-fund tycoon behind the Trump presidency. *New Yorker*.
Milanovic, B. (2013). Global income inequality in numbers: In history and now. *Global Policy, 4*, 198–208.
Milkoreit, M., Hodbod, J., Baggio, J., Benessaiah, K., Calderón-Contreras, R., Donges, J. F., et al. (2018). Defining tipping points for social-ecological systems scholarship – An interdisciplinary literature review. *Environmental Research Letters, 13*, 033005. https://doi.org/10.1088/1748-9326/aaaa75
Miller, C. C., & Parlapiano, A. (2023). The U.S. built a European-style welfare state. It's largely over. *New York Times*. https://www.nytimes.com/interactive/2023/04/06/upshot/pandemic-safety-net-medicaid.html
Moody, K. (2017). *On new terrain: How capital is reshaping the battleground of class war*. Haymarket Books.
Morel, L. (2022). *Analyzing the house price boom in the suburbs of Canada's major cities during the pandemic*. Bank of Canada. https://www.bankofcanada.ca/2022/06/staff-analytical-note-2022-7/
Murray, C. (1984). *Losing ground: American social policy, 1950–1980*. Basic Books.
Nicholson, K. (2024). 2023 was the hottest year on record, but scientists are already worried about 2024. *HuffPost UK*. https://ca.news.yahoo.com/2023-hottest-record-scientists-already-163508170.html?guccounter=1
OECD (Organisation for Economic Co-operation and Development). (2011). *Divided we stand: Why inequality keeps rising*. OECD. https://doi.org/10.1787/9789264119536-en
OECD (Organisation for Economic Co-operation and Development). (2015). In it together: Why less inequality benefits all. OECD. https://doi.org/10.1787/9789264235120-en
OECD (Organisation for Economic Co-operation and Development). (2020). *Paid sick leave to protect income, health and jobs through the COVID-19 crisis*. OECD.https://read.oecd-ilibrary.org/view/?ref=134_134797-9iq8w1fnju&title=Paid-sick-leave-to-protect-income-health-and-jobs-through-the-COVID-19-crisis
Office for National Statistics. (2022). *UK house price index: December 2021*. ONS. https://www.ons.gov.uk/economy/inflationandpriceindices/bulletins/housepriceindex/december2021
Page, J., & Soss, J. (2021). The predatory dimensions of criminal justice. *Science, 374*, 291–294. https://doi.org/10.1126/science.abj7782
Parolin, Z., & Filauro, S. (2023). The United States' record-low child poverty rate in international and historical perspective: A research note. *Demography, 60*, 1665–1673. https://doi.org/10.1215/00703370-11064017
Pickett, K. (2024). The spirit level at 15 – Technical appendix. *Equality Trust*. https://media.equality-trust.out.re/uploads/2024/07/Technical-Appendix-20-07.pdf
Pickett, K. E., & Wilkinson, R. G. (2015). Income inequality and health: A causal review. *Social Science & Medicine, 128*, 316–326. https://doi.org/10.1016/j.socscimed.2014.12.031

Pickett, K., Gauhar, A., & Wilkinson, R. (2024). The spirit level at 15. *Equality Trust*. https://media.equality-trust.out.re/uploads/2024/07/The-Spirit-Level-at-15-2024-FINAL.pdf
Piketty, T. (2014). *Capital in the twenty-first century*. Belknap Press of Harvard University Press.
Piketty, T., & Saez, E. (2014). Inequality in the long run. *Science, 344*, 838–843. https://doi.org/10.1126/science.1251936
Plehwe, D. (2009). Introduction. In P. Mirowski & D. Plehwe (Eds.), *The road from Mont Pèlerin: The making of the neoliberal thought collective* (pp. 1–42). Harvard University Press.
Preserving rainforests: The rule of saw. (2023, March 4). *The Economist*, 52–54.
Price, K. (2023). A quarter of GPs have private medical insurance. *Pulse Today*. https://www.pulsetoday.co.uk/news/practice-personal-finance/a-quarter-of-gps-have-private-medical-insurance/
Price, C. C., & Edwards, K. A. (2020). *Trends in income from 1975 to 2018*. Working Paper No. WR-A516-1. RAND Corporation. https://www.rand.org/content/dam/rand/pubs/working_papers/WRA500/WRA516-1/RAND_WRA516-1.pdf
Przeworski, A., Bardhan, P., Bresser Pereira, L. C., Bruszt, L., Choi, J. J., Comisso, E. T., et al. (1995). *Sustainable democracy*. Cambridge University Press.
Rajagopal, B., & De Schutter, O. (2024). *Breaking the cycle: Ending the criminalization of homelessness and poverty: Report of the Special Rapporteur on extreme poverty and human rights*. A/HRC/56/61/Add.3. United Nations. https://www.ohchr.org/sites/default/files/documents/hrbodies/hrcouncil/sessions-regular/session56/advance-versions/a-hrc-56-61-add-3.pdf
Reducing poverty: When policy works. (2021, September 18). *The Economist*, 39–40.
Regilme, S. S. (2023). Crisis politics of dehumanisation during COVID-19: A framework for mapping the social processes through which dehumanisation undermines human dignity. *The British Journal of Politics and International Relations, 25*, 555–573. https://doi.org/10.1177/13691481231178247
Rieff, D. (1993). *Los Angeles: Capital of the Third world*. Phoenix.
Rolnik, R. (2020). Housing under the empire of finance. In J. Knox-Hayes & D. Wójcik (Eds.), *The Routledge handbook of financial geography* (pp. 189–207). Routledge.
Roosevelt, F. D. (1936, October 31). Address at Madison Square Garden, New York City. *The American Presidency Project*. https://www.presidency.ucsb.edu/documents/address-madison-square-garden-new-york-city-1
Saez, E. (2024). Gabriel Zucman: Winner of the 2023 Clark medal. *Journal of Economic Perspectives, 38*, 227–244. https://doi.org/10.1257/jep.38.2.227
Sassen, S. (2009). When local housing becomes an electronic instrument: The global circulation of mortgages – A research note. *International Journal of Urban and Regional Research, 33*, 411–426. https://doi.org/10.1111/j.1468-2427.2009.00868.x
Sassen, S. (2015). Beyond inequality: Expulsions. In S. Gill (Ed.), *Critical perspectives on the crisis of global governance: Reimagining the future* (pp. 69–88). Palgrave Macmillan UK.
Scheidel, W. (2017). *The great leveler: Violence and the history of inequality from the stone age to the twenty-first century*. Princeton University Press.
Schraff, D., & Pontusson, J. (2024). Falling behind whom? Economic geographies of right-wing populism in Europe. *Journal of European Public Policy, 31*, 1591–1619. https://doi.org/10.1080/13501763.2023.2278647
Schrecker, T. (2022). Building back worse? The prognosis for health equity in the post-pandemic world. In L. Dalingwater et al. (Eds.), *The unequal costs of Covid-19 on well-being in Europe* (pp. 21–39). Springer International Publishing. https://doi.org/10.1007/978-3-031-14425-7_2
Searles, M. (2025, January 13). Corridor care 'normalised' as 12-hour trolley waits hit record high. *Telegraph*. https://www.telegraph.co.uk/news/2025/01/13/corridor-care-normalised-12-hour-trolley-waits-record-high/
Shorrocks, A., Davies, J., & Lluberas, R. (2019). *Global wealth report 2019*. Credit Suisse Research Institute. https://www.credit-suisse.com/media/assets/corporate/docs/about-us/research/publications/global-wealth-report-2019-en.pdf

Shorrocks, A., Davies, J., & Lluberas, R. (2022). *Global wealth report 2022*. Credit Suisse Research Institute. https://www.credit-suisse.com/media/assets/corporate/docs/about-us/research/publications/global-wealth-report-2022-en.pdf

Sirleaf, M. (2022). We charge vaccine apartheid? *Journal of Law, Medicine & Ethics, 50*, 726–737. https://doi.org/10.1017/jme.2023.14

Smith, F. (2023). Three quarters of Britons support wealth taxes on millionaires. *YouGov UK*. https://yougov.co.uk/politics/articles/45044-three-quarters-britons-support-wealth-taxes-millio

Smith, C., Baker, J. C. A., & Spracklen, D. V. (2023). Tropical deforestation causes large reductions in observed precipitation. *Nature, 615*, 270–275. https://doi.org/10.1038/s41586-022-05690-1

Søndergaard, N., de Sá, C. D., & Platiau, A. F. B. (2023). Introduction: The sustainability challenges of Brazilian agriculture. In N. Søndergaard et al. (Eds.), *Sustainability challenges of Brazilian agriculture: Governance, inclusion, and innovation* (pp. 1–16). Springer International Publishing. https://doi.org/10.1007/978-3-031-29853-0_1

Sowula, J., Gehrig, F., Scruggs, L. A., Seeleib-Kaiser, M., & Ramalho Tafoya, G. (2024). The end of welfare states as we know them? A multidimensional perspective. *Social Policy & Administration, 58*, 785–799. https://doi.org/10.1111/spol.12990

Stedman Jones, D. (2012). *Masters of the universe: Hayek, Friedman, and the birth of neoliberal politics*. Princeton University Press.

The Amazon: On the brink. (2019, August 3). *The Economist*, 14–16.

Therborn, G. (2020). Sweden's turn to economic inequality, 1982-2019. *Structural Change and Economic Dynamics, 52*, 159–166. https://doi.org/10.1016/j.strueco.2019.10.005

Toplensky, R. (2018). Multinationals pay lower taxes than a decade ago. *Financial Times*. https://www.ft.com/content/2b356956-17fc-11e8-9376-4a6390addb44

Tørsløv, T., Wier, L., & Zucman, G. (2023). The missing profits of nations. *Review of Economic Studies, 90*, 1499–1534. https://doi.org/10.1093/restud/rdac049

Turchin, P. (2023). *End times: Elites, counter-elites and the path of political disintegration*. Penguin.

UNCTAD (United Nations Conference on Trade and Development). (2020). *Trade and development report 2020: From global pandemic to prosperity for all: Avoiding another lost decade*. United Nations. https://unctad.org/en/PublicationsLibrary/tdr2020_en.pdf

UNDESA (United Nations Department of Economic and Social Affairs). (2022). *World economic situation and prospects 2022*. United Nations. https://desapublications.un.org/file/728/download

van Holsteyn, J. J. M., & Galen, A. (2025). The Dutch parliamentary elections of November 2023. *West European Politics, 48*, 464–477. https://doi.org/10.1080/01402382.2024.2397629

Vanderklippe, N. (2025, January 17). Trump's 'pivot counties.' [Toronto] *Globe and Mail*. https://www.theglobeandmail.com/world/article-trump-counties-that-once-backed-obama-are-the-picture-of-an-aggrieved/

Wamsley, D. (2019). Neoliberalism, mass incarceration, and the US debt-criminal justice complex. *Critical Social Policy, 39*, 248–267. https://doi.org/10.1177/0261018318779477

Ward, K., & England, K. (2007). Introduction: Reading neoliberalization. In K. England & K. Ward (Eds.), *Neoliberalization: States, networks, people* (pp. 1–22). Blackwell.

Warner, M., & Zaranko, B. (2023). *Implications of the NHS workforce plan*. IFS Green budget 2023. Institute for Fiscal Studies. https://ifs.org.uk/sites/default/files/2023-08/R272-Implications-of-the-workforce-plan-IFS%20%282%29.pdf

Warner, M., & Zaranko, B. (2024). *The past and future of NHS waiting lists in England*, IFS Report No. 302. Institute for Fiscal Studies. https://ifs.org.uk/sites/default/files/2024-02/The-past-and-future-of-NHS-waiting-lists-in-England-IFS-report-R302.pdf

Watts, J., Greenfield, P, & van der Zee, B (2023, June 2). The multinational companies that industrialised the Amazon rainforest. *Guardian*. https://www.theguardian.com/global-development/2023/jun/02/the-multinational-companies-that-industrialised-the-amazon-rainforest

Weisman, J. (2025, January 5). How the Democrats lost the working class. *New York Times*. https://www.nytimes.com/2025/01/04/us/politics/democrats-working-class.html

Wetzstein, S. (2017). The global urban housing affordability crisis. *Urban Studies, 54*, 3159–3177. https://doi.org/10.1177/0042098017711649
Wilkinson, R., & Pickett, K. (2010). *The spirit level: Why equality is better for everyone*. Penguin.
Wrenn, M. (2024). Coming of age: Think tanks and the rise of right-wing populism. In J. Komlos (Ed.), *Neoliberal economic policy and the rise of right-wing populism: Western civilization at the crossroads* (pp. 203–221). Springer Nature Switzerland. https://doi.org/10.1177/0042098017711649

Canadian political scientist Ted Schrecker is Emeritus Professor of Global Health Policy at Newcastle University (UK). He moved to the UK in 2013, returning to Canada in retirement in 2022. The second, expanded edition of his co-authored book *How Politics Makes Us Sick: Neoliberal Epidemics* was published by Palgrave in summer 2025. His research has been published in many leading social science and health journals. He coordinated the knowledge network on globalization that supported the WHO Commission on Social Determinants of Health, and from 2014 to 2019 he served as co-editor of the *Journal of Public Health* (Oxford University Press).

Part II
Health and Well-being in Educational Settings

Chapter 3
From "Health" to "Health and Well-being": A Study of the Emerging Discourse of Well-being in Indian Education Policy

Rachna Sikarwar

Abstract Governments worldwide, including India, recognize schools as vital platforms for promoting population health. Indian education policies have consistently incorporated health provisions since independence. Recent health initiatives, such as the School Health Program under *Ayushman Bharat*, have placed a significant emphasis on "well-being" and "wellness" within educational settings. The increasing focus on well-being is part of the expansion of the concept of "health," which has gradually progressed over time through successive policies. National Education Policy 2020 frequently mentions the term well-being in contrast to earlier policies—National Education Policy 1968 and 1986, where its presence was more limited. Despite this increased focus, the interchangeable use of the terms "wellness" and "well-being" has led to conceptual ambiguity, complicating its effective implementation. The broad scope of "well-being" risks turning it into a catch-all term, reducing it to a rhetoric rather than a concrete, actionable framework. Additionally, intense academic competition, high student–teacher ratio, and existing gaps between well-being initiatives and core curriculum content, all hinder progress. While well-being has become more closely linked to health-related initiatives in education, developing a clear and structured framework remains a critical challenge. Ensuring consistent definitions and measurable outcomes will be essential for translating policy aspirations into tangible outcomes.

Keywords Well-being · National Education Policy · Wellness · School Health Program · NCERT

R. Sikarwar (✉)
Centre for South Asian Studies, Jawaharlal Nehru University, New Delhi, India

© The Author(s), under exclusive license to Springer Nature Switzerland AG 2025

L. Dalingwater et al. (eds.), *Structural and Systemic Perspectives on Health and Well-being*, Human Well-Being Research and Policy Making,
https://doi.org/10.1007/978-3-031-99924-6_3

3.1 Introduction

The importance of promoting well-being in schools is increasingly acknowledged in public policy (Konu & Matti, 2002; Kilgour et al., 2015). Schools are viewed as institutions for imparting knowledge while also nurturing individuals' overall well-being. This perspective underscores a holistic vision of education emphasizing the overall development of individuals. It has led to international efforts to incorporate well-being into educational policies and curricula (Graham, 2011). For instance, the UK's *Every Child Matters* policy, Scotland's *Curriculum for Excellence*, and Australia's *Kids Matter* program all emphasize well-being in school settings.

In India, the recognition of well-being in educational settings has gained traction through various initiatives focusing on promoting health and holistic development. In 2010, the Central Board of Secondary Education (CBSE) released a school health manual which emphasized promoting wellness and well-being in schools. CBSE, a national-level education board established in 1962 by the Government of India, sets educational standards and guidelines for both private and public schools across the country. Another example is the School Health Program launched in 2018 as part of the *Ayushman Bharat* program, a major healthcare initiative by the Ministry of Health and Family Welfare aiming to improve healthcare access and affordability for vulnerable communities. Its School Health Program emphasizes well-being alongside health, signaling a shift toward expansion of the concept of health. Furthermore, well-being has been integrated into the teacher training package, National Initiative for School Heads' and Teachers' Holistic Advancement (NISHTHA) released by the National Council of Educational Research and Training (NCERT), in 2019. NCERT, an apex institution of the Government of India, serves as a clearinghouse for educational ideas and information and acts as an advisory body on educational matters for both central and state governments. Additionally, the National Education Policy (NEP) 2020 released by the Ministry of Education suggests promoting health and well-being within school settings, further indicating the growing importance of well-being in national-level educational discourse.

Health has been in focus in Indian educational policies since independence, but over time, its scope has gradually expanded to include well-being. As a result, the term "well-being" now appears frequently alongside health in policy documents, reflecting its growing prominence in educational discourse. For example, earlier national education policies such as those of 1968 and 1986 mentioned well-being, but its occurrence was sporadic, appearing only a handful of times in entire documents and often without clear emphasis or definition. In contrast, the National Education Policy 2020 shows a significant increase in the frequency of the term "well-being," suggesting a growing recognition of its importance.

In the context of health-related educational initiatives, two key ministries are involved at the national level: the Ministry of Education is responsible for framing educational policies, while the Ministry of Health and Family Welfare oversees public health policies. For certain national-level initiatives, such as the School Health Program of *Ayushman Bharat*, both ministries collaborate. National-level initiatives aim to promote health and well-being through a standardized framework, generally adopted by CBSE-affiliated schools that follow the NCERT curriculum. At the same time, India's federal structure grants autonomy to states in educational matters, resulting in variations in state policies and how state boards may adopt approaches for promoting well-being in their school settings. As education falls under the Concurrent List of the Indian Constitution, both Union and state governments contribute to the development and execution of education-related policies and initiatives. The central government develops overarching national educational policy frameworks, while state governments tailor and implement these initiatives based on regional requirements and available resources. As a result, while national-level policies offer a broad framework of health and well-being that reflects India's overarching vision, state-level variations highlight diverse approaches shaped by regional contexts, all contributing to the larger landscape of health and well-being in India.

This paper traces the journey of the term "well-being" within Indian educational policies, examining why the focus has expanded from health, alone, to encompass well-being in these policies. It studies what prompted this shift, and what implications it holds for school-level implementation. Further, this paper examines whether the incorporation of well-being in Indian educational policies constitutes a substantive shift or merely a rebranding of existing health initiatives. The scope of the paper is limited to national-level initiatives and their implications. State-level variations are not addressed, except for the Delhi government's *Happiness Curriculum*, which serves as a notable localized effort aimed at integrating well-being within school settings. The paper is divided into the following key sections. The first section delves into the concept of well-being, discussing its definition and significance. The second section traces the journey of how the concept of "health" has gradually expanded to include well-being in various national education policy documents and school health programs of India. The third section analyzes the implementation of health and well-being initiatives across schools, and the fourth section highlights the challenges faced in implementing them in Indian contexts. The fifth section concludes with key arguments and recommendations, addressing identified challenges such as the need for standardized assessment methods to measure well-being and the integration of well-being into core curricula and textbooks.

3.2 Understanding Well-being

In educational policies, the term "well-being" is frequently used alongside "health," underscoring their interrelation. Connection between the two concepts merits closer examination, as it aligns with global discussions that frequently refer to the World Health Organization's definition of health as "a state of complete physical, mental, and social well-being, not merely the absence of disease or infirmity," given in 1948 (WHO, 2020, p. 1). Underdown (2011) appreciates the WHO's expansive view of health for its holistic approach, as it extends understanding of health beyond the physical dimension to encompass emotional, mental, and social dimensions and their interconnections. However, Konu and Matti (2002) argue that WHO's emphasis on well-being in the definition introduces ambiguity, as defining health in terms of well-being blurs the distinction between the two concepts. WHO has also faced criticism for emphasizing "complete well-being" in its definition of health, setting an unachievable ideal of perfect health (Armitage, 2023). Critics argue that WHO's idealistic stance renders health an unattainable goal, questioning the practical applicability of the definition. Schramme (2023) addresses these critiques by suggesting that the term "complete" in the WHO's definition can be interpreted in two ways: qualitatively and quantitatively. A quantitative interpretation implies an ideal of perfect health, which is often unattainable. Alternatively, "complete" can be understood as encompassing all aspects of well-being—physical, mental, and social—without requiring absolute perfection in each area. This distinction can be framed as the difference between aspirational and operational definitions. The quantitative interpretation represents an aspirational ideal, yet an unattainable vision. In contrast, the holistic view moves toward an operational framework. An operational definition, crucial for public policy, requires that concepts are defined in terms of measurable indicators (Ereaut & Whiting, 2008). While the notion of "perfect health" serves as an aspirational target, it may not be practical for policy implementation. In contrast, the holistic interpretation is more suitable for political and public health objectives, as it creates the possibility of setting achievable and measurable goals. While the WHO's 1948 definition has been criticized for its perceived idealism, it has played a pivotal role in recognizing the inextricable link between health and well-being, influencing the contemporary relationship between both concepts.

In addition to health and well-being, the term "wellness" is also actively used, often alongside these concepts in policy discourse. In the academic literature, discussions of health, well-being, and wellness often see health through a deficit-focused framework, rooted in medical interventions and pathology, primarily concerned with identifying diseases and addressing them through treatment, while the notions of well-being and wellness have broader implications. The concept of wellness reflects a shift from a narrowly defined medical perspective to a more expansive and positive understanding of health. Wellness is commonly defined as a multidimensional concept, encompassing various interconnected dimensions like physical, psychological, emotional, social, intellectual, spiritual, occupational, and environmental, all contributing to an individual's overall health. Roscoe (2009) points out that wellness is also a subjective construct, with its dimensions and definitions varying among authors. One of the earliest contributions to the conceptualization of wellness was made by Dunn (1959), who defined wellness as the maximization of health across various dimensions, aiming for harmony of body, mind, and spirit. The subjective nature of wellness, with its multiple definitions and dimensions, possibly contributes to its frequent interchangeable use with well-being, as observed by McCallum and Price (2010). However, scholars like Roscoe (2009) and Ciziceno (2022) emphasize that well-being is a broader concept, encompassing aspects of wellness while maintaining a distinct separation. Ciziceno (2022) argues well-being focuses more on life satisfaction, fulfillment, and subjective experiences, in contrast to wellness. It emphasizes not only the positive dimensions of health but is closely tied to fundamental questions about the human condition and what constitutes a meaningful life, aiming for a good life (Ereaut & Whiting, 2008).

The concept of well-being lacks a universally agreed-upon definition (Carter & Andersen, 2023), reflecting its inherent complexity and subjective nature. Its meaning is shaped by cultural contexts, individual perspectives, and the disciplinary frameworks within which it is examined. For instance, philosophical perspectives may emphasize purpose and meaning, while psychological perspectives often focus on mental health and emotional fulfillment. Cultural influences also play a significant role: some cultures value material success and the pursuit of individual goals, whereas other cultures may prioritize spiritual growth, collective harmony, and shared achievements. Thus, defining and understanding well-being requires a nuanced approach that acknowledges the complex interplay of diverse factors. Graham (2011) describes well-being as a "complex construct that concerns optimal experience and functioning" (p. 4). This notion of optimal functioning is relative rather than absolute, as it is shaped by individual perceptions of their own aspirations. Despite the lack of consensus on its definition, there is widespread agreement on the importance of promoting well-being. Well-being can be understood through two important approaches: hedonic and eudemonic (Carter & Andersen, 2023; Ciziceno, 2022; Graham, 2011; Lindert et al., 2015). The hedonic approach defines well-being in terms of happiness, emphasizing the reduction of pain and discomfort while maximizing pleasure and positive emotions. In contrast, the eudemonic approach focuses on living a meaningful and fulfilling life by fostering personal growth and self-realization.

The subjective nature of well-being presents significant measurement challenges because aspirations, values, and cultural contexts all influence how well-being is experienced and expressed (Lindert et al., 2015). To operationalize well-being and move beyond these definitional challenges, researchers have developed measurable frameworks. One prominent example is Diener and Ryan's (2009) tripartite model of subjective well-being which combines three elements: life satisfaction, positive affect, and negative affect. The element of life satisfaction in the model reflects focus on the meaning and long-term well-being derived from personal growth and fulfillment, while positive affect and negative affect align with emphasis on maximizing positive emotions (like joy and contentment) and minimizing negative emotions (like sadness and pain), thus integrating both hedonic and eudemonic approaches (Lindert et al., 2015). More relevant in the educational context is the holistic model developed by McCallum and Price (2010), which promotes holistic well-being by ensuring the well-being of learners, educators, and the community. It identifies key components and strategies, including: positive relationships (building and sustaining healthy relationships), strengths development (nurturing individual and group strengths), positive communication (establishing effective and safe communication strategies), positive behavior (promoting a sense of belonging), positive emotions (nurturing emotional well-being), and positive leadership (fostering well-being through democratic leadership).

Educational policies embrace multidimensional approaches to well-being to address different aspects of child development. For instance, Graham (2011) outlines six dimensions of child well-being: "material well-being, health and safety, education, peer and family, behavior and risks, and young people's own subjective sense of well-being" (p. 7). This comprehensive framework, often referred to as the child-centered approach, aims to holistically support the overall development of children. Similarly, Ministry of Education in India has integrated 11 themes to promote health and well-being:

> growing up healthy, emotional well-being and mental health, interpersonal relationships, values and citizenship, gender equality, nutrition, health and sanitation, prevention and management of substance abuse, promotion of healthy lifestyle, reproductive health and HIV prevention, safety and security against violence and injuries, [and the] promotion of safe use of internet and social media behavior. (NCERT, 2020, p. xxiii)

This multidimensional framework of health and well-being aims to encompass different aspects of a child's life. However, the broad inclusion of well-being, as endorsed by NCERT, has led to a situation in which almost everything falls under the umbrella of well-being. The rationale behind limiting the themes to 11 remains unclear: why not include more or fewer? The fundamental issue with such a broad conceptualization is that any attempt to establish boundaries or prioritize certain aspects of well-being appears arbitrary. For example, if inclusivity is the guiding principle, then there are always new dimensions to consider other than gender, such as language, race, caste, or even socioeconomic status. Determining where to draw the line is a formidable challenge that risks marginalizing certain groups even with an inclusive framework. Without a structured framework to delineate its scope, well-being risks becoming an overly broad and ambiguous concept.

The following section outlines the development of educational policies in India, tracing the gradual expansion of the concept of health within the education system. Initially, health-focused educational policies and initiatives emphasized on basic medical services, sanitation, nutrition, and health education. Over time, the concept of health has aligned with broader educational goals, leading to incorporation of concepts such as personality development, life skills, and overall well-being. Eventually, the 11-theme framework of health and well-being was introduced, reflecting adoption of a more comprehensive approach. The section highlights the key milestones in the integration of well-being in education policies.

3.3 Tracing Well-being in Educational Policies and School Health Initiatives

The Indian government has identified schools as critical platforms for health interventions, as a significant portion of the population spends a substantial part of their formative years in schools (NIOS, 2019). The report of the Health Survey and Planning Committee (1959–61) published by the Ministry of Health emphasized the importance of integrating schools with primary healthcare centers within the public health distribution system to improve standards of health and nutrition among children. As primary institutions for student development, schools offer a strategic entry point for interventions, making them a cornerstone of public health strategy.

India has faced significant public health challenges among children, such as high rates of child mortality, malnutrition, diarrhea, pneumonia, anemia, and infectious diseases (NCERT, 2006d). In response, school health programs were developed as early as the 1940s to address these pressing concerns. These school health programs provided a framework for government action within the domain of public health, targeting issues like nutrition, infection control, and physical growth and development (NCERT, 2006d). The 1940s school health programs emphasized four key elements: access to medical care within schools, nutritive school lunches, a safe and healthy learning environment, and the learning of health and physical education (NCERT, 2005). These foundational recommendations catered to India's basic health needs and became the basis for subsequent school health initiatives. Over the period of time, various committees such as Bhore Committee and 1953 Secondary Education Commission aligned themselves with these early recommendations, integrating and expanding them to address broader health concerns.

The Health Planning and Development Committee, also known as the Bhore Committee, established under the chairmanship of Indian civil servant Sir Joseph William Bhore in pre-independent India, submitted its report in 1946. It conducted surveys on the health conditions of the Indian population and existing health infrastructures and made recommendations for their betterment. The committee is well-regarded for its pivotal role in shaping health provisions as well as in setting benchmarks for subsequent health-related policy recommendations. The committee made significant recommendations to promote health in schools (NCERT, 2006d). In its recommendations, it continued to emphasize the four key elements of the school health program: medical care, school lunches, hygienic learning environments, and physical education. Additionally, it placed greater emphasis on promoting a culture of sports, games, and other recreational activities that encourage physical engagement among students. This focus on promoting sports was intended to support the physical development of students.

The Secondary Education Commission report released by the Ministry of Education, Government of India (1953) continued to emphasize the four key elements of the 1940s school health program and highlighted the importance of integrating health with education. What stands out is its alignment with the broader objective of personality development. It underscored the idea that health-related initiatives should contribute to the overall development of students. This comprehensive approach laid the foundation for linking health promotion with broader educational goals. The report emphasized health education as a means to promote good health habits and introduced the concept of holistic growth. Holistic growth, as defined in this report, involved development not only at the personal levels (physical, mental, emotional), but also at the social levels. By linking health with holistic growth, the report advanced the idea that education should encompass the complete development of individuals across multiple dimensions.

In 1968, the first national-level education policy was released by the Ministry of Education. In the domain of health, it briefly addressed the inclusion of games and sports in schools, emphasizing physical fitness. This limited focus was due to the different priorities of the time, which centered on national development and nation-building. As the country's first post-independence education policy, its primary focus was on establishing a standardized national education system. The 1968 policy aimed to educate individuals who could contribute to the country's growth and prosperity by developing a skilled human resource base. Its objectives, shaped by the needs of a newly independent nation, also guided the formulation of the National Curriculum Framework (NCF) 1975. Both NEP 1968 and NCF 1975 demonstrated limited attention to health initiatives, as their primary focus lay in fostering national integration, modernizing society, promoting social justice, and cultivating moral and spiritual values. Early education policies in newly independent India primarily focused on collective aims, emphasizing nation-building, societal integration, and cultivating responsible citizens who could contribute to the country's growth and prosperity (Ministry of Education, Government of India, 1968; NCERT 1975).

The National Education Policy (NEP) of 1986 kept the nation-building aspect of earlier NEP 1968, and also included the concept of holistic development. It ensured that education remained not merely a tool for national progress but also became a means to foster the personal growth and development of individuals. The NEP 1986 defined holistic development as encompassing physical, mental, emotional, social, and moral dimensions, reflecting a broader understanding of education's role in helping the overall growth of individuals. However, references to well-being in 1986 NEP remained sparse and were addressed in a general context. What stands out is the policy's commitment to health and holistic development that laid a foundation for future education policies, gradually expanding the scope of health to include broader concepts of well-being (MHRD, Government of India, 1986). This shift toward holistic development in the 1986 education policy was further solidified in the NCF of 2005, which was based on the same policy. The NCF 2005 explicitly introduces and frequently used terms like "mental well-being," "emotional well-being," "social well-being," and "physical well-being": a notable departure from earlier curriculum documents, including the National Curriculum for Elementary and Secondary Education (NCESE) in 1988 (NCERT, 1988). NCESE 1988, which was also based on the NEP 1986, did not mention well-being. In NCF 2005, the term "well-being" is discussed in conjunction with mental, emotional, social, and physical aspects, reflecting a broader and more integrated understanding of the term. The conception of well-being in NCF 2005 underscores its commitment to the holistic development of children, reinforcing the policy's broader educational goals (NCERT, 2005).

The expansion of the concept of health occurred not only in educational policies but also within school health programs. In 2010, Central Board of Secondary Education (CBSE) released the *Comprehensive School Health Teachers Activity Manual* in collaboration with the World Health Organization (WHO) India. CBSE's (2010) school health program revolved around six key initiatives: understanding one's body, maintaining a balanced diet and proper nutrition, practicing personal hygiene, ensuring cleanliness and sanitation, engaging in regular physical activity for fitness, fostering responsibility through safe behaviors, and adopting important life skills. Notably, the inclusion of safe behaviors and life skills represents a significant expansion from earlier school health programs. Safe behaviors ensure students understand behaviors that promote safety on both physical and mental levels, such as preventing accidents and maintaining emotional health. Life skills education equips students with essential abilities like critical thinking, empathy, and other abilities that contribute to personal growth, resilience, and effective problem solving in everyday situations. Life skills are important for navigating challenges and essential for leading a fulfilling life. CBSE's health manual reflects the understanding of health as a multidimensional concept influenced by biological, physical, psychological, social, economic, and cultural factors.

Health has been a topic of discussion in school health programs in India, but well-being was not given the same level of importance. For instance, the 2006 paper by NCERT entitled *Health and Physical Education* provides an overview of health programs that have existed within the education system in India. Interestingly, the paper does not mention the term "well-being" even though it focuses on health-related initiatives in schools. This omission highlights that the term "well-being" was until recently not tightly associated with health-focused programs in schools.

The 2018 school health program launched under the School Health and Wellness component of the *Ayushman Bharat* marked a significant shift by integrating well-being more prominently into school health programs. Under this program, the NCERT released three key documents: *Curriculum on Health and Wellness of School-going Adolescents, Training and Resource Material of Health and Wellness of School-going Children,* and the *Facilitator Guide for School Health Program.* These documents marked a significant shift from earlier school health program materials by placing well-being and wellness at the forefront, highlighting their integral roles in students' overall development. For instance, the *Curriculum on Health and Wellness of School-going Adolescents* includes "wellness" in its title. The Curriculum also aims "to enhance health and well-being of school going children" (NCERT, 2018, p. 4). Meanwhile, the *Training and Resource Material of Health and Wellness of School-going Children* emphasizes "health and well-being as an important investment in children for their overall development" (NCERT, 2020, p. 9). These documents emphasize gender inclusivity, preventive care, emotional intelligence, life skills, and digital literacy to empower students with knowledge, values, and skills necessary for holistic development. They primarily bring together various aspects of health education and unify and integrate existing initiatives and topics under the broader theme of well-being. For instance, topics like HIV awareness, which were traditionally included in the subject of Biology, are now consolidated within these documents.

The *Curriculum on Health and Wellness of School-going Adolescents* introduces a comprehensive framework centered around 11 areas to support the health and well-being of children. It emphasizes that health, wellness, and life skills are essential for the holistic development of school-children. This comprehensive framework does not introduce entirely new elements, but rather organizes and aligns already-existing efforts under a cohesive framework of health and well-being. Earlier health-related initiatives in education were fragmented, and NCERT (2006d) specifically sought to align programs related to adolescent education programs, health, and environmental safety implemented by several bodies such as CBSE, NCERT itself, and other State Boards. The Health and Wellness Curriculum of NCERT builds on this effort by attempting to unify these diverse concepts under a single cohesive theme. This integration has been a longstanding goal of building a more coordinated and comprehensive approach to health and well-being in education.

The emphasis on holistic development has continued to shape education policies since 1986. For instance, recent initiatives such as CBSE's *Handbook on Joyful Learning (CBSE,* 2020*)* and Delhi government's *Happiness Curriculum,* published by the State Council of Educational Research and Training (SCERT, DoE, 2019), illustrate an emphasis on holistic development. The *Joyful Learning* initiative focuses on fostering joy to improve academic achievements. It emphasizes that cultivating positive emotions in children leads to both individual growth and societal benefit by developing knowledgeable, productive, and emotionally healthy individuals. While the *Joyful Learning* handbook aims to center education around the learner, it does not explicitly engage with the concept of well-being. In contrast, the *Happiness Curriculum* explicitly emphasizes health and well-being in its framework by recognizing happiness as an overarching framework for enhancing learning outcomes and promoting individual health and well-being. This signifies a noteworthy expansion of well-being into state-level educational policies. While both frameworks share a child-centered pedagogical approach, their foci differ slightly. The *Happiness Curriculum* aims to balance individual and collective goals, identifying happiness, itself, as a fundamental objective, both for personal well-being and societal harmony. Meanwhile, *Joyful Learning* is more oriented toward creating an emotionally positive environment that enhances academic performance. Together, these initiatives underscore the importance of integrating emotional well-being into education to nurture well-rounded individuals who contribute meaningfully to society.

The latest National Education Policy (NEP) released in 2020 frequently mentions well-being and wellness in conjunction with health, using phrases like "health and well-being" or "health and wellness" (MHRD, GoI, 2020). Analysis of the term health across the education policy documents and committee reports reveals a progressive expansion of its scope, transcending its original narrow definition. Historically, health primarily connoted a physical dimension, but its meaning has since broadened to include emotional, mental, and social aspects, exemplified by the incorporation of wellness and well-being. This inclusive expansion is apparent in NCERT documents, where health now encompasses a multidimensional approach. The integration of well-being into the concept of health underscores this shift, acknowledging the interconnectedness of various aspects of human health. This term's inclusion demonstrates a continuous refinement, rather than a sudden shift, reflecting an increasingly comprehensive understanding of human health.

The concept of well-being has evolved into an expansive multifaceted framework that encompasses nearly every aspect of education. It has grown so broad in scope that it aligns seamlessly with the ideals of a progressive welfare society. Traditional concerns such as inequality, which have long been a focus of Indian education as reflected in the National Curriculum Framework 2005 and subsequent textbooks (Syeed, 2018), are now integrated with discussions of well-being. The latest 2018 curriculum on health and wellness further extends this integration, addressing constitutional values like liberty, justice, fraternity, and human dignity under value-based education (NCERT, 2018). As a result, any initiative aimed at promoting social inclusivity or fostering human flourishing can be contextualized within this paradigm, framing well-being as an umbrella concept that pervades every facet of education. It has become a catch-all term, risking its reduction to mere rhetoric in policy action.

Meanwhile, the increased usage of the term "well-being" is not accompanied by conceptual clarity or uniformity. For example, the terms "health" and "well-being" are often used interchangeably in policy documents and their usage lacks consistency. At times, the focus is on "physical health," while in other instances, it shifts to "physical well-being." Similarly, references are made to "mental health" or "mental well-being." This inconsistent terminology creates confusion about when the term "health" is appropriate and when "well-being" should be used, highlighting the absence of a clear conceptual distinction between the two. Similarly, the documents released under the *Ayushman Bharat* School Health Program reveal similar patterns of inconsistency. The *Facilitator Guide and Curriculum on Health and Wellness* frequently refer to "wellness" and "well-being," yet the terms are often used interchangeably without a clear conceptual distinction. For instance, the *Facilitator Guide* in its initial sections refers to "well-being" but later abruptly shifts to "wellness," treating both terms as interchangeable. Similarly, despite the fact that the title of the document, the *Curriculum on Health and Wellness*, emphasizes "health and wellness," its key goals and objectives are framed in terms of "health and well-being," reflecting yet another inconsistency. This inconsistency in use of the terms like "health," "well-being," and "wellness" is evident across various documents. This suggests a blurred distinction between these concepts and a lack of clarity or coherence in how these concepts are constructed and communicated across different policy frameworks.

While analyzing policy documents, a noticeable inconsistency emerges in the emphasis of the term "well-being." For instance, "well-being" is discussed in the *National Curriculum Framework for School Education* 2023 (National Steering Commitee for National Curriculum Frameworks, 2023), while it is notably absent from the *National Curriculum Framework for Foundational Stage 2022 (National Steering Committee for National Curriculum Frameworks,* 2022*)*. This is when both frameworks are based on NEP 2020. This is interesting because "well-being" is talked about at the Secondary stage but not at the Primary stage, even when there is established research in favor of early intervention to promote health and well-being in individuals (Underdown, 2006). A similar pattern is observed in NCERT's *Learning Outcomes* document, where the term "well-being" is mentioned for the Secondary stage but not at the Primary stage. For instance, in NCERT's *Learning Outcomes at the Secondary Stage* released in December 2019 (NCERT, 2019b), the term "well-being" is mentioned in various contexts such as physical well-being, health and well-being, social well-being, and mental and emotional well-being.[1] However, the term "well-being" does not appear in NCERT's earlier document entitled *Learning Outcomes at the Elementary Stage,* published in April 2017 (NCERT, 2017).[2] This variation in the frequency and context of its use highlights a lack of coherence in addressing well-being across educational stages and policies. The concept of well-being is inconsistently addressed across educational documents and policies and unevenly prioritized across policy initiatives.

This section has traced the trajectory of the term "well-being" within Indian health-related educational policy. It highlights that the term remains vague and inconsistent, with a broad framework that risks making it a catch-all term. The next section focuses on the implementation of health and well-being in schools through various initiatives.

3.4 From Policy to Practice: Health and Well-being Implementation

Educators play a crucial role in implementing well-being initiatives, a fact widely acknowledged in educational discourse (NCERT, 2006d). Therefore, efforts to enhance well-being in schools often start with equipping teachers with the necessary knowledge and skills. Under the *Ayushman Bharat* program, existing teachers are appointed and trained as Health and Wellness Ambassadors to deliver health and well-being education. These ambassadors act as facilitators and coordinators, organizing expert talks and related activities, as well as delivering an hour-long weekly class focusing on themes of health and well-being (NCERT, 2019a).

Despite the development of training manuals and the recognition of teachers' central role, a significant gap exists between policy and practical implementation. By 2023, nearly 3 years after the launch of the *Ayushman Bharat* School Health and Wellness Program, less than half of India's states had initiated the recommended weekly classes. Challenges contributing to the shortfall in program implementation vary among states. In Delhi, for instance, teachers are overburdened with implementing multiple curricula such as the *Happiness Curriculum*, *Desh Bhakti Curriculum*, and *Entrepreneurship Mindset Curriculum*, leading to the perception of Health and Wellness education as an additional activity (Porecha, 2023). Consequently, program implementation is undermined by teacher shortages or overburdening, leading to disinterest and the perception of health and well-being education as an additional burden on schools.

[1] This comprehensive guide outlines key curricular expectations, pedagogical processes, and learning outcomes for classes IX and X, enabling educators and other stakeholders to understand and achieve these goals.

[2] This document also serves as a reference guide for educators to assess learning achievements and competencies of students but for classes I to VIII.

Apart from the *Training and Resource Material: Health and Wellness of School-going Children* (NCERT, 2020), in 2019 NCERT published a NISHTHA teacher training module focused on health and well-being. NISHTHA, the National initiative for School Heads' and Teacher' Holistic Advancement is a capacity building program launched by the Ministry of Education to improve the quality of school education through integrated teacher training. NCERT has emphasized the importance of teacher training—both pre-service and in-service—to address the unique requirements of health education. NISHTHA Module-5 (NCERT, 2019c) equips teachers with the skills to identify signs of distress among students and support their well-being. It has elements of strength-based approaches to promoting well-being. There are two ways to promote well-being: strength-based and deficit-focused approaches (Graham, 2011). The deficit-focused approach emphasizes what is lacking, while the strength-based approach focuses on empowering students by building their capability for well-being. The strength-based approach is reflected in Module-5 (NCERT, 2019c), as it encourages educators to ask learners to discuss in groups and identify and articulate verbal expressions that indicate a state of well-being, distress, or illness. This reflexive activity aims to create awareness among students and equip them to recognize signs of emotional and mental states in themselves and in others. The training aims to equip teachers with strategies to guide these discussions effectively. For instance, one of the methods outlined in the manual involves using linguistic tools to help students articulate their feelings and identify potential signs of distress. An example of this is the theme of violence, where a pictorial representation is provided in the curriculum. This depiction is discussed with students, followed by questions and activities designed to help them understand violence and develop the language to talk about it. Such approaches are designed to foster a supportive classroom environment where early signs of emotional discomfort can be addressed.

It is important to note that teachers do not simply implement policies in a mechanical manner; rather, they bring their own interpretations, experiences, and values, which can influence how they adopt, adapt, or even reject certain aspects of the policies. This is particularly significant when considering strength-based frameworks, as educators are central to translating these concepts into classroom practice. In this context, an optimal student–teacher ratio becomes essential for effective implementation of the concept of well-being (Konu & Matti, 2002). When teachers can provide adequate attention, support, and engagement to each student, it fosters a more conducive environment for holistic growth. However, Indian schools often have a higher teacher–student ratio (Education GPS, OECD, 2022). This structural limitation poses a significant challenge: no matter how progressive the concepts may be, foundational issues like overcrowded classrooms hinder their practical application. This contradicts the fundamental principles of well-being promotion, as teachers, recognized as essential components of the school community (McCallum & Price, 2010), cannot effectively promote well-being when their own well-being is compromised.

In India, textbooks serve as primary tools for implementing education policy. NCERT is the key institution responsible for creating textbooks at the national level.

While various textbooks are used across different schools, NCERT textbooks are particularly significant and are primarily used in CBSE government schools. Other educational boards, especially state-level boards, develop their textbooks to align with their curricula. Despite the presence of these diverse resources, NCERT textbooks are highly regarded (Advani, 2009) and widely used, reaching approximately 15% of school students nationwide (Kumar, 2011). Their widespread distribution and government production make them more accessible for students from various socioeconomic backgrounds. NCERT's 1962 report (Syeed, 2018) highlighted the unique challenges faced by the nation, specifically a large population with significant rural and under-privileged sections. In such a context, textbooks were assigned a central role as tools for disseminating knowledge in educational institutions (NCERT, 2005). This over-reliance on textbooks is often referred to as the "textbook problem," where the textbook effectively becomes the curriculum, rather than being one of many instructional resources. They are popular in classroom settings and have become synonymous with the curriculum, itself. Thus, to assess whether policies are effectively implemented, or aligned with intended outcomes, one must closely examine the content and structure of textbooks.

A review of the NCERT's high school textbooks based on the NCF (2005) reveals that the concept of well-being is predominantly confined to Health and Physical Education textbooks, which were introduced in 2016 (NCERT, 2016). The core subjects textbooks (English, Indian Language, Social Science, Science, Mathematics) do not even mention the term "well-being" (NCERT, 2006a, b, c; NCERT 2007a,b). This lack of integration of well-being into the core curriculum suggests that it remains an additional component rather than a foundational principle. NCERT (2006d) recommended that health education textbooks be taught at all levels and be given equal importance alongside core academic subjects. Furthermore, the recommendation proposed making physical education a compulsory subject up to the 10th grade, treating it as on par with core academic subjects. Despite the NCF 2005 also recommending that Health and Physical Education be compulsory subjects, these subjects are still not treated on par with core subjects (NCERT, 2006d). Health and Physical Education are frequently treated as supplementary rather than core subjects. Given India's diverse population, the true test of its reach lies in its integration within core subjects and the emphasis on Health and Physical Education. Although this integrated approach is a key recommendation of *Ayushman Bharat's* School Health Program (NCERT, 2019a) it is yet to be fully implemented, as the new NCERT textbooks have not been published. Its successful implementation will depend on various factors, including policy priorities and resource allocation, given that curriculum change is inherently a political activity (Syeed, 2018). Therefore, whether health and well-being will be effectively integrated into mainstream subjects remains uncertain and may be influenced by shifting priorities and practical challenges.

This section analyzed the implementation strategies for well-being education, with a particular focus on *Ayushman Bharat's* School Health Program. The subsequent section will address the wider challenges encountered by schools in promoting health and well-being across the country.

3.5 Building Well-being in Schools: Challenges and Concerns

School health programs have been launched to address critical health concerns, yet persistent challenges hinder their effectiveness. In post-independent India, poor nutritional status and high prevalence of communicable diseases necessitated targeted interventions. Recognizing that mere awareness about a nutritious diet was insufficient when many children lacked access to food, free school lunches were incorporated into these programs. However, implementation of these lunch programs was uneven across states. While Tamil Nadu successfully implemented a robust mid-day meal scheme, most states only adopted it in a fragmented manner, reflecting diverse local contexts and resource constraints. To address this inconsistency and ensure nationwide coverage, the Government of India's (GoI) centrally sponsored Mid-day Meal Scheme was launched in 1995. Even then, implementation remained inconsistent until a landmark Supreme Court judgment in 2001 mandated its introduction in all primary schools within 6 months. This directive transformed the program into a critical initiative for addressing hunger, a major contributor to child malnutrition. Nevertheless, the Mid-day Meal Scheme continues to grapple with significant challenges. Food inflation impacts meal quality and quantity, and there is a lack of corresponding budgetary increases to compensate for these rising costs (Dash et al., 2024). Additionally, inadequate funding, logistical difficulties, and disparities in food quality and distribution further limit its impact.

Despite the implementation of several strategies within school health programs, including the crucial Mid-day Meal Scheme, the overall performance of these initiatives remains inadequate. The 2019–21 National Family Health Survey (NFHS) data reveal a concerning trend: while child mortality and malnutrition have generally declined, rates of anemia have increased (Raushan et al., 2022). This persistent anemia, among other health issues, indicates that the collective impact of school health programs is not meeting the intended goals. Moreover, marginalized caste groups, particularly Scheduled Castes (SC) and Scheduled Tribes (ST), continue to bear the highest burden of mortality and malnutrition, with minimal improvement over the decades (Acharya, 2018). Contributing to this is the fragmented implementation and limited coordination between the Ministry of Health and the Ministry of Education, which has resulted in these programs functioning primarily as vertical initiatives under the Ministry of Health, with minimal integration into the broader educational framework (NCERT, 2006a, b, c, d). Further, it is crucial to note that these initiatives are primarily limited to government schools. Approximately half of India's total students study in private unaided schools, which operate with significant autonomy and are largely outside the purview of these programs (Jakasania et al., 2023). Private schools may contribute to promoting school health, but their efforts are mostly limited to high-fee institutions, making them inaccessible to broader masses.

Suboptimal performance of school health programs raises critical concerns about India's ability to successfully integrate well-being as an outcome within the school system. If school health programs continue to face challenges in addressing issues like malnutrition and anemia, as evidenced by fragmented implementation and minimal improvement in health outcomes for marginalized communities, the effective prioritization and achievement of well-being—a far more complex and multifaceted goal—becomes a significant undertaking. Well-being encompassing cognitive, psychological, social, physical, and material dimensions demands a level of systemic integration and equitable resource distribution that has proven elusive in past health initiatives. The entrenched disparities indicate that while policy initiatives aimed at improving health outcomes are being implemented, they are not reaching all communities equitably. Thus, achieving a comprehensive well-being framework, and making it a tangible outcome within schools, necessitates not only robust assessment mechanisms but also a deeper understanding of the social determinants of health, including caste-based disparities and resource inequalities.

India currently lacks a standardized framework for assessing well-being among school students. Traditionally, child health has been measured using metrics such as child mortality rates and disease incidence and prevalence. These parameters, while crucial, focus primarily on tangible and specified epidemiologic outcomes, making them easier to quantify and track over time. However, when a broader and more abstract concept like well-being is introduced into the framework of health, it presents significant challenges. Unlike disease or mortality rates, well-being encompasses subjective and multidimensional factors that are harder to define and measure. The introduction of well-being into health policies requires a rethinking of measurement frameworks. Traditional epidemiologic indicators, while still essential, must be supplemented with qualitative and holistic approaches: inclusion of well-being calls for innovative tools and methodologies to measure its objective and subjective dimensions, ensuring that well-being is not just an aspirational concept but a measurable and achievable goal.

While some initiatives have touched upon well-being, they remain limited in scope. For instance, the Global School-based Student Health Survey (GSHS), conducted in collaboration with the World Health Organization (WHO) and the US Centers for Disease Control and Prevention, was carried out in India in 2007. This survey, which included CBSE schools, aimed to provide data on health-related behaviors among students, including mental health indicators (CDC et al., 2007). However, it did not comprehensively address broader well-being components like cognitive, social, or material well-being. India could learn from the 2015 well-being framework used in the Program for International Student Assessment (PISA), conducted by the Organization for Economic Co-operation and Development (OECD). However, India's reluctance to participate in international assessment further complicates the situation. India participated in PISA 2009 which tested students' skills in mathematics, science, and reading but performed poorly, ranking 73rd out of 74 countries (Mohanty, 2025). The poor performance led India to withdraw from subsequent PISA assessments, citing cultural biases and the non-alignment of the test with the Indian education system. However, this decision also meant that India missed out on valuable insights that could have been gained from the PISA 2015 well-being framework. It assesses well-being across five dimensions: cognitive, psychological, physical, social, and material (Borgonovi & Pál, 2016) and could have provided valuable data to guide policy developments. The absence of an assessment framework hampers efforts to evaluate policies aiming to address student well-being.

Beyond the systemic challenges and the absence of an assessment framework, the very culture cultivated within Indian schools, characterized by intense academic pressure and competition, often stands in opposition to promoting well-being. Education in India is highly valued, with academic excellence often seen as the primary determinant of success. As a result, schools place significant emphasis on academic performance, sometimes beginning as early as primary school. This intense focus on scholastic achievement fosters a highly competitive environment, where students are constantly measured against their peers (Pathak, 2024). Recognizing the pressures created by such a culture, policymakers introduced a comprehensive grading system into the high school level. This reform aimed to reduce direct competition by eliminating ranks and absolute scores, instead promoting grade-based evaluation of students' performance. However, while this change sought to alleviate some of the competitiveness within schools, the persistence of high-stakes competitive exams after grade 12 continues to reinforce the culture of academic pressure. Entrance exams for prestigious institutions, such as engineering and medical colleges, are particularly intense due to the limited number of available seats, making these exams a source of immense pressure for students (Gupta & Pandit, 2024). The significance of these exams is further amplified by the widespread media coverage of exam toppers—students who secure the highest score in board exams or competitive entrance tests like the IIT-JEE for engineering and the NEET for medical admissions. This competitive environment is perhaps best exemplified by Kota, a city in Rajasthan known as India's coaching hub, where thousands of students relocate each year to undergo rigorous training for these exams. In such an environment, where the goal is securing a top rank rather than fostering a love for learning, it becomes increasingly difficult for schools to fully embrace and implement the concept of well-being.

3.6 Conclusion

Well-being is frequently mentioned along with health in official education-related documents, highlighting its tight association with health-related concepts and initiatives. The trajectory of Indian education policies highlights a gradual yet significant expansion of the concept of health, moving from a narrow medical perspective, to a holistic, child-centered approach. Over time, policies have moved beyond addressing physical health through medical interventions, to incorporating mental, emotional, and social well-being. The gradual expansion of the concept of health is reflected in key official documents, such as the 1953 *Secondary Education Commission* report, the 1968 and 1986 *National Education Policies*, the 2005 *National Curriculum Framework*, and the 2020 *National Education Policy*. The recent initiative of the School Health Program under the *Ayushman Bharat* (2018) reinforces the trend of expanding health-related initiatives in school education. Traditionally, school health programs were limited to medical services, sanitation, hygiene, and physical education. Building on this, the *Ayushman Bharat* has further broadened the scope of school health programs to include citizenship values, gender inclusivity, safe behaviors, and interpersonal relationships, all under the umbrella of health and well-being.

Well-being has emerged as an important concept in Indian education, yet its implementation is hampered by conceptual ambiguity. Policy documents often conflate "wellness" and "well-being," lacking a clear framework. It creates conceptual ambiguity that hinders effective implementation. This is exemplified by the *Ayushman Bharat* School Health Program, where well-being is emphasized in curriculum, but the operational guidelines focus primarily on wellness (MoHFW & MHRD, 2018), highlighting a critical disconnect. Furthermore, the broad scope of well-being risks it becoming a catch-all term for any initiative related to health or education. To address this challenge, it is essential to distinguish between the philosophical aspirations of well-being and its operational definition, as analyzed within UK government documentation (Ereaut & Whiting, 2008). While philosophically, well-being is a holistic vision, its operationalization requires concrete indicators and assessment frameworks. The inherent gap between these two aspects requires continuous negotiation and refinement. Currently, the designation of teachers as "Health and Wellness Ambassadors" to deliver weekly sessions—though well-intentioned—is limited by the competitive and exam-oriented education system, marginalizing well-being as a supplementary activity. Integrating well-being into core curricula and textbooks, as recommended by the *Ayushman Bharat* program and historically effective for other concepts, offers a solution. To address this, textbooks as well as examinations should incorporate well-being-related questions and scenarios, embedding it within the standard teaching and assessment structure. This integration, however, hinges on political will and prioritization. Ultimately, while India's education policies have made considerable strides in broadening the scope of student health and well-being, ensuring their effective implementation remains a critical challenge.

Beyond the integration of well-being into curricula, a critical need exists for developing tailored surveys to assess the effectiveness of well-being policies. Systematic research and learning from existing frameworks, such as the PISA well-being scale, could help in developing a comprehensive assessment model suited to India's context. Such surveys would allow policymakers to evaluate the progress of policies and identify areas for improvement. While training manuals and professional development aim to equip teachers with necessary skills, their effectiveness is often undermined by workload and lack of individualized student attention.

Addressing these structural barriers, including the high student–teacher ratio and excessive teacher workload, is essential to translating these well-being principles into practical and meaningful outcomes for students. Ultimately, effective implementation requires sustained efforts, clear policy language, and a consistent, well-defined framework that bridges the gap between aspiration and operation, and that does not confuse wellness with well-being. Recognizing the unique challenges posed by India's societal diversity and competitive academic culture, the introduction of well-being concepts could be a crucial first step toward lasting change.

References

Acharya, S. S. (2018). Health equity in India: An examination through the lens of social exclusion. *Journal of Social Inclusion Studies, 4*(1), 104–130. https://doi.org/10.1177/2394481118774489

Advani, S. (2009). *Schooling the national imagination: Education, English, and the Indian modern*. Oxford University Press. https://doi.org/10.1093/acprof:oso/9780198062752.001.0001

Armitage, R. (2023). The WHO'S definition of health: A baby to be retrieved from the bathwater? *The British Journal of General Practice, 73*(727), 70–71. https://doi.org/10.3399/bjgp23x731841

Borgonovi, F., & Pál, J. (2016). *A framework for the analysis of student well-being in the PISA 2015 study: Being 15 in 2015*. OECD Education Working Papers No. 140.

Carter, S., & Andersen, C. (2023). *Wellbeing in educational contexts* (2nd ed.). University of Southern Queensland. https://usq.pressbooks.pub/wellbeing/

CBSE. (2010). *Revised school health manual: Comprehensive school health teacher's activity, Vol. 1*. https://cbseacademic.nic.in/web_material/HealthManual/HEALTH%20MANUAL%20VOL%201.pdf

CBSE. (2020). *Handbook of joyful learning*. https://cbseacademic.nic.in/web_material/Manuals/handbook-joyful.pdf

Centers for Disease Control and Prevention (CDC), Central Board of Secondary Education (India), & World Health Organization (WHO). (2007). *India global school-based student health survey 2007*. World Health Organization. https://extranet.who.int/ncdsmicrodata/index.php/catalog/41/get-microdata

Ciziceno, M. (2022). The conceptions of quality of life, wellness and well-being: A literature review. In P. Corvo & F. M. Verde (Eds.), *Sport and quality of life: Practices, habits and lifestyles* (pp. 11–27). Springer. https://doi.org/10.1007/978-3-030-93092-9_2

Dash, J., Saurabh, S., & Ira, D. (2024). India's high food inflation leaves less in lunch boxes of poor school children. *Reuters*. https://www.reuters.com/world/india/indias-high-food-inflation-leaves-less-lunch-boxes-poor-school-children-2024-10-11/

Diener, E., & Ryan, K. (2009). Subjective well-being: A general overview. *South Africa Journal of Psychology, 39*(4), 391–406. https://doi.org/10.1177/008124630903900402

Dunn, H. L. (1959). High-level wellness for man and society. *American journal of public health and the nation's health, 49*(6), 786–792. https://doi.org/10.2105/ajph.49.6.786

Education GPS, OECD. (2022). *Ratio of student to teaching staff (OECD indicators on the Learning Environment)*. https://gpseducation.oecd.org

Ereaut, G., & Whiting, R. (2008). *What do we mean by 'well-being'? And why might it matter?*. Report Research DCSF-RW073 prepared for the Department for Children, Schools, and Families, London, UK. https://dera.ioe.ac.uk/id/eprint/8572/1/dcsf-rw073%20v2.pdf

Graham, A. (2011). *Strengthening young people's social and emotional wellbeing*. Background Briefing Series, no. 7 prepared for the Centre for children and young people, Southern Cross University, Lismore.

Gupta, K., & Pandit, A. (2024). Impact of competitive exam on anxiety and stress level of students studying in senior secondary schools. *International Journal for Innovative Research in Multidisciplinary Field, 10*(5), 97–102. https://www.ijirmf.com/wp-content/uploads/IJIRMF202405014-min.pdf

Jakasania, A., Lahariya, C., Pandya, C., Raut, A. V., Sharma, R., Mundra, A., Kapoor, J. P., Khajuria, S., & Gupta, S. S. (2023). School health services in India: Status, challenges, and the way forward. *Indian Journal of Pediatrics, 90*(Suppl 1), 116–124. https://doi.org/10.1007/s12098-023-04852-x

Kilgour, L., Matthews, N., Christian, P., & Shire, J. (2015). Health literacy in schools: Prioritising health and well-being issues through the curriculum. *Sport, Education and Society, 20*(4), 485–500. https://doi.org/10.1080/13573322.2013.769948

Konu, A., & Matti, R. (2002). Well-being in schools: A conceptual model. *Health Promotion International, 17*(1), 79–87. https://doi.org/10.1093/heapro/17.1.79

Kumar, K. (2011). Curriculum reforms in India. In K. N. Pannikar & M. B. Nair (Eds.), *Emerging trends in higher education: Concepts and practices* (pp. 156–168). Dorling Kindersley.

Lindert, J., Bain, P. A., Kubzansky, L. D., & Stein, C. (2015). Well-being measurement and the WHO health policy health 2010: Systematic review of measurement scales. *The European Journal of Public Health, 25*(4), 731–740. https://doi.org/10.1093/eurpub/cku193

McCallum, F., & Price, D. (2010). Well teachers, well students. *The Journal of Student Wellbeing, 4*(1), 19–34. https://doi.org/10.21913/JSW.v4i1.599

Ministry of Education, Government of India. (1953). *Report of the secondary education commission, Mudaliar commission report, October 1952 to June 1953.* https://indianculture.gov.in/reports-proceedings/report-secondary-education-commission

Ministry of Education, Government of India. (1968). *National Policy on Education, 1968.* https://www.education.gov.in/sites/upload_files/mhrd/files/document-reports/NPE-1968.pdf

Ministry of Health & Family Welfare (MoHFW) & Ministry of Human Resource and Development (MHRD). (2018). *Operational guidelines on school health programme under Ayushman Bharat.* https://nhm.gov.in/New_Updates_2018/NHM_Components/RMNCHA/AH/guidelines/Operational_guidelines_on_School_Health_Programme_under_Ayushman_Bharat.pdf

Ministry of Human Resource and Development (MHRD), Government of India. (1986). *National policy on education, 1986.* https://ncert.nic.in/pdf/nep/Policy_1986_eng.pdf

Ministry of Human Resource and Development (MHRD), Government of India. (2020). *National education policy, 2020.* https://www.education.gov.in/sites/upload_files/mhrd/files/NEP_Final_English_0.pdf

Mohanty, K. B. (2025). Daunting power of PISA. *The Telegraph Online.* https://www.telegraphindia.com/india/daunting-tower-of-pisa-centre-balks-at-global-exam-as-learning-gaps-linger/cid/1929530

National Institute of Open Schooling (NIOS). (2019). *Senior secondary course 373- Physical education and Yog.* https://www.nios.ac.in/media/documents/Physical_Education_and_Yog_373/Book-1-373.pdf

National Steering Committee for National Curriculum Frameworks. (2022). *National curriculum for foundational stage.* https://ncert.nic.in/pdf/NCF_for_Foundational_Stage_20_October_2022.pdf

National Steering Committee for National Curriculum Frameworks. (2023). *National curriculum framework for school education (NCFSE).* https://ncf.ncert.gov.in/webadmin/assets/ba0dd5d8-b8f9-4315-9e14-403752acdc26

NCERT. (1975). *The curriculum for the ten year school: A framework.* https://ncert.nic.in/pdf/focus-group/NCF_10_Year_School_eng.pdf

NCERT. (1988). *National curriculum for elementary and secondary education: A framework.* https://ncert.nic.in/pdf/focus-group/NCESE_1988.pdf

NCERT. (2005). *National curriculum framework.* https://ncert.nic.in/pdf/nc-framework/nf2005-english.pdf

NCERT. (2006a). *Social science contemporary India II: Textbook in geography for class X* (1st ed.). https://ncert.nic.in/textbook.php?jess1=ps-7
NCERT. (2006b). *Science: Textbook for class X* (1st ed.) [English]. https://ncert.nic.in/textbook.php?jesc1=ps-16
NCERT. (2006c). *Understanding economic development: Social science textbook for class* X (1st ed.). https://ncert.nic.in/textbook.php?jess2=ps-5
NCERT. (2006d). *Position paper national focus group on health and physical education*. https://ncert.nic.in/pdf/focus-group/health_prelims_final.pdf
NCERT. (2007a). *Democratic politics II: Textbook in political science for class X*. https://ncert.nic.in/textbook.php?jess4=ps-8
NCERT. (2007b). *India and the contemporary world II: Textbook in history for class X* (1st ed.). https://ncert.nic.in/textbook.php?jess3=ps-5
NCERT. (2017). *Learning outcomes at the elementary stage*. https://ncert.nic.in/pdf/publication/otherpublications/tilops101.pdf
NCERT. (2018). *Curriculum on health and wellness of school-going adolescents*. https://nhm.gov.in/New_Updates_2018/NHM_Components/RMNCHA/AH/Training_Materials/Curriculum-on-Health-and-Wellness-of-School-Going-Children-English.pdf
NCERT. (2019a). *Facilitator guide for school health program*. https://nhm.gov.in/New_Updates_2018/NHM_Components/RMNCHA/AH/Training_Materials/Facilitator-Guide-for-School-Health-Programme-English.pdf
NCERT. (2019b). *Learning outcomes at the secondary stage*. https://ncert.nic.in/pdf/notice/learning_outcomes.pdf
NCERT. (2019c). *Module 5: Health and well-being in schools*. https://itpd.ncert.gov.in/mss/course_content/Module%205%20%20Health%20and%20Wellbeing%20in%20Schools.pdf
NCERT. (2016). *Health and physical education: Textbook for class IX* (1st ed.). https://ncert.nic.in/textbook.php?iehp1=0-14
NCERT. (2020). *Training and resource material: Health and wellness of school-going children*. https://ncert.nic.in/pdf/announcement/Training_Resource_Material_english.pdf
Pathak, A. (2024). It's time to rethink education. *The Tribune*. https://www.tribuneindia.com/news/comment/its-time-to-rethink-education-638256/#:~:text=In%20a%20way%2C%20the%20prevalent,anguish%20that%20arouses%20my%20critique
Porecha, M. (2023). Ayushman Bharat school health and wellness programme has less than 50% uptake. *The Hindu*. https://www.thehindu.com/news/national/ayushman-bharat-school-health-and-wellness-programme-has-less-than-50-uptake/article66417309.ece
Raushan, R., Acharya, S. S., & Raushan, M. R. (2022). Caste and socioeconomic inequality in child health and nutrition in India. *CASTE: A Global Journal on Social Exclusion, 3*(2), 345–364. https://doi.org/10.26812/caste.v3i2.450
Roscoe, L. J. (2009). Wellness: A review of theory and measurement for counselors. *Journal of Counseling & Development, 87*(2), 216–226. https://doi.org/10.1002/j.1556-6678.2009.tb00570.x
Schramme, T. (2023). Health as complete well-being: The WHO definition and beyond. *Public Health Ethics, 16*(3), 210–218. https://doi.org/10.1093/phe/phad017
State Council of Educational Research and Training (SCERT), Delhi & Directorate of Education (DoE). (2019). *Happiness curriculum*. SCERT, Delhi. https://www.edudel.nic.in/welcome_folder/happiness/HappinessCurriculumFramework_2019.pdf
Syeed, E. (2018). Conflict between covers: Confronting official curriculum in Indian textbooks. *Curriculum Inquiry, 48*(5), 540–559. https://doi.org/10.1080/03626784.2018.1546099
Underdown, A. (2006). *Young children's health and well-being*. McGraw-Hill Education.
World Health Organization (WHO). (2020). *Basic documents: 49th ed (including amendments adopted up to 31 May 2019*. https://apps.who.int/gb/bd/pdf_files/Bd_49th-en.pdf

Rachna Sikarwar works at the intersection of health and education, exploring how both are shaped by political processes. She earned her PhD from the Centre for South Asian Studies, Jawaharlal Nehru University, India, where her research focused on the politics of medicine and educational spaces. Her work examined how the practice of medicine is inherently political, analyzing India's influence in shaping Ayurvedic education and practice in Sri Lanka and Nepal. She is particularly interested in how political dynamics mold health and education discourses.

Chapter 4
The Case for Caring Compassionately for the Well-being of Others in the University

Paul Gibbs

Abstract Higher education is being sought by growing numbers of students whose ambitions are various but at their core there seems to be an economic imperative to improve their well-being rather than caring about those who make up the higher education community and beyond. The neoliberal consensus on the necessity of market capitalism has led to the dominance of rights and duties around choice, independence and personal achievement, as well as competition, selfishness, and the pursuit of profit, status, and power. Construing the purpose of the university primarily in economic terms limits a wider contribution it can make as a social institution to framing and forming futures. To achieve that I suggest that, among other things we need to be more compassionate to ourselves and to others. Compassion gives rise to altruism, generosity, social connectedness, and kindness toward oneself and others focused on others, which naturally results in greater social connectedness. This is surely a good thing but those of us who have the privilege to facilitate the well-being goals of the university also have other civic responsibilities. In this chapter, this distinction is explored through the weaving of a transdisciplinary attitude to care and the role of the university community.

Keywords Caring · Compassion · Transdisciplinarity · Universities · Student well-being

---

P. Gibbs (✉)
Middlesex University, London, UK
e-mail: P.Gibbs@mdx.ac.uk

© The Author(s), under exclusive license to Springer Nature Switzerland AG 2025
L. Dalingwater et al. (eds.), *Structural and Systemic Perspectives on Health and Well-being*, Human Well-Being Research and Policy Making,
https://doi.org/10.1007/978-3-031-99924-6_4

4.1 Introduction

The neoliberal consensus on the necessity of market capitalism has led to the dominance of values around choice, independence and personal achievement, as well as competition, selfishness, and the pursuit of profit, status, and power or perhaps worse, in the author's opinion, the objectifying of entities as things used by or ways of using entities as things. This is a point echoed powerfully by Parfitt et al. who write that "to carry compassion forward into the post-pandemic university, taken-for-granted individualism and self-seeking behavior have to change, and a new stance toward our relational selves be adopted" (2021, p. 188). Any evidence of such changes being systematically embedded in higher education institutional practices seems to the author to be slight.

The COVID-19 pandemic had offered some hope for permanent positive changes, especially for the well-being of others and developed regulations, and protocols for institutionalized caring practices triggered by certain contexts, as I will argue, as a normative response to well-being. The text highlights that an ethic of care presented as being concerned with perfunctory actions ascribed to roles such as lecturer, student body, or administration makes no sense for care as a moral imperative. It is better framed as ontic response to caring which differs from ontological care which is not just caring practices but as a way of being. This is caring for the well-being of others as individuals and recognizing their and one's own common needs and vulnerability. What is needed, and proposed here is a transdisciplinary dialogue first realized through the realization of the values of others, their world views, and their wisdoms. This is a radical revision of the university relationship with those who constitute it, putting centrally their well-being through care and compassion.

This may be achieved through an emergent moral disposition in those who are members of the community and should become an important, interrelated, and relational concept of higher education with a purpose to engage the flourishing potentiality of the student and faculty. It will need an ethos of care of well-being to be infused into institutional cultures and practices through the Heideggerian sense[1] of disclosing, at a deeper level than the functional or ontic experience of care; a care that is about authenticity, and not the totalization of the oneself or the other. This requires spaces in which our care flourishes and is provided for the self as it is presented to students and staff. It is where, according to Clouston, academics, "embody their own caring values in terms of care and compassion toward the student body and their colleagues" (2018, p. 1018). Furthermore, Herring suggests that caring involves meeting the well-being needs of another "in a way that respects them as a person, which involves acknowledging the responsibilities that come with caring, and which must be understood in the context of a mutual relationship" (Herring,

[1] Heidegger addresses Care in Chap. 6 of *Being and Time* (1963). There, in his analyses in response to his own question, 'how can the totality of that structural whole we have pointed out be defined in an existential-ontological manner?' (p. 225), he reveals the unity of care as being. He states that the fundamentals of this entity 'are existentiality, facticity, and being fallen' (p. 235).

2017, p. 159). He continues "compassion and care are closely linked, but most understandings of care will primarily focus on activities, rather than motivations, while most understandings of compassion primarily focus on emotions leading to care" (ibid).

Such caring for the well-being of others does require compassion, and it requires accepting responsibility for the self and others and can be motivated by "the painful emotion occasioned by the awareness of another person's undeserved misfortune" (Nussbaum, 2001, p. 301). Moreover, following this line, an ethic of care is premised not only on the singularity of individuals but on their commonality, that commonality which allows us to feel empathy and compassion by recognizing the vulnerability of others. Once care is adopted as an ontological reality, complete autonomy is revealed as illusory, emphasizing the importance of the relational, creating caring environments which support all individuals in meeting their caring needs. In this sense compassion is a deep concern for the well-being of others.

4.2 Caring as the Dialogue of Caring for the Well-being of the Other

Buber[2], in his *I and Thou*, argues that humans engage with the world in two ways. One is with the attitude of an "I" as an "It," creating a separation, a standing apart, or an objectification of beings as objects to be experienced or used. The other arrangement which he discusses is an attitude of an "I" toward a "Thou," where the self enters into real relation with other people, or nature, through dialogue of which listening is a critical part and true dialogue. It is an "I lived continually in the relation with man which is bodied forth in dialogue" (1950, p. 65). Moreover, such genuine dialogic is at the core of transdisciplinarity and requires bravery—*Respondo etsi mutabor*—I respond, although I will be changed. This sentiment is at the core of genuine caring in transdisciplinary agency. It entails "a risk, the 'danger' that by truly listening to the other one might, indeed, be changed, transformed cognitively and existentially" (Mendes-Flohr, 2014, p. 3).

This is caring relationship which seeks reciprocity and symmetry but not the same as which cannot be covered in any obligation to functionally care (by adding

[2] I draw attention to the perceived incompatibility of using Buber and later Heidegger at this early stage in the chapter and explain my case. Their philosophical difference is complex but Mendes Flohr, in this extended quote gives a good indication, "Crucial for Buber would be the distinction between "the experience of thought"—that is, the experience of the thinking "I," which Heidegger sets apart from the apperceptive self—and the experience *(Erfahrung)* of the latter self that is conscious of itself in relation to a reality external to itself. There are similar differences with the work of Buber and Levinas. However, all three fundamentally see the self as contingent on the other and it is this under this premise and the clarity of Buber on this point that I use them both at different stages of my argument.

it to the job description of academic for instance) but emerges from authenticity in the well-being of others.

Caring needs to be experienced as ontological over time to emerge more readily from those exhibiting moral virtues, which I suggest ought to be woven into the fabric of the university's ethos. To care is a dispositional aspect of being which is different from, albeit related to, caring as a series of perfunctory actions. It is seeing the vulnerability in oneself and in others and not conceptualizing "vulnerable" as a collective adjective which is objectified through the act of caring. If we care, we don't need to frame people in terms of deficits to expect to cultivate the compassionate, and making people feel inadequate and incompetent is a wasted and corrupting endeavor. We need to find time to recognize our needs and those of the vulnerable to care authentically, by enacting that care in an intended practice of caring. Here we see the subject in need of care not as a member of a homogeneous student community but as individuals whose similarities and their differences are important in our recognition of them. This is achieved through dialogic and specially with listening to their world views, not filtering it through our own.

Caring, when used to describe an individual or an institution, implicitly assumes a person who cares about something, perhaps themselves, their role, or their inauthenticity, rather than, in the sense used by Heidegger, caring as becoming. Heidegger's[3] distinction between the ontic, the factual transactions of life—which can be assessed, legitimized, and controlled—and the ontological—the becoming of caring—is even more than enacting good acts, it is about caring for the person from one who acts.[4] In this sense to care cannot be reducible in empirical evaluation to cause and effect nor can it be adequately predicted as some form of evolution. Certainly, there are conditions that enable caring to emerge, and Held (2006) suggests these might include attentiveness, sensitivity, and responding to others (which are susceptible to teaching), but it is not just an extension of these, rather it is caring in an ontological phenomena of emergence of the common good, and, as Held suggests, the care ought to be seen as "practice and value" (Ibid.). Care is transformative and ontologically emergent (it is not supervenient) and is perhaps ordinarily irreversible, and it reveals itself in the presence and being of the parties who are caring.

Caring can be an everyday activity, and we do not need compassion or solicitude to elicit caring behavior toward our work or our personal integrity and well-being especially if we hold the "thou" as an "it." Caring does not need to be

[3] I recognize the philosophical and political concerns of discussing Heidegger, especially in an essay built on the relational not the individual; but suggest that his tripartite woven structure of care (sorge) (existentiality, facticity and being-fallen) is a fundamental ontology that offers something to the debate. His statement, "care is always concern and solicitude" (1963: 238) relates to the contemporary discussion of an ontology of vulnerability, stemming from our anxiety of being thrown into the world (see Heidegger 1.6, 41), consisting of care for oneself (Besorgen) and solicitude (Fürsorge) and the failures of these which prevent the actualization of potentials, but I do not take it further here. For wider discussion of Heidegger and care theory see Stevens (2022).

[4] See Buber, *I and Thou*.

compassionate, it can be functional, as it is when it is for obligation to act, as is the case with our nurses, doctors, social workers, teachers, and parents.

Care and compassion do not have to be mutually exclusive and, indeed, are usually better when both are aligned, but they do not have to be and indeed can be separated and can still make a positive contribution to caring for others This leads to three possible states: (a) a person who cares may not act in a caring way, (b) a person who does not care might act in a caring way, and (c) a person who cares may act in a caring way. The following chapter will explore the optimum option—(c)—as I believe that, to be realized, care might have a more central part in higher education.

Elley-Brown and Pringle suggest that viewing the care "through Heideggerian philosophy can provide a more nuanced understanding of the care ethic" (2019, p. 24), especially its ability to open up possibilities, rather than find solutions or results. For Heidegger, "Care is always concern and solicitude, even if only privately" (1963, p. 238), and this operates as an ontological dyad structuring the fundamental conduct of caring. Solicitude has two extreme possibilities; these are described as "leaping in," as when out of concern, a caregiver takes over another person and solves the problem on the other's behalf, and "leaping ahead" (ibid., p. 158). The person receiving this kind of care experiences freedom, increased meaningfulness, new insights, and consequently feels more fully human. Care, as described as "leaping in" by Heidegger, is our ontic view, and "leaping ahead" is our ontological view. These form summaries of care when Elley-Brown and Pringle state "although both are positive, the first results in a person becoming dependent and dominated, whereas the second results in a person becoming enabled and experiencing meaningfulness. 'Leaping in' tends to be concerned with the present, whereas 'leaping ahead' has a greater sense of possibility and future-focus" (2019, p. 27). Further, Verdera suggests that, in leaping ahead, "caring must originate in the needs stated by the person receiving the care, either expressly or through their behavior, but not in the needs inferred from financial or cultural demands or any others that try to direct the work of teaching" (Verdera, 2019, p. 88).

4.3 Well-being as Compassionate Caring

To build a better understanding of a transdisciplinary caring disposition which is essential in the caring person, I wish to introduce three issues that underpin this concept. These threefold notions are:

(a) transindividual mutuality where I discuss, albeit briefly, the myth of a single consistent and enduring identity unaffected by context;
(b) ontological emergences with the need to explore a little more clearly a way of acting in the world.
(c) vulnerability as a special care of those in need of a caring dialogue.

This is what is attempted in the next few and short sections before drawing the issues together in a notion of transdisciplinary care.

4.3.1 Transindividual Mutuality

Using the notion of Thou discussed earlier Buber suggests that the thou "is the I of pure intercourse with nature; nature gives herself to it and speaks unceasingly with it, revealing her mysteries to it but not betraying her mystery" (Buber, 1950, p. 57). It is also, I suggest, the basis of trans-individualism as an emerging ontology dialogue within oneself for, rather than seeking to totalize oneself as an identity for the benefit of others, we are encouraged to do that to others when we talk of one student body or referring to all student views in the singular (student voice), or assessing a student with a good grade to satisfy an administrator's desire for high progression rates. It forces us to see the individual in their context, not as a part of the collective but to encourage us to engage in "careful" dialogue where we recognize and respect the interlocutor as they wish to be heard. Further, it asks us to question the totalization of our own self as independent of, and thus unaffected by, our dialogues with others which is never the case in true dialogue. This understanding argues for a notion of self that transcends a coherent and consistent individualism.

Balibar (1997, 2018) and Simondon (2007) have pointed out that there is potential in Spinoza's (1677/1992) work to conclude that the ever-changing intersectionality of selves and other, both animate and inanimate, of thought and extension, means that no separation between a subject of knowledge and its object can subsist (likewise Nicolescu, 2002). In this way, the materialism of Spinoza may better be understood as a unification seeking the individualization as spiritual materialism. Moreover, thought and extension are just two of the infinite attributes of the unique substance, leading to a multitude of separate entities with a common genus. Taking such an ontological stance, individual things exist only because of the existence of other individual things (Spinoza, 1992) with which they participate in an infinite network of connections (Balibar, 1997; see also Nicolescu, 2002, 2014).

Further, as Bottici noted, "causality must not be understood in the sense of a linear succession of events, but rather as a multiplicity of connections linking individuals, which are made up of simpler and more complex individuals all causally related" (2019, p. 438). Consequently, every individual is constantly composed and decomposed by other individuals with whom they enter into contact through a process of individuation, which involves infra-individual, inter-individual, and supra-individual levels (Balibar, 1997). To render this complexity meaningful, Balibar argued, individuality must be understood as a *transindividuality*—a "transindividual process of individuation" (1997, p. 12).

For clarification, an individual is "fixed, essence-like, and interior. A transindividual is the product of a continual process of individuation in response to its external environment" (Taylor, 2021, para. 5). Balibar suggested that the individual essence, "which by definition is a *self-affirmation,* should also immediately mean a *resistance* to its potential destruction by other things, therefore *intrinsically* requiring a combination or coalition with some other 'similar' or 'convenient' things against other things which are 'adverse'" (1997, p. 10). Further, Balibar said that "the concrete concept of transindividuality therefore implies that relationships between individuals, or parts of the individuals' Minds and Bodies are considered *in the transition* from Imagination to Reason, i.e., from a lesser to a greater power to act" (1997, p. 31).

4.3.2 Ontological Emergences

Emergence can be considered as synchronic or diachronic. Synchronic emergence considers "the emergent phenomenon to exist simultaneously with the features from which it emerges… In contrast, diachronic emergence takes emergent phenomena to develop over time from the pre-existing state of a system" (Humphreys, 2016, p. xviii–xix). The conditions for ontological emergence are dependent upon it being relational and resulting from something else not previously existing in the parties to the relationship, and that these emergent properties are characterized by their novelty and usually have a coherence within the world (Ibid). It assumes that entities are not endowed with a fixed and definable set of absolutely intrinsic properties, being qualitatively immutable through extrinsic relations, but assumes, as Santos states, that "the identity and the causal behavior of any emergent systemic property can only be conceived, and explained, as constructed by and through specific networks of qualitatively transformative relational processes" (1915, p. 429).

Transdisciplinarity assumes the presence of such emergence, where the emergent is not simply a consequence of a logical production process but has its own ontological status, identity, and causal efficacy (Santos, 1915; Humphreys, 2016). This creates new knowledge ecologies which embrace ontological emergent forms of knowledge at different levels of reality while also incorporating disciplinary generative forms at lower levels, liberated from the constraints and rules of a Foucauldian interpretation of disciplinarity. It is the inclusion of different levels of reality which allows the understanding of the emergent object, which in turn allows for different systems to pertain at the higher levels or ontological emergence, resulting in a phenomenon of woven, open systems of levels of reality and, importantly, for the higher level to causally change the lower levels. Strong, ontological emergence requires such engagements to create the conditions where new modes and forms of knowledge are emergently revealed into our understanding and where relationality as an extension of specific forms of knowledge and power favoring certain paradigms of causality, as are implicit in disciplines,[5] are unnecessary to reach transdisciplinary outcomes.

[5]This counters the assumption that Aristotelian gnoseology is challenged by transdisciplinary understanding.

4.3.3 Vulnerability

Vulnerability conceptually embraces all kinds of human fragilities that manifest in individuals differently. If "people are recognized for the vulnerabilities they encounter, and then they are assisted in such a way that their vulnerabilities are attended to caringly" (Waghid, 2019, p. 124), then compassionate care means attending and responding to vulnerability, where vulnerability is defined as "susceptibility to harm, need, loss, coercion, domination, or other ills or blights" (Engster, 2019, p. 106). Moreover, care is personally reflecting on difference, not sameness, and in a Heideggerian sense, the expression of care means "an existential and basic ontological phenomenon which nevertheless is not simple in its structure" (1962, p. 240). As part of Heidegger's ontological care structure, I would suggest we consider that anxiety is a disclosure of Being and the inherent anxiety around "our potentiality-for-being-in-the-world" (ibid., p. 235) is ontologically revealed in our vulnerability. I further want to suggest that it is concern about our own vulnerability, as well as that of others, as simultaneous acts of empathy, which reveals care as ontological phenomena rather than a functional (ontic) one, but both are necessary for an interpretation of care.

The power to act, however, is not universally distributed and declines in the vulnerable in their actions and their voices and it can result in "learned helplessness." Power which is not equally distributed across the collective of the university can encourage such a phenomena, even if unintentionally, through lectures, seminars, and assessments which have at their core a premise of failure rather than enhancing student identity. If a university is a place with such an ethos it compounds the fragility and vulnerability of others even if it claims a caring mission with plenty of student support mechanisms. As individuals, we make our being feasible by questioning the reality of our everyday experiences in the context of the knowledge we have of ourselves and others through a preparedness and courage to imagine, accept, and create new knowledge. To do this we have to care for ourselves and for others—facing and rejecting self-deceit and bad faith in ourselves and others, and in so doing we make ourselves vulnerable as well as responding to the vulnerability of others in their singularity. In doing so and in recognizing our self in others we are called upon to care for others in their existential being. Freedom resides in our choice to act on our potential, and potentialities are aligned with the properties of our individuality that determine powers to act. However, not all the properties of a thing are equally important to the understanding of the specific activities, relationships, and commitments, which give meaning to an individual's identity, yet which also contribute to our potentialities.

The exploration of our being provides the potential for us to understand our life project and to seek it; to understand being as our becoming is not deterministic but is emergent. It is not unencumbered; it requires a blending of knowledge and realities in order that we might have the power to reflect and deliberate about the potential impact of our actions. These expressions of individuality are not primarily self-absorbed, for, as Johnson suggests, individuality is "grounded in an ethical existential commitment to work out one's identity in relation to greater surrounding forces that comprise the individual's horizons of significance" (2014, p. 71). Most importantly, this process is not static but is in constant motion, in flow with complexity and causation. The acceptance of a dominant societal discourse restricts and enframes our ability to see the openness available to us and imposes an existential horizon where none need be.

4.4 Transdisciplinarity as the Care for the Well-being of Others

The premise of this chapter is that transdisciplinarity is an emergent phenomenon which, to quote Nicolescu, Morin, and de Freitas "is the semantic and practical unification of the meanings that traverse and lie beyond different disciplines" (1994). The essence of transdisciplinarity is therefore about working together across difference; openness to listening to the perspectives of the other; consensus rather than compromise and the dialogue of knowledges to arrive at what the particularity of local culture needs in order to thrive for the benefit of the individual and the collective in a world of complexity. The inherent difficulties of such models are the experience of a multiplicity of realities which are not fixed but flow rhythmically under the influence of complexity and intra-reality causation yet deny causation between realities. The rhythm of realities forms an open system in which possible worlds emerge and realities are (a) perceived as independent yet indeterminate and (b) realized and dependent on the location of the becoming being. To view these open systems in which becoming is the realization as potentiality (both internally natural and externally elicited as), energy and power that enables the capacity to bring about change in another thing or in itself aligns with Aristotle's fourth and final cause.

The interweaving of disciplinary perspectives and methodologies encourages an epistemological restructuring of knowledge, but the interacting disciplines retain their epistemological independence and so fail to recognize the ontological nature of transdisciplinary knowledges to produce collective and comparatively novel solutions which might be found through bringing together disciplines and problems as a systematic and complex whole. These connections might usefully be identified as the transrational (Barrett, 2013), which is non-theoretical, non-rational, and is achieved through the incorporation of, for example, visions and dreams. It includes knowing from indigenous peoples as a legitimate form of knowledge generation. Even the aggregability of interdisciplinarity might provide methodological sources to explore a problem and may, as developed below, create conditions for weak emergence. This is where two or more disciplines with different epistemological groundings are utilized to view a problem; a mechanical engineering and a psychological which may give insight but the basic premises of these disciplines are not changed even if aspects of their methodology are shared. This is in contrast to strong emergence where the nature of the investigation changes. For example, the processes that use the same pixels forming different television images with the essence of the pixel not changing in the transformation of the different image or murmurings of starlings flocking in which the birds remain unchanged. In strong emergence the result is a permanent changed entity, thoughts, or creation where the parts are insufficient to explain the new entity and that entity is not reducible to its parts. Examples are consciousness itself, which somehow creates thoughts, creativity, and the ways market actually react. This is a distinction that is not clearly made in the extant literature and has significant structural issues for the university, due in part to the irreducibilities of disciplinary discourses and the tension this creates within the vortex of complex systems.

In contrast, the emergence of new and open in vivo knowledge within a transdisciplinary framework embraces "factual knowledges," whether they be positivistic-derived or from the imagination, or mysticism or faith generative but in their essence are essential ontologically caring, where everyone develops an approach to resetting problems in order to reveal solutions where they are within the diverse collectives' capacity to understand them. It requires an Heideggerian understanding of a mode of presence and care which orientates spatial and temporal phenomenological experiences of events which stand before and shapes both time and space that is Being. It is a move that Heidegger sees as a counter to the nihilistic materialism which is overrunning the cultures of the university and denying the common good. Heidegger also draws attention to the modern contrasting of mythos and logos, offered a different appreciation of the unfolding of the being in conjunction with logos rather than the current domination of logos.[6] This deeper ontological Being is hidden by the ontic and first needs us to see how what we care to attend to might be considered appropriately compassionately caring. This reveals what care is directed to their attention during the course of a certain practice by caring beings or those who perform the acts designated as caring, presence, or the event of attention.[7] For example, take Heidegger's use of the temple as a space in the Origins of the World of Art. The temple provides the space for the emergence of the mystery of the divine.

How can the above discussion be used to help build a moral rather than instructional imperative in the higher education community? In recent years in the UK[8] the need for more care for the well-being of its community has become more evident and indeed discussions at the highest levels of government have been concerned with the level of suicides of students and have been discussed by Gibbs and Dalingwater (2024). The full argument is not rehearsed again but it is important to set this chapter briefly in that context of caring actions and building a futural, Buberian dialogue.

---

[6] See Heidegger in *Parmenides* (1998: 6).

[7] For example, the scandals in the nursing and aged care homes in the UK.

[8] I recognize that the argument I will make is brief and therefore lacks the intellectual depth provided in the appropriate literature, but I hope to be clear enough to ground my subsequent arguments (*Create statutory legal duty of care for students in Higher Education—Petitions) (parliament.uk)*.

An ethics of care implies that there is moral significance in the fundamental elements of relationships and dependencies in human life; dependencies revealed through the attentiveness of the carer to the needs of the vulnerable as they, the vulnerable, individually are conceived. In this context, care ethics seek to maintain relationships by contextualizing and promoting the well-being of caregivers and care-receivers in a network of social relations.[9] This approaches the realities of the singularity of the vulnerable person, not the impartiality derived from a Kantian duty of care and that implicit in statutory duties, for it is not an ethic of empathy but of difference. The premise of impartiality in the universal Kantian imperative (and also utilitarianism) is, as Ferraresse suggests, no more than a "fetish of generality which is a powerful mechanism of indifference to others" (2021, p. 15). It is "a rhetorical tool used to confer legitimacy on a homogenizing moral viewpoint grounded in abstract duty" (Ibid., p. 18).

Along the same theme, Brugère (2019) reveals a distinction between the moral and the ethical: "Morality is related to the necessity of justice established with the framework of a reference to neutral, impersonal subjects who guarantee the perspective of equality" (2019, p. 33), whereas the ethical approach is an approach to others' vulnerability "in their singularity" (Ibid., p. 33). Ethics is thus embodied in the rational process of solicitude as a condition of respect and compassion in asymmetrical relations which "moral principles and law render inextricable and imperceptible" (Ibid., p. 34).

4.5 Concluding Comments: Caring for the Well-being of Those in Higher Education

These issues raise the condition of the very motivation of compassion as an emotive and a rational call to action and how it is applicable to higher education; principles that in the higher education press, and more widely, are not being discussed. Ferrarese argues that such an approach will often deny the dignity of the individual by homogenizing it as a moral viewpoint which is grounded in abstract duty, thus quietening the voice of the individual who suffers. Care for the well-being of students, staff, and fellow academics within their academic lives and their circumstances beyond the institution has proven to be critical to the way in which students respond to the institution and to their own responsibility to study. This is care that is not restricted by any obligatory action of care, which emerges from authenticity in accepting empathically the well-being of others, and the informal distribution of

[9]The main work on developing a distinct moral theory is usually attributed to Gillian (*A Different Voice*, 1982), Noddings (*Caring: A Feminine Approach to Ethics and Moral Education*, 1982) and Tronto (*Moral Boundaries: A Political Argument for an Ethic of Care,* 1994) and Caring. Their work is well known, and in this paper I want to explore two more contemporary philosophers: Ferrarese (*The Fragility of Concern for Others*, 2021) and Brugère (*Care Ethics: The Introduction of Care as a Political Category*, 2019).

such care can lead to the carer themselves being vulnerable. Forms of academic assessment developed for a distinctive set of skills and abilities often alienate others with different ways of being in the world. Respecting diversity, equality, and inclusion is about understanding the vulnerability of change and its unexpected consequences; it is about merit and recognition, both of which respect the talented but not at the expense of those less able. Care cannot, whereas caring might, be contracted, although it can be facilitated by organizations' structures and procedures. Moreover, an ethics of care warns against a well-ordered control through structural dependencies that give a face to a simulacra of care which, essentially, transforms care into functionality within a legal entity under statute. Instead, it is about leaping ahead through listening and responding to the becoming of those who we are caring for, that goes beyond the vulnerable to us all.

By considering the issues of sameness and individualism, with the aim of identifying ways in which universities address both concepts through their educational and service provisions, I begin with an understanding of the difference between sameness and individuality and will try to resist reducing "difference" to disqualification and exclusion rather than inclusion and absorption. Further, as Deleuze (2014) suggests, difference is distinguished from diversity and otherness by its inter-genus nature and by the resemblance upon which it depends. Within the university there is a need for a genuine ethic of care, where a student-centered pedagogical ethos seeks to facilitate, at different levels, both the sameness in terms of collective cooperation (in that students choose to become forms of engineers, physicians, teachers, artists, etc.) and the way in which students might generate their self-identity, as they perceive it, in their individual "becoming." Confronting such dependency works through the attentiveness of the carer to the need of the vulnerable as they conceptualize and live them for themselves not empathically but as our own thoughts and emotions. To hear the other directly we need to provide for their self-expression and give space for self-creation of her own identity; one which is more than an example of "a student" and is a unified and distinct entity in its own right, though it may share certain features with the ubiquitous other. Brugère's perspective is insightful here, when she states that the ethics of care "deconstructs the possibility of a collective master narrative that involves each and every individual in an impersonal and indiscriminate way" (2019, p. 41).

It is creating an ethos where caring is recognized as a relational essential in our being and then developing and supporting staff to help to create an organizational structure that has processes, networks, and policies to facilitate them. Caring for students' well-being, both within their academic lives and for their circumstances beyond the institution, has proven to be critical to the way in which students respond to the institution and to their own authentic responsibilities as social actors. It requires considerable moral courage as well as creativity for it will change the hegemonies within the university, directly affecting its positioning in society and within political policy and, in so doing, radically change the power structures that pervade contemporary institutions. Such an institutional ethos would directly affect the institution's attention to its students and its wider community as a moral agent, not just as a provider of knowledge and skills to benefit society. It would lead to more heads of institutions embracing the transdisciplinary and focusing not on the barriers to engagement with others to retain their competitive positions but on in-depth and authentic collaborations. Its impact on curriculum and assessment would bring into context the societal and political goods needed for communities to flourish and stop the deceptions encouraged by the need to compete, not for solutions to problems but for financial rewards. It would help students to become more critical of the world in which they live and encourage them to act. Research would be more focused on the "good" needed for all in societies, approaching altruistically major issues facing humanity with focus and a credo of social justice. In many cases, such action may be evident in universities, and where it occurs, this is clearly positive but, with the drift in universities from public to private concerns, this is far from universal. Rather, the subject–object fusion is not merely the alteration of the organism but the fusion of pan-experiential reality. We thus do not simply observe realities, we become one within the emotive, purposive, creative realities operating around and through us: "Thus, as disclosed in the fundamental essence of our experience, the togetherness of things involves some doctrine of mutual immanence… We are in the world and the world is in us" (Whitehead, 1967, p. 62). Indeed, what we take as radical creativity are the emergent properties of the complex system by which we would become caring beings.

References

Balibar, E. (1997). Spinoza: from Individuality to Transindividuality. In *Medelingen vanwege het Spinozahauis*, 3–36. Delft: Eburon.

Balibar, E. (2018). Philosophies of the Transindividual: Spinoza, Marx, Freud. *Australasian Philosophical Review, 2(1): 5–25.*

Barrett, M. J. (2013). Enabling hybrid space: Epistemological diversity in socio-ecological problem-solving. *Policy Sciences, 46*(2), 179–197.

Brugère, F. (2019). *Care ethics: The introduction of care as a political category*. Peeters.

Buber, M. (1950). *I and thou* (R. G. Smith, Trans.). T & T Clark Ltd. (Original work published 1923)

Clouston, T. (2018). Transforming learning: Teaching compassion and caring values in higher education. *Journal of Further and Higher Education, 42*(7), 1015–1024. https://doi.org/10.1080/0309877X.2017.1332359

Deleuze, G. (2014). *Difference and repetition*. Bloomsbury. (Original work published 1968)

Elley-Brown, M. J., & Pringle, J. K. (2019). *Sorge*, Heideggerian ethic of care: Creating more caring organizations. *Journal of Business Ethics, 168*(1), 23–35.

Engster, D. (2019). Care ethics, dependency, and vulnerability. *Ethics and Social Welfare, 13*(2), 100–114. https://doi.org/10.1080/17496535.2018.1533029

Ferraresse, E. (2021). *The fragility of concern for others*. Edinburgh University Press.

Gibbs, P., & Dalingwater, L. (2024). Is student wellbeing better served by an ethic of care or a duty of care? A perspective on the current debate in English higher educational establishments. *The International Journal of Health, Wellness and Society, 14*(3), 31–43. https://doi.org/10.18848/2156-8960/CGP/v14i03/31-43

Heidegger, M. (1963). *Being and time*. Wiley-Blackwell. (Original work published 1927)

Held, V. (2006). *The ethics of care: Personal, political, global*. Oxford University Press.

Herring, J. (2017). Compassion, ethics of care and legal rights. *International Journal of Law in Context, 13*(2), 158–171. https://doi.org/10.1017/S174455231700009X

Humphreys, P. (2016). *Emergence: a Philosophical Account*, Oxford: Oxford University Press.
Johnson, A. (2014). Authenticity and self-cultivation as learning to be: The hermeneutics of lifelong education. *Philosophical Studies in Education, 45*, 66–73.
Mendes-Flohr, P. (2014). Martin Buber and Martin Heidegger in dialogue. *The Journal of Religion, 94*(1), 2–25.
Nicolescu, B. (2002). *Manifesto of Transdisciplinarity*, New York: SUNY.
Nicolescu, B. (2014). *From Modernity to Cosmodernity*. Albany: SUNY Press.
Nussbaum, M. (2001). *Upheavals of thought: The intelligence of emotions*. Cambridge University Press.
Parfitt, A., Read, S., & Bush, T. (2021). Can compassion provide a lifeline for navigating coronavirus (COVID-19) in higher education? *Pastoral Care in Education, 39*(3), 178–191. https://doi.org/10.1080/02643944.2021.1952645
Santos, G. (1915) Ontological Emergence: How is That Possible? *Towards a New Relational Ontology Foundations of Science, 20(4):429–446.*
Simondon, G. (2007). *L'individuation Psychique et Collective*. Paris: Editions Aubier.
Stevens, R. (2022). An existential foundation for an ethic of care in Heidegger's *Being and Time*. *The Journal of Ethics, 26*, 415–431.
Taylor, D. (2021). Book review: *Spinoza, the Transindividual* by E. Balibar. *Marx and Philosophy Review of Books*. https://marxandphilosophy.org.uk/reviews/18671_spinoza-the-transindividual-by-etienne-balibarreviewed-by-dan-taylor/
Verdera, V. V. (2019). Care ethics in universities: Beyond an easy "add and stir" solution. *Encounters in Theory and History of Education, 20*, 83–101.
Waghid, Y. (2019). *Towards a philosophy of caring in higher education: Pedagogy and nuances of care*. Palgrave Macmillan.
Whitehead, A. N. (1967). *The Aims of Education*. London: The Free Press.

Paul Gibbs is Emeritus Professor of Middlesex University and founder of the Centre for Education Research and Scholarship. He is a visiting professor at UTS Sydney, Azerbaijan, East European and Tbilisi State Universities. He is a fellow of the Academy of Transdisciplinary Learning & Advanced Studies (ATLAS) and of the Centre for Higher Education Policy, New College, Oxford.

Chapter 5
Implementing Approaches to Improve the Well-being of First-Year Students at the University of the Witwatersrand During the COVID-19 Lockdown: From Access to Success

Busisiwe Nkala-Dlamini, Zintle Ntshongwana, and Roshini Pillay

Abstract The COVID-19 pandemic had a global impact and severely affected the well-being of students in higher education. This chapter illustrates how the application of the ethics of care approach helped identify first-year social work students' threats to their well-being and achieving academic success and examines how this collaborative approach assisted students facing urgent needs. The purpose of higher education is to prepare graduates to respond to local realities. However, not all students who enroll in institutions of higher learning adjust easily to university life. Support structures to ease students' challenges require an understanding of the unique circumstances of the students and a caring philosophy. We provided comprehensive support to students in overcoming socio-economic challenges, which helps cultivate a conducive learning environment. Using reflection and ethics of care, we examined the period before, during, and after the COVID-19 pandemic to describe our observations, actions, decisions, and processes in providing care and support for first-year students. In any specific context, understanding students' unique circumstances at the start of the academic year is paramount to help students achieve success and thrive in higher education despite a global lockdown and a rapid pivot to emergency online learning.

Keywords Approaches · First-year students · COVID-19 · Lockdown · Well-being · Access · Success

B. Nkala-Dlamini (✉) · Z. Ntshongwana · R. Pillay
University of the Witwatersrand, Johannesburg, South Africa
e-mail: busisiwe.nkala-dlamini@wits.ac.za; roshini.pillay@wits.ac.za; zintle.ntshongwana@wits.ac.za

© The Author(s), under exclusive license to Springer Nature Switzerland AG 2025

L. Dalingwater et al. (eds.), *Structural and Systemic Perspectives on Health and Well-being*, Human Well-Being Research and Policy Making,
https://doi.org/10.1007/978-3-031-99924-6_5

5.1 Introduction

Education is an essential driver of societal development, enhancing individuals' physical and mental well-being and promoting a healthier society. The United Nations' Sustainable Development Goal 4 states that "education liberates the intellect, unlocks the imagination, and is fundamental for self-respect" (United Nations, 2015). Higher education, recognized as key to prosperity, plays a pivotal role in enhancing economic growth, optimizing the use of resources, and supporting sustainable development. Moreover, societal progress relies heavily on educated individuals who possess both the skills and capacity to address complex problems. Education significantly enhances the potential for positive, meaningful change in communities, groups, and individuals.

A Times Higher Education article by Bhardwa (2017) cited ten reasons why students attend university, with the top three being passion for their subject (58.4%); continuation of learning and development (58%); and a desire to pursue their career (55.2%). Despite their ambition to improve their knowledge, lives, and sense of purpose, many aspiring students face barriers to accessing university or other higher education providers (Ige et al., 2017)—the very institutions considered essential for improving their social well-being. Several scholars (Kuh et al., 2006; Lalendle & Mgijima, 2018; Weatherton & Schussler, 2021) contend that universities' criteria for defining success based on degree completion rates overlook the sociocultural processes shaping student success. While access to higher education remains crucial for building inclusive learning communities and university environments (Walton et al., 2019), even those who gain admission to these institutions often encounter obstacles that are difficult to overcome.

Social work education faces the challenge of preparing graduates for local realities while considering rapid national, regional, and global transitions that profoundly affect people's lives (CHE, 2015; Walker & Fongwa, 2017). This paper shares the perspectives and learning experiences of first-year coordinators and lecturers who supported social work students over a four-year period before and during the COVID-19 pandemic (2018–2021). Rather than presenting research findings or highlighting successes, we describe our process of observation, action, decision-making aimed at creating an environment conducive to learning for first-year students.

This chapter explores the nature of student support provided by the Department of Social Work at Wits University in Johannesburg, South Africa. We present this experience as a potential model for promoting students' sense of purpose and social integration. Hettler (1984) posited that identifying and addressing barriers would help students remain in their programs and improve their learning experiences. It is with this purpose in mind that we have reflected on our engagement and intervention. COVID-19 was also a key factor in our reflections on processes, engagements, and resources employed.

5.2 Literature Review

Roberts and Danoff-Burg (2010) highlighted a marked increase in students experiencing psychological distress, depression, and anxiety, a trend that has continued to escalate since. In South Africa, the Department of Higher Education and Training's 2018–19 annual report revealed that 8% of tertiary education students experienced food insecurity. This translates to approximately 82,960 students struggling to maintain adequate nutrition (SA's university students faced, 2020)—the same students who were expected to adjust and thrive in a new learning environment (Sikakana, 2010). In response, Sikakana (2010, p. 922) called for institutions of higher learning to provide "comprehensive support" to students, encompassing academic, emotional, psychological, and socio-economic assistance.

During the 2020 COVID-19 pandemic, universities worldwide transitioned to online teaching in response to lockdown restrictions that limited movement to essential activities, such as buying groceries or seeking medical care (World Health Organization, 2025). While the shift to digital learning strategies helped mitigate the pandemic's impact on the academic year, students faced significant challenges in adapting to online learning management systems and new teaching methods (Amoah & Le Roux, 2024; Naidoo & Moonasamy, 2022; Onwuegbuzie & Ojo, 2021). In many cases, digital access enabled teaching and learning to continue with no major disruptions to the academic year. However, a study across Israel, Kosovo, Ukraine, Cyprus, and Germany documented widespread disruptions in higher learning institutions (Pat-Horenczyk et al., 2022).

During this time, students faced additional challenges, primarily arising from the absence of physical human interaction. At the same time, the pandemic exposed existing social inequalities, as some students lacked the necessary devices and had never used digital technologies before entering university (Czerniewicz et al., 2020; Ige et al., 2017). A study conducted in South Africa's Gauteng province revealed that students did not have adequate resources, such as laptops, to support their online studies during the lockdown (Olowoyo et al., 2022).

Both physical contact and social support in higher education institutions play a vital role in mitigating mental health risks (Motala & Menon, 2020), as evidenced by elevated stress levels among university students during the pandemic, compromising their general sense of well-being. This could be attributed to the fact that students did not receive the same personal and interactive support they had become accustomed to while on campus full-time. However, because of COVID-19 lockdown regulations, physical contact was restricted and students' feelings of loneliness and anxiety escalated (Sifunda et al., 2021).

According to a study in Spain by Gómez-García et al. (2022), some students, particularly those living in rural areas, had difficulties accessing the internet due to poor network connectivity, making remote learning problematic. The study also revealed that students struggled to reach their lecturers, particularly via email (Gómez-García et al., 2022). This stood in stark contrast to the prompt responses they received from their lecturers when on campus. However, a study in the United

States suggested that a substantial proportion of students received adequate support from their lecturers and tutors (Minkos & Gelbar, 2021). Weuffen et al. (2021) advocated for diversified academic support by creating contextually relevant opportunities that catered to the needs of students from diverse socio-economic backgrounds.

Notwithstanding the struggles students endured during the pandemic, some South African universities offered supporting interventions, which included funding data bundles to help students attend online classes and submit their coursework, transport for students to return home for the lockdown period, and, in some cases, refunded them for their university term of university housing costs (Sifunda et al., 2021). Moreover, some students financed by South Africa's National Student Financial Aid Scheme (NSFAS) were provided with laptops (Olowoyo et al., 2022). As lockdown restrictions eased and COVID-19 seroprevalence rates started declining, some universities arranged for the physical delivery of study materials (Minkos & Gelbar, 2021). This was helpful for students who did not have access to laptops or for students from disadvantaged backgrounds. Additionally, the students reported that their institutions provided support by screening and referring students who presented COVID-19 symptoms (Sifunda et al., 2021).

A majority of students received social and emotional support from their families and friends (Sifunda et al., 2021), who played a crucial role in fostering an environment in which they could perform well academically.

Online learning was not an entirely new concept for South African universities. Many had introduced digital platforms during the "#FeesMustFall movement" in 2015, when student protests over tuition fees disrupted academic activities (Akpojivi, 2023). The movement emerged from students' frustration with their inability to pay registration and tuition fees in full and on time at the beginning of each academic year (Mathebula & Calitz, 2018, p. 171). This prior experience suggests that some were already familiar with the available academic assistance and support options when transitioning from face-to-face to online learning.

Philosophical Framework: The Ethics of Care

The ethics of care emphasizes relationships and compassion (Adhariani et al., 2017) and is rooted in an individual's sense of connection with others. Moreover, it prioritizes interactive communication and interpersonal engagement—for resolving ethical conflicts. What distinguishes the ethics of care is its focus on attachments, issues of self-sacrifice, and selflessness. It highlights the co-dependence of human beings, emphasizing other people's needs, while asserting that moral responsibility is reflected in the voices of women (Adhariani et al., 2017).

An ethic of care speaks of the ability to see people as unique individuals beyond just warm bodies with a student number. It requires caring educators who take the time to get to know the person and is student-centered. Thus, during lockdown it required a better understanding of home circumstances such as access to devices, access to Wi-Fi and data so students could engage in emergency remote online learning. Another view is seeing the ethic of care as supporting the well-being of the student and encouraging learning so that responsive empathic relations are sustained (Keeling, 2014). Salazar (2013) sees the ethic of care as being part of a humanizing pedagogy that allows students to bring with them the treasures they have from their culture, history, and experiences. There is recognition and understanding of the unique aspects of individual students and in so doing fostering academic resilience.

The ethics of care focuses on responsibility toward the needs of people who depend on assistance, including prioritizing the well-being and dignity of vulnerable populations (Maio, 2018). The first-year university students discussed in this paper would be considered vulnerable, according to Townsend and Dawes's (2013) definition, which considers environmental and economic factors that predispose an individual to substantial risk of harm. If these predisposing factors were not addressed, these students risked an inability to focus on their studies, university dropout, course failure, and mental health challenges.

According to Beauchamp and Childress (2001), the ethics of care reinforce sympathy, moral emotions, and experiences, which translate into care and helping. They posited that caring involves being open and responding to the needs of others. This philosophy focuses on emotions more than the reason for them when examining the challenges surrounding people's situations. Hume, as cited in Beauchamp and Childress (2001), stated that "emotions motivate us and tell us much about the person's character, but human understanding directs us in choosing a path of action" (p. 374).

Additionally, the ethics of care does not follow a deductive model, which entails applying general principles to specific cases. Instead, it recognizes the singularity of the situation (Maio, 2018), and as such, aims to create a supportive and inclusive environment that helps people to thrive. In the context of this paper, this would mean considering each student's uniqueness, their unique situations, backgrounds, needs, and circumstances. Creative resolutions to conflicts are fundamental in the ethics of care, which acknowledges immediate perspectives and prioritizes relationships. By fostering open dialogue and empathy we can seek solutions to address the issues and strengthen the relationships between those involved. Research shows that ethics of care gives preference to emotional knowledge. According to Maio (2018), ethics of care also focuses on education, with the emphasis on students' well-being.

Drawing on this framework, we developed supportive interventions based on the ethics of care to help students thrive in the learning environment. These interventions addressed not only academic needs but also emotional, social, and financial aspects—elements that Sikakana (2010) identified as crucial for creating an environment conducive to learning. Our approach was distinctive in its timing and scope: we engaged with students during their first week of university life, exploring their individual contexts and circumstances from the outset. We engaged students in various group activities to induct and orient them into social work education, the department of Social Work and the university community. This early intervention gave us an opportunity to understand students' needs and circumstances, as well as the challenges they faced when they first encountered the university environment. We believed that addressing obstacles at this crucial early stage would enable students to focus on their academic work without being hindered by problems that had attainable solutions. Our observations revealed that removing these barriers required intentional efforts to create interculturally sensitive support alongside culturally sensitive pedagogy.

Faculty have an ethical responsibility to speak on behalf of voiceless students whose opinions are often ignored (Agherdien et al., 2022). The care we provide includes amplifying the voices of the students. In this paper, we argue that going beyond speaking on behalf of students—by reflecting on our engagement with them and acting on their behalf—serves social justice ideals. Social justice, in this context, meant recognizing and addressing the systemic barriers that students faced on account of their socio-economic backgrounds and was the lens through which we viewed our responsibility. By operationalizing this approach, we actively identified and removed obstacles. In this way, we endeavored to create an equitable learning environment that would enhance all students' academic success.

5.3 Methodology

The three authors of this paper are lecturers in Wits University's first-year program. Each reflected on the four-year period of practical interventions with first-year students. The first author taught the first-year social work class from 2018 to 2022, the second author held the position of course coordinator from 2021 to 2022, and the third author fulfilled the role of first-year course coordinator starting before COVID-19 and during the COVID-19 lockdown (2018–2020). Course coordinators serve as the primary liaisons with teaching staff and ensure the accuracy of class lists, preparation of course or program outlines, year grades, and record-keeping for extensions, anomalies, and student issues. They also oversee quality assurance and mark entries, while the lecturer is responsible for teaching a module or course. All three authors engaged with students through the personal information forms and induction to assess their needs.

Wits University is situated in Johannesburg, South Africa, a vibrant, leading commercial city on the African continent. The university has 5 faculties and 33 schools, with student enrollments totaling 42,175 per year (University of Witwatersrand, 2022). Wits has in the region of 6000 employees, including approximately 1500 academics and 2500 joint staff. It offers a wide variety of residence housing or housing, encompassing single-gender residences, catering residences (those that provide food for students), and mixed-gender residences.

For the purposes of this paper, we drew upon reflection as a tool for promoting action (Schön, 1983, 1987) as part of our approach to student learning. Reflective practice is a powerful tool in student–teacher relationships, which entails critically examining past experiences to inform the future (Pinsky et al., 1998). Specifically, we employed reflective practice to examine our own observations, actions, and decisions, as well as the processes we engaged with in supporting first-year students. We used reflection tools such as self-assessment journals, guided reflection questions, and group discussions to help structure this process.

The Bachelor of Social Work Degree's qualification leads to a practice-based profession (Ife, 1997) that integrates theoretical knowledge with field practice throughout the four-year program in South Africa (Sewpaul & Lombard, 2004). Wits University enrolls an average of 60 students every year. The individuals discussed in this paper were first-year students, representing a cohort for each of the 4 years covered by the reflection.

The first teaching semester, particularly the first day of class, is a period when many students are still navigating uncertainties related to funding, housing, and adjusting to their new environment. At our institution one in five students find housing in one of the university residences, an average of just 20% of all the students enrolled for their first year of study. In our experience, when faced with such uncertainties, class attendance is sporadic, and even when students do attend, their attention is often divided, which is not conducive to learning. These challenges were further exacerbated by the COVID-19 pandemic, which necessitated a shift from in-person to online learning.

Our reflection will be presented in a sequence of observation, action, decision-making, and finally, reflection-in-action (Greenwood, 1993; Tubbs, 2000). This sequence was influenced by Tronto's (1993) four-phase ethics of care model, which comprises four elements: recognition of need, willingness to respond, direct action, and reaction to care and process. The main thrust of this paper—reflection-in-action—will look back on our actions and what we have learned. According to Schön (1983), reflection-in-action is a deliberate process of thinking about what happened, why it happened, and how it can be improved in the future.

5.3.1 Recognition of Need

Typically, during their first interaction with the institution and the department, students are given essential information about the university and the program, as well as a resource list. Prior to the COVID-19 pandemic (2018–2019), the information was provided in hardcopy, distributed during face-to-face classes. During the COVID-19 reporting period, this information was made available on the university's learning management system, SAKAI (before COVID-19 and in 2020), and ULWAZI (from 2021).

Information is disseminated to first-year students in the following three stages:

1. When students receive their acceptance to study at the university, they are given a link to university resources which includes access to the learning management platform.
2. During the Social Work Department's three-day induction program, which takes place before the start of the teaching program, students receive a list of support services, as well as talks by various people at the university such as campus health and Counselling and Careers Development Unit (CCDU) and the writing center, provided by the university.

3. In the first week of the academic program, all students who missed the induction program are offered a list of support services.

Each year, students are required to complete a Department of Social Work form, capturing personal details, next-of-kin contact information, term-time addresses, and any additional information students feel is important, such as medical conditions. During our reflections, we reviewed these forms—identifying any issues students had raised—and prioritized the circumstances. Some challenges were not documented in the form provided; however, students volunteered further information following a debriefing session with course coordinators.

5.3.2 Willingness to Respond

Table 5.1 summarizes the problems with which students presented, which will be addressed in the discussion later in this paper, along with how each problem was tackled.

Summary of the circumstances, in 2020 there were many requests for laptops and network connectivity. The number decreased between 2021 and 2022 with fourteen (14) to seven (7) requests for laptop, respectively. By April 2020, almost 5000 laptops had been delivered to homes of students including those in rural areas (SAnews, 2020). The following is a communication from the management in beginning of the year 2021:

> We received more applications than the laptops available in the loan bank. (The situation was worsened by the delay in NSFAS decisions, as the NSFAS learning allowance is now available towards students purchasing their own laptops) Given this, I urgently raised the

Table 5.1 Classification of student circumstances

Socio-economic issues	*Academic support*
• Housing—traveling long distances • Financial difficulties—transport, owing fees, awaiting response from NSFAS • Family responsibilities • Limited access to printing resources • Lack of food • Cost of data • Access to devices	• Computer literacy • Writing skills • Field practice sites • Academic performance • Computer • Laptop • Data • Network access
Health issues	*Personal issues*
• Illness—severe headache, hearing aid • Emotional stress—death in the family • Disability	• Family issues • Court appearances • Isolation in classes • Lack of confidence • Family violence • Loss of family members • Not coping with new environment

> challenge at (Senior executive Team) SET, and SET approved the acquisition of some 2500 additional laptops on a fast-tracked basis. My understanding is that the additional laptops would arrive this week for urgent distribution to students. In the meantime, we agreed that at least for those students who are able to, computer labs would be opened to give them access to on campus facilities.

Receiving devices such as laptop was not sufficient to address the online class attendance, some students did not have internet access as per quotations from the students below:

Student email communication in March 2021:

> I applied for the wits laptop but I could not get it because they said that students who are covered by NSFAS will get learning allowance, even now NSFAS has not approved and we have started with assignments of which laptops will make it easier to write. Your intervention will be highly appreciated.

In 2022 alone, the university distributed food parcels containing non-perishables to 837 students throughout the whole university, and 96,000 hot meals per month through the food bank (Integrated Report, 2022). According to the institution report, 48% of students come from both rural and Black townships. The social work department's trend is that of 68% students from urban areas, while 32% is from rural areas. Of note is that almost 50% of the students are first in their family to attend university.

5.3.3 Direct Action

Sixty-seven first-year social work students enrolled at Wits in 2018, 55 in 2019 and 59 in 2020. During this period, their problems centered on the uncertainty of funding, preventing most from securing housing. In desperation, some students awaiting confirmation of housing or for funding approval resorted to sleeping in the library.

It should be noted that most students who struggled with housing were from outside of Johannesburg. While the university prioritizes housing for students from outside the province, those without funding are not allocated housing before arriving in the city.

The lecturers assisted students by informing them about the Wits Student Representative Council (SRC), a formal structure that supports students across the entire university, and by referring them to the fees office and the NSFAS. We directed students with financial problems, whose financial aid was insufficient to meet their day-to-day needs, to the director of the food bank. Students reporting a lack of confidence in their abilities to produce scholarly writing were referred to the writing center for assistance.

We invited students facing extreme personal issues to meet with us one-on-one. Some circumstances were so urgent and risky that we had to liaise with other university departments on their behalf. For example, a female student reported sharing a room with her brother's male friend. She expressed extreme discomfort and had missed several lectures before our intervention. In this case, we engaged with the Dean of Students and the Housing Office, advocating for immediate housing to be provided.

At this juncture, it is important to note that the processes on which we reflected have been ongoing since 2016 and continue to be implemented. The process of collecting data from students began in 2016, initially to obtain students' next-of-kin details for emergencies. Over time, the form was amended to include students' term-time addresses and other pertinent information. We also revised the form during the COVID-19 pandemic to include a section on the need for a laptop. However, it was only in 2018—following the incident involving the female student living with her brother's male friend—that we began conducting more in-depth analyses of students' information.

These interventions were necessary to support students' learning. However, we had to ensure that the boundaries around involvement with students with emotional risks were maintained within the lecturer–student relationship, to prevent dependency while facilitating learning and teaching.

In 2020 and 2021, students' problems were exacerbated as the landscape of their education was about to undergo a sudden and challenging turn. In 2020, we began by distributing personal forms to the 59 newly enrolled students, analyzing their situations, and intervening in the same manner as we had done from 2018 to 2019. However, the situation changed in mid-March 2020 with the COVID-19 emergency response. Students living in university residences were instructed to vacate within 72 h and return home. This directive, issued by the South African President in compliance with the World Health Organization and the National Institute for Communicable Diseases, led to an immediate change in how care and support for first-year students were provided. We had to adjust how we collected personal data, intervened to resolve their problems, and helped students settle into a new online learning environment.

The 2020 academic year posed a multitude of challenges, exposing gaps highlighted by COVID-19, including students' lack of access to technology (Mtshweni, 2022). This was not a new revelation in our case; we were already aware that many of our students came from resource-constrained backgrounds. However, the shift to online learning added further strain, as many lacked essential devices, such as computers or laptops, and stable internet access.

Our intervention involved reaching out to all our social work students to determine their access to a computer or laptop. After establishing that certain students did not have access to digital devices, and therefore could not attend online classes, the university immediately made laptops available to all students who needed them. These laptops were delivered to even the most remote areas in South Africa. In 2020, 34 laptops were distributed, while in 2021 only 14 students needed them. In the process of resolving the laptop issue, our attention was drawn to other barriers. For some students in remote areas, device access, electricity, water, conducive workspaces, and high data costs presented significant constraints to accessing their courses, support, and learning resources.

One student shared the following message:

> I've been unable to attend classes mainly because I struggle with data connection. I have downloaded the Canvas app [a mobile app for accessing course materials, submitting assignments, viewing grades, and participating in discussions] on my Mobicel phone. However, when I try to access files or download files or lecture slides it [the app] is unable to do so. When I try to use the link sent via email, it says I'm unauthorized to use this app (sent 19 March 2021 10:17).

In response to messages like these, several universities made large-scale data purchases for all students, identified digitally excluded students, and provided data.

5.3.4 Reaction to Care and Process

During the reporting period, we remained attentive to students' needs, explored their contexts, and identified barriers to a conducive learning environment. Our efforts extended beyond merely recognizing these needs—what Tronto (1993) described as the first phase in the ethics of care. We moved from probing and identifying need to actively respond to the issues that emerged from our assessment of students' contexts. In aligning our approach with Tronto's (1993) model, we considered the resources available to students and the extent to which this information was accessible to them. While we were aware of students' socio-economic backgrounds, we had not fully understood how these circumstances shaped their experiences within the university environment. Without this process, we would not have grasped the impact of socio-economic background at key stages: during the application process, upon acceptance, and after enrollment. It allowed us to make direct contact with students to offer support.

Since information about the resources for support was available on the website, provided during induction, and reiterated in the first week, we assumed this would be translated to use. However, this was not necessarily the case. Therefore, our direct action focused on helping students access and use the information. Most importantly, we facilitated connections between the students and resources such as the food bank.

We also discovered during the lockdown that providing laptops to assist students in accessing online classes was not enough. We later learned that students also needed reliable internet access to engage with online platforms, something we had not initially considered.

Our continued goal was to ensure that the university environment was conducive to learning. Throughout this process, we strived to improve the connectedness between lecturers and students. Care was achieved not through good intentions, alone; it required us to act and assist students when they needed our help. In line with Ricoeur's (1992) view, providing care to students not only supported them but also helped us as lecturers. It challenged us to reconsider how we viewed students' contexts, and it pushed us to continually improve our assessment practices and support strategies.

5.4 Discussion

Successful pedagogical engagement depends upon a well-prepared lecturer–student working relationship that is free from obstacles that hinder effective communication and learning. This paper presents how we used our reflections on the implementation of student support interventions during three different periods: pre-COVID-19 pandemic, during the COVID-19 emergency response, and post COVID-19 lockdown. We reviewed a brief period between 2018 and 2022, during which we responded to the needs assessment of a cohort of first-year students over four successive years. While we have not presented formal evaluation indicators, our approach was shaped by ongoing feedback from students, faculty, and staff, along with our own reflections on the challenges students face. We believe the success of our efforts is evident in the increased engagement with and support for students. However, we recognize that incorporating more formal evaluation metrics could provide a clearer understanding of the impact of our approach.

We have argued that students' environments and situations cannot be ignored in the quest to help them adapt to, remain in, and succeed in academia. We shifted from a reactive stance to proactively applying the ethics of care, identifying both existing and potential challenges, and working alongside students to remove additional hindrances to learning. We employed a social justice approach to address both current and future barriers to their learning.

Our interventions demonstrate that while students do have a voice, that voice needs to be amplified. Attending to students' basic needs at the beginning of the academic year supported their success and their adjustment to the university environment. Identifying and intervening in dire circumstances further aligned staff expectations with the goal of helping students meet their academic obligations. We engaged in a process of learning as we implemented the intervention. Our personal information form evolved from initially asking about health-related issues and next-of-kin to addressing hunger, housing-related concerns, and later incorporating questions on technological devices, transport, and internet connectivity. This continuous improvement led to reflection, through which we consciously learned from students' situations and refined our approach to probing and our areas of focus.

The strength of our interventions was that we did not profile students or categorize them based on their socio-economic backgrounds. Instead, we provided a platform for all students to identify and communicate with the areas in which they required support. Heydenrych and Case (2016) cautioned against implementing interventions that categorized students according to race or remedial status, arguing that such interventions tended to overlook students from previously disadvantaged and marginalized backgrounds (Warren, 2002). Our approach revealed several ways for faculty to understand the issues or problems students experienced. Crucially, some issues required practical interventions, while others necessitated psychological and emotional engagements with students, or, in some cases, both. Whether issues were practical or emotional, if left unattended, they would hinder students' ability to engage with pedagogy and fully benefit from teaching and learning practices.

We demonstrated several methods through which students were able to voluntarily share information about their current and perceived future struggles. In our case, students could volunteer information to a staff member. Alternatively, staff could observe certain behaviors and inquire about students' concerns or proactively seek information by requesting students to complete the personal information form. Furthermore, students were made aware of the existing resources during their induction into the social work program. Concerned classmates were also at liberty to report matters to lecturers. These methods formed the basis for assessing students' needs and allowed for further assistance or intervention. This moved away from systems that were rooted in dated pedagogical approaches (Warren, 2002). Heydenrych and Case (2016) noted that of the interventions implemented in institutions of higher learning to assist students, some are remedial, some perpetuate segregation, and others promote wellness (Gieck & Olsen, 2007). The strength in our approach lay in its ability to make the learning environment conducive to all, based on the premise that each individual student had specific needs, irrespective of their socio-economic background.

What also distinguished our intervention is that it existed before COVID-19 and continued after the pandemic restrictions were lifted. In-person classes resumed in January 2021, implying a transition back to traditional learning environments. These interventions remain relevant, irrespective of whether students attend classes face-to-face or remotely, and connecting students to resources remains an ongoing practice.

The COVID-19 pandemic served as a reminder of the fractures in our society along racial, class, location, and gender lines (Hettler, 1984). Applying the ethics of care as a guiding philosophy for our interventions assumed that individuals had varying degrees of dependence and interdependence on one another (Dykes, 2012). Given the emphasis on education as a liberator of society, it stands to reason that identifying factors that assist in student success and helping them access and complete their studies is vital. We posit that a conducive environment contributes to students' adjustment to university and further to their success. Our interventions offered academic, emotional, psychological, and socio-economic support. Through our approach, we have shaped an enabling support system to improve students' learning experience. It was our deeper commitment to provide support, over and above approaches to teaching and learning pedagogy, that led to our involvement in the intervention and its continuation.

Without the resources provided by Wits University, our intervention would not have been possible. Ongoing reflection on current and past experiences serves to inform future directions. We used lessons learned from these practices to inform further practice and institutional policies, such as providing laptops to students. Prior to COVID-19, the personal information form did not include a question about laptops, but we added it and continue to inquire, even after returning to face-to-face teaching.

Reflecting on our experiences continues to enhance our interventions, enabling us to continuously adapt to changing social challenges. As learning to teach is an ongoing process, so is learning to support students in adapting to teaching and learning. Our reflective experiences regarding socio-economic and well-being support for students are an essential component of developing professionals within our field.

5.5 Limitations

The limitations of this paper lie in its focus on the authors' reflections on their actions and engagements with students' issues. Data were not collected with the intention of quantifying the input, output, or successes. Additionally, the discussion was centered on a single program at a university and involved only first-year students within that program.

5.6 Conclusion

The interventions provided to the first-year cohort in our department offered an opportunity to continue with the academic year with minimal disruption from socio-economic challenges. These interventions succeeded in connecting students to available resources within the institution while helping them self-reflect by identifying their own needs, which, when met, would facilitate their access, retention, and focus on their studies. In addition, applying the ethics of care approach opened opportunities for students to engage remotely with the academic institution, thereby facilitating their learning. Academic institutions have a valuable opportunity to support and invest in student services while ensuring sustainability. While graduate completion rates are a measure of success, quality education requires a nurturing environment for students to thrive. As a caring profession, we cannot distance ourselves from providing care. Our efforts demonstrate that embracing a holistic approach to student support, moving away from the idea that lecturers are simply professionals, and acknowledging both academic and psychosocial needs enhance the educational environment and optimize conditions for student success across all socio-economic backgrounds.

UNIVERSITY OF THE WITWATERSRAND, JOHANNESBURG

SCHOOL OF HUMAN AND COMMUNITY DEVELOPMENT
SOCIAL WORK

STUDENT PERSONAL DETAILS (CONFIDENTIAL INFORMATION)

A. Identifying Particulars

1. Surname:	
2. Name:	
3. Date of birth:	
4. Student number:	
5. SACSSP Registration number:	
6. E-mail address:	
7. Contact number(s):	
8. Address during term time:	
9. Home physical address:	
10. Home postal address:	
11. Address of next of kin:	
12. Contact number(s) of next of kin:	
13. Relationship to next of kin:	
14. Home language:	
15. Which other languages you can speak?	
16. Name of mother	
a. Contact details.	
b. Occupation of mother	
17. Name of father a. Contact details. **b.** Occupation of father	

Umthombo Building - Basement, Room USW-8, Braamfontein East Campus, Private Bag 3, WITS 2050
T +27 11 717 4472 | E socialwork.SHCD@wits.ac.za | W www.wits.ac.za/shcd/social-work

100 1922 2022

18. Name of guardian a) Contact details. b) Occupation of father	
19. Are you the first in your family to attend higher education?	YES NO
20. Do you have a cell phone that can connect to the internet?	YES NO
21. Do you have friends or family members at Wits?	Names and contact details, if yes…

B. Academic Record

1. Name of Secondary School attended:	
2. In which town or city and province is the school?	
3. What year of study are you at WITS?	
4. List the courses (per semester or year) you are registered for in 2023	

C. Financial Support for Studies

1. Please indicate how you are funding your studies (Tick the appropriate box)

DSD Scholarship	
NSFAS Loan	
Self-Funded	
Student Loan from a financial Institution	
Other bursary/scholarship or loan	

2. If you have a DSD Scholarship, please provide the following information:

Name the province	
Contact number of contact person	
E-mail address of contact person	

3. If you have a DSD scholarship or NSFAS loan, what is your scholarship/loan amount for this year?

DSD Scholarship	
NSFAS Loan	
Other Loan	

D. Medical History (Tick appropriate box)

1. Do you suffer from any medical condition?

Yes	
No	

2. If yes, state the condition
…………………………………………………………………………………………………
…………………………………………………………………………………………………
……………………………………………………

3. Do you have any mental health difficulties?

Yes	
No	

4. If yes, state the difficulty …
…………………………………………………………………………………………………
…………………………………………………………………………………………………
…………………………………………………

5. Do you have any other special needs or information you feel we should know about?

Yes	
No	

6. If yes, state
…………………………………………………………………………………………………
…………………………………………………………………………………………………
…………………………………………………………………………………………………
…………………………………………………………………………………………………
…………………………………………………………………………………………………

E. General

If there is any other information you would like to share with us to support you during your studies this year at WITS please state
…………………………………………………………………………………………………
…………………………………………………………………………………………………
…………………………………………………………………………………………………

Signature of students: … ……………………………………

Date completed by student………………………………….

For Official Use

Name of course coordinator: ______________________________

Signature and date seen by of course coordinator: ______________________________

Name of Field Instruction Coordinator: ______________________________

Signature and date see by Field Instruction Coordinator: ______________________________

Comments: ______________________________

References

Adhariani, D., Sciulli, N., & Clift, R. (2017). An introduction to the ethics of care. In *Financial management and corporate governance from the feminist ethics of care perspective* (pp. 17–48). Palgrave Macmillan. https://doi.org/10.1007/978-3-319-33518-6

Agherdien, N., Pillay, R., Dube, N., & Masinga, P. (2022). What does decolonising education mean to us? Educator reflections. *Scholarship of Teaching and Learning, 6*(1), 55–78. https://journals.uj.ac.za/SOTL/index.php/sotls/article/view/204

Akpojivi, U. (2023). *Social movements and digital activism in Africa*. Palgrave Macmillan. https://doi.org/10.1007/978-3-031-30207-7_3

Amoah, C., & Le Roux, L. (2024). Students' challenges with online remote teaching and learning in South Africa. *International Journal of Construction Education and Research, 1–21*. https://doi.org/10.1080/15578771.2024.2423632

Beauchamp, T. L., & Childress, J. F. (2001). *Principles of biomedical ethics* (5th ed.). Oxford University Press.
Bhardwa, S. (2017). Why do students go to university and how do they choose which one? *THE Student*. https://www.timeshighereducation.com/student/news/why-do-students-go-university-and-how-do-they-choose-which-one
CHE. (2015). *Higher education qualifications sub-framework: Qualification standard for bachelor of social*. Council on Higher Education. https://www.che.ac.za/publications/standard-reviews/qualification-standards-bachelor-social-work
Czerniewicz, L., Agherdien, N., Badenhorst, J., Belluigi, D., Chambers, T., Chili, M., de Villiers, M., Felix, A., Gachago, D., Gokhale, C., Ivala, E., Kramm, N., Madiba, M., Mistri, G., Mgqwashu, E., Pallitt, N., Prinsloo, People, Solomon, K., Strydom, S., et al. (2020). A wake-up call: Equity, inequality and COVID-19 emergency remote teaching and learning. *Postdigital Science and Education, 2*(3), 946–967. https://doi.org/10.1007/s42438-020-00187-4
del Carmen Salazar, M. (2013). A humanizing pedagogy: Reinventing the principles and practice of education as a journey toward liberation. *Review of Research in Education, 37*(1), 121–148. https://doi.org/10.3102/0091732X12464032
Dykes, G. (2012). Phronesis and adverse childhood experiences of social work students. *The Social Work Practitioner-Researcher, 24*(3), 331–349. https://doi.org/10.25159/2415-5829/2257
Gieck, D. J., & Olsen, S. (2007). Holistic wellness as a means to developing a lifestyle approach to health behavior among college students. *Journal of American College Health, 56*(1), 29–35. https://doi.org/10.3200/JACH.56.1.29-36
Gómez-García, G., Ramos-Navas-Parejo, M., de la Cruz-Campos, J. C., & Rodríguez-Jimenez, C. (2022). Impact of COVID-19 on university students: An analysis of its influence on psychological and academic factors. *International Journal of Environmental Research and Public Health, 19*(16), 10433. https://doi.org/10.3390/ijerph191610433
Greenwood, J. (1993). Reflective practice: A critique of the work of Argyris and Schon. *Journal of Advanced Nursing, 18*(8), 1183–1187. https://doi.org/10.1046/j.1365-2648.1993.18081183.x
Hettler, B. (1984). Wellness: Encouraging a lifetime pursuit of excellence. *Health Values, 8*(4), 13–17.
Heydenrych, H., & Case, J. M. (2016). Academic development in the mainstream: A case study in an undergraduate engineering programme in South Africa. *South African Journal of Higher Education, 29*(5), 179–200. https://doi.org/10.20853/29/-5-523
Ife, J. (1997). *Rethinking social work: Towards critical practice*. Longman.
Ige, B. O., Amosun, S. L., & Hartman, N. (2017). Widening student access and participation in allied health sciences: A critical reflection. *South African Journal of Higher Education, 31*(5), 65–89. https://doi.org/10.20853/31-5-1554
Integrated Report. (2022). https://www.wits.ac.za/media/wits-university/about-wits/documents/IntegrateReport,2022_20June_web.pdf
Keeling, R. P. (2014). An Ethic of Care in Higher Education: Well-Being and Learning. *Journal of College and Character, 15*(3), 141–148. https://doi.org/10.1515/jcc-2014-0018
Kuh, G. D., Kinzie, J., Buckley, J. A., Bridges, B. K., & Hayek, J. C. (2006). *What matters to student success: A review of the literature*. National Postsecondary Education Cooperative.
Lalendle, L. L., & Mgijima, M. (2018). Trends and challenges in measuring student success: A South African perspective. In H. M. Fardoun, K. J. Downing, & M. Mok (Eds.), *The future of higher education in the Middle East and Africa* (pp. 167–185). Springer. https://doi.org/10.1007/978-3-319-64656-_15
Maio, G. (2018). Fundamental of an ethics of care. In F. Krause & J. Boldt (Eds.), *Care in healthcare: Reflections on theory and practice*. Palgrave Macmillan. https://doi.org/10.1007/978-3-319-61291-1-4
Mathebula, M., & Calitz, T. M. (2018). #Feesmustfall: A media analysis of student's voices on access to universities in South Africa. In M. Case & A. Paul (Eds.), *Higher education pathways. South African undergraduate education and the public good* (pp. 177–191). African Minds. https://doi.org/10.5281/zenolo/1920793

Minkos, M. L., & Gelbar, N. W. (2021). Considerations for educators in supporting student learning in the midst of COVID-19. *Psychology in the Schools, 58*(2), 416–426. https://doi.org/10.1002/pits.22454

Motala, S., & Menon, K. (2020). In search of the 'new normal': Reflections on teaching and learning during COVID-19 in a South African University. *Southern African Review of Education, 26*(1), 80–99. https://doi.org/10.10520/ejc-sare-v26-n1-a6

Mtshweni, B.V. (2022). COVID-19: Exposing unmatched historical disparities in the South African Institutions of higher learning. *South African Journal of Higher Education, 36*(1), 234–250. https://doi.org/10.20853/36-1-4507. eISSN 1753-5913.

Naidoo, G. M., & Moonasamy, A. R. (2022). Digital learning challenges experienced by South African university students during the COVID-19 pandemic. *The Independent Journal of Teaching and Learning, 17*(2), 76–90. https://journals.assaf.org.za/index.php/ijtl/article/view/17999/21087

Olowoyo, M. M., Ramaila, S., Mavuru, L., & Mugivhisa, L. (2022). The impact of the COVID-19 pandemic on students' learning at universities in the Gauteng Province, South Africa. *Africa Education Review, 19*(1), 143–159. https://doi.org/10.1080/18146627.2023.2197152

Onwuegbuzie, A. J., & Ojo, E. (2021). University students' experiences of learning in an online environment in COVID-19 pandemic: A meta-methods research study of perceptions and attitudes of South African students. *Journal of Pedagogical Research, 5*(4), 1–18. https://doi.org/10.33902/JPR.2021472164

Pat-Horenczyk, R., Schiff, M., Arënliu, A., Zasiekina, L., Kagialis, A., Ferreira, N., Nesterko, Y., Glaesmer, H., Fernández-Alcántra, M., & Benbenishty, R. (2022). Challenges faced by university students during the COVID-19: An international study in five countries during the early phase of the pandemic. *International Journal of Psychology, 57*(5), 547–558. https://doi.org/10.1002/ijop.12846

Pinsky, L. E., Monson, D., & Irby, D. M. (1998). How excellent teachers are made: Reflecting on success to improve teaching. *Advances in Health Sciences Education, 3*(3), 207–215. https://doi.org/10.1023/A:1009749323352

Ricoeur, P. (1992). *Oneself as another*. University of Chicago Press.

Roberts, K. C., & Danoff-Burg, S. (2010). Mindfulness and health behaviors: Is paying attention good for you? Journal of American College Health, 59(3), 165–173.https://doi.org/10.1080/07448481.2010.484452

SA's university students challenges faced. (2020, August 18). *George Herald*. https://www.georgeherald.com/News/Article/National-News/challenges-faced-by-sa-s-university-students-202008181019

Schön, D. A. (1983). *The reflective practitioner: How professionals think in action*. Temple Smith.

Schön, D. A. (1987). *Educating the reflective practitioner: Toward a new design for teaching and learning in the professions*. Jossey-Bass.

Sewpaul, V., & Lombard, A. (2004). Social work education, training and standards in Africa. *Social Work Education, 23*(5), 537–554. https://doi.org/10.1080/0261547042000252271

Sifunda, S., Mokhele, T., Manyaapelo, T., Dukhi, N., Sewpaul, R., Parker, W.-A., Parker, S., Naidoo, I., Jooste, S., Ramlagan, S. Gaida, R., Mabaso, M., Zuma, K., & Reddy, P. (2021). Preparedness for self-isolation or quarantine and lockdown in South Africa: Results from a rapid online survey. *BMC Public Health, 21*, Article 580. https://doi.org/10.1186/s12889-021-10628-9

Sikakana, C. N. (2010). Supporting student-doctors from under-resourced educational backgrounds: An academic development programme. *Medical Education, 44*(9), 917–925. https://doi.org/10.1111/j.1365-2923.2010.03733.x

Townsend, L., & Dawes, A. (2013). Individual and contextual factors associated with the sexual abuse of children under 12: A review of literature. In L. Richter, A. Dawes, & C. Higson-Smith (Eds.), *Sexual abuse of young children in southern Africa* (pp. 55–94). HSRC Press.

Tronto, J. C. (1993). *Moral boundaries: A political argument for an ethic of care*. Routledge.

Tubbs, N. (2000). From reflective practitioner to comprehensive teacher. *Education Action Research, 8*(1), 167–178. https://doi.org/10.1080/09650790000200113

United Nations, Department of Economic and Social Affairs, Sustainable Development. (2015). *Transforming our world: The 2030 Agenda for Sustainable Development: Department of Economic and Social Affairs*. https://sdgs.un.org/2030agenda

University of the Witwatersrand. (2022). *Facts & figures: 2021/2022*. https://www.wits.ac.za/media/wits-university/about-wits/documents/WITS%20Facts%20and%20Figures%202022%20Web-Ready.pdf

Walker, M., & Fongwa, S. (2017). Graduate employability, global shifts and local realities. In M. Walker & S. Fongwa (Eds.), *Universities, employability and human development* (pp. 29–51). Palgrave Macmillan. https://doi.org/10.1057/978-1-137-58452-6_2

Walton, E., Carrington, S., Saggers, B., Edwards, C., & Kimani, W. (2019). What matters in learning communities for inclusive education: A cross-case analysis. *Professional Development in Education, 48*(1), 134–148. https://doi.org/10.1080/19415257.2019.1689525

Warren, D. (2002). Curriculum design in a context of widening participation in higher education. *Arts and Humanities in Higher Education, 1*(1), 85–99. https://doi.org/10.1177/1474022202001001007

Weatherton, M., & Schussler, E. E. (2021). Success for all? A call to re-examine how student success is defined in higher education. *Life Sciences. Education, 20*(1), es3. https://doi.org/10.1187/cbe.20-09-0223

Weuffen, S., Fotinatos, N., & Andrews, T. (2021). Evaluating sociocultural influences affecting participation and understanding of academic support services and programs (SSPs): Impacts on notions of attrition, retention, and success in higher education. *Journal of College Student Retention: Research, Theory & Practice, 23*(1), 118–138. https://doi.org/10.1177/1521025118803847

World Health Organization. (2025). *COVID-19 response in South Africa – Country brief*. https://www.afro.who.int/countries/south-africa/publication/COVID-19-response-south-africa-country-brief

Busisiwe Nkala-Dlamini is an associate professor. University of the Witwatersrand, School of Human and Community Development, Department of Social Work. Research in socio-behavioral research, parental involvement, and international collaborative interdisciplinary research in teenage boys' exposure to and involvement in gender-based violence. Currently working on community engagements on air pollution. Holds a PhD in Development Studies, a Master of Health Science in Bioethics from the University of Toronto, and a Bachelor of Arts in Social Work from the University of the Witwatersrand. Recipient of the Fogarty International Scholarship, NRF Sabbatical Grant and Female Academic Leaders Fellowship Grant.

Zintle Ntshongwana is a lecturer in the Social Work Department at the University of the Witwatersrand. She holds a PhD, a Master's and Bachelor of Social Work from the University of Fort Hare. She is a Female Academic Leaders Fellow (FALF) and earned the Emerging Scholar Award at the International Conference on Health, Wellness & Society in both 2022 and 2023. In 2023, she received a Faculty of Humanities Research Recognition and is a Mellon Catalyst recipient. Her research interests include family social work, child welfare, foster care, gender-based violence, and disability.

Roshini Pillay is an associate professor at the University of the Witwatersrand. Her research interests encompass group work, technology-enhanced learning in social work education, social justice, and Occupational Social Work. She has a passion for people and has worked in both in the public sector and non-governmental sectors. Currently, she leads the podcast, "Social Work Khuluma." She is the principal investigator on a National Research Fund Project called Social Work education Post COVID 19-Course Redesign/rediscovering new ways of learning and teaching in South Africa.

Chapter 6
Designing Healthier Cities: A Pilot Program in the Architectural Design Studio

Stéphane Sadoux and Cecilia Di Marco

Abstract This paper focuses on a pedagogic pilot program aiming to integrate health-related issues into the architectural and urban design studio. The paper first sets out the context in which this test curriculum took place as part of the AE&CC Master of Architecture program (*Architecture, Environment & Cultures Constructives*) at Grenoble School of Architecture. It then provides a critical analysis of learning outcomes, which were revealed through a series of interviews with six students and three teachers. Pedagogical outputs are illustrated through a selection of student work. The broad theoretical framework used as a basis for this research is the revised Bloom's taxonomy of educational objectives, produced by Anderson and colleagues (Anderson et al., *A taxonomy for learning, teaching, and assessing: A revision of Bloom's taxonomy of educational objectives*. Longman, 2001). The paper concludes with an identification of challenges for the further development of health-based approaches in urban and architectural design education.

Keywords Health · Architecture · Urbanism · Design · Pedagogy

6.1 Introduction

In a paper published in the *Journal of Architectural Education*, Renée Cheng suggested that the challenges students training in architecture are facing today are more complex and urgent than those with which previous graduates had to deal. Globalization, climate change, and digital tools are quoted both as drivers of the transformation of the profession and as challenges requiring "multifaceted and multidisciplinary responses" (Cheng, 2014). This point of view is somewhat difficult to dispute, as a plethora of academic publications continuously points to the wide

S. Sadoux (✉) · C. D. Marco
Univ. Grenoble Alpes, ENSAG, AE&CC, Grenoble, France
e-mail: stephane.sadoux@univ-grenoble-alpes.fr

© The Author(s), under exclusive license to Springer Nature Switzerland AG 2025

L. Dalingwater et al. (eds.), *Structural and Systemic Perspectives on Health and Well-being*, Human Well-Being Research and Policy Making,
https://doi.org/10.1007/978-3-031-99924-6_6

range of environmental, economic, and cultural issues designers nowadays have to address. Architectural education is consequently subject to pressures for continuous institutional improvement and student learning, which, as Bachman and Bachman (2009) remind us, result in a need to develop empirically measurable outcomes.

As future practitioners, students must be encouraged to address architectural and urban design in the light of an increasingly wide range of health-related challenges. Teaching curricula should provide them with theoretical and methodological tools to help them understand how designers can contribute to fostering healthier environments. This paper provides an overview of the ways in which health has been introduced in the final year design studio of one of the Grenoble School of Architecture's master's programs (*Architecture, Environment & Cultures Constructives*, hereafter referred to as MArch AE&CC).

Firstly, we summarize some of the key design issues made necessary in pursuit of health. We then briefly describe the organization of the MArch AE&CC program and its recent transformation which aims to address health-related issues. Underpinning this paper is the revised taxonomy of educational objectives, developed by Anderson and colleagues (Anderson & Krathwohl, 2001) based on Bloom's pioneering work (Bloom et al., 1984). The latter was originally designed as a means of "facilitating the exchange of test items among faculty at various universities in order to create banks of items, each measuring the same educational objective" (Krathwohl, 2002). The revised taxonomy produced by Anderson is used in this paper: it is particularly well-suited to design pedagogy given the fact that it draws in creativity, which is presented as the highest form of learning. Semi-structured interviews were carried out in 2018 with six students and three members of teaching staff in order to understand how they, respectively, dealt with health issues throughout the learning and design process. The paper is illustrated through a selection of students' work.

6.2 Health in Urban Design

According to the World Health Organization definition, health is a state of complete physical, mental, and social well-being and not merely the absence of disease or infirmity (WHO, 1948). Well-being results from the interaction between humans and the biological, chemical, physical, psychological, and social agents in their environments. Environmental determinants of health are thus significant, and addressing populations' health in a proactive way requires a multidisciplinary and cross-sectoral approach. Well-being depends not only on the quality of the health-care system but also on living conditions, on the social, environmental, and economic determinants: the environment is a major determinant of health (Barton & Grant, 2006). Thus, policies and practices for the management, control, and prevention of environmental factors affect the health of present and future generations.

An increasing number of studies have suggested that some illnesses, such as respiratory disease (Halloran, 2011; Suglia et al., 2011), obesity (Papas et al., 2007; Coombes et al., 2010; Townshend & Lake, 2017), diabetes (Pasala et al., 2010), cancers (Morelli et al., 2016; Widziewicz & Rogula-Kozłowska, 2018), and mental disorder (Kuo & Faber, 2004; Song et al., 2019), are influenced by the built environment, air quality, and greenness. Through urban and architectural design, actions aiming to improve the environment, such as reducing air and water pollution, increasing green areas, developing infrastructure for soft mobility (non-motorized), or endorsing spacious and comfortable homes for everyone, can contribute to behavioral change in terms of physical activity and social relations. Raising students' awareness of the possible contributions of urban and architectural design to address health issues is therefore crucial.

6.3 The AE&CC Master's Program

6.3.1 Urban Design in the School of Architecture

The Master of Architecture offered by the School of Architecture of Grenoble is an illustration of what Carmona has referred to as the immersed model, whereby urban design is "not recognized as a separate discipline but is instead part and parcel of a larger discipline—typically architecture—in which design at the urban scale is addressed" (Carmona, 2016). Although until 2023 the Grenoble School of Architecture ran a specific master of urban design in partnership with the university's Institute of Urban Planning and Alpine Geography, urban design, as a cross-disciplinary field, has also always been addressed within the architecture curriculum. As part of their final Master of Architecture (MArch) project, students of the AE&CC program are required to produce an architectural design project framed within a wider urban and regional context.

The MArch AE&CC program runs over a two-year period. The first year is underpinned by a design-build studio, which allows students to work on materials and construction techniques as part of a process which ends with the building of a real scale building (Zawistowski et al., 2020). Examples of recent projects have over the years included the Terra Nostra demonstrator built as part of the Terra world congress on earthen architecture (2016), a community center ("Maison pour tous") for the village of Four (2019) and more recently the retrofitting and transformation of the Magdeleine Durand House and Park in Autrans-Méaudre in the Vercors mountains (2022, in progress). During the second year, students focus on the production of their final year project. The design studio is complemented by a seminar in which teaching staff provide students with methodological and theoretical inputs through lectures and seminars, which draw content from their own research. This specific input is, as far as health is concerned, related to a major cross-disciplinary research project focusing on health trajectories. The LIFE[1] project was led by the Grenoble Alpes University Hospital and the Institute for Advanced Biosciences. The AE&CC research unit was a member of the consortium and as part of this research it focused on the environmental determinants of health trajectories, the latter referring to changes in health patterns over time. The overall goal of this project was to examine the determinants of disease trajectories by capturing underestimated yet crucial contributing factors including access to care, socioeconomic factors, environmental exposures, and the quality of the built environment.

6.3.2 Teaching Technique

In order to understand how health was explicitly integrated into the master's program, it is useful to summarize some of the main teaching techniques used within it. Overall, MArch AE&CC seeks to encourage students to think of architectural and urban design in ways that contribute to reducing fuel energy dependency and that promotes social and environmental justice for all. In order to achieve this, it relies on a range of teaching methods as well as on certain design precedents, which the teaching staff see as useful to encourage students to think critically about contemporary challenges.

6.3.3 Garden City as a Case Study: Precedents and Futures

Pedagogic delivery partly relies on the theory and history of architectural and urban design, through an examination of precedents. Since 2014, research has focused on garden cities and new settlements, both in terms of their history and of their current resurgence, most notably in the United Kingdom where a number of the so-called new garden settlements are being built in an attempt to address the housing shortage. In order to question the possible relevance of the garden city model in the light of current urban design debates, students have been required to carefully analyze a range of existing new settlements in Britain (garden cities and new towns), as well as the range of proposals developed as part of the 2014 Wolfson Economics Prize[2] and the National Health Service (NHS) Healthy New Towns Program.[3] The latter,

[1] LIFE (is MaDE of ChoiCes): Leveraging Multidimensional Information for curbing LIFE-course trajectories of Multimorbid Chronic Diseases: Integrating Environment, socioeconomic factors and urban planning with Clinical data and biomolecular Mechanisms.

[2] The competition invited contestants to show how they would 'deliver a new garden city that which would be visionary, economically viable and popular'.

[3] Program launched by the British National Health Service in 2015. As part of this initiative, ten demonstrator sites were selected throughout the country and several are referred to as garden settlements—Barton Park garden suburb in Oxford being one of them.

which was launched in 2015, aimed to "dramatically improve population health, and integrate health and care services, as new places are built and take shape"; it is suggested the scheme will allow to "rethink how health and care services can be delivered," and that it offers "a golden opportunity to radically rethink how we live," thus taking "an ambitious look at improving health through the built environment."[4] In similar vein, projects submitted for the Wolfson Economics Prize in 2014 have been put forward as examples of the various ways in which the garden city theory, as an early twentieth century precedent, can be subject to reinterpretation in the light of contemporary challenges. The intention is of course not to encourage students to replicate the original garden city model. Rather, the aim is to highlight the relevance of the garden city theory as a precedent that addresses a wide range of social, environmental, political, spatial, and economic issues in a systemic way. But above all, garden cities offer a particularly relevant case study to think about the role of design in addressing health issues (Sadoux & Di Marco, 2020; Sadoux et al., 2022).

As part of their undergraduate training, students were taught urban and planning history and were therefore aware of Ebenezer Howard's major contribution to improving living conditions in the early twentieth century through his garden city theory and the new settlements that were built on its basis, most notably Letchworth and Welwyn. This process allows students to think about the specific health issues that current public policy seeks to address from a spatial perspective. The intention here is to show that, although the health issues which Howard sought to address in his time are very different from those tackled today, the current health and garden city convergence is worth examining based on the assumption that some design principles may be as valid today as they were a century ago.

6.3.4 *Travel and Immersion Experience*

Architectural and urban design cannot only be learned in the classroom. The built environment is something that everyone experiences, and architectural training must therefore involve onsite activities, not least to allow students to gain a better understanding of the spaces and places they are required to address as part of their designs.

In a recent paper, Lara and Evans-Cowley pointed out that there is a great variability in the instructional content of urban design programs throughout the world and that "many faculty members adopt innovative learning techniques that include case study analysis combined with travel/immersion experiences, studio work and fieldwork" (Lara & Evans-Cowley, 2016). The MArch AE&CC program relies on such a range of techniques. Between 2015 and 2018, the first week of the final year was spent abroad as part of a field trip abroad, in the UK. The seven-day trip organized for students included visits of "original" garden cities (Letchworth or

[4] https://www.england.nhs.uk/ourwork/innovation/healthy-new-towns/

Welwyn), an early garden suburb (Hampstead), a post-war new town (Hatfield) and a recent development by Healthy New Town, Barton Park Garden Suburb in Oxford. During these field trips, students carried out surveys of the areas and met a number of key local stakeholders, including residents, local authorities, business representatives, and academics involved in a range of disciplines, such as architecture, urban planning, engineering, transport, and health. As Lara and Evans-Cowley (2016) have pointed out, encouraging students to think about foreign historical precedents is beneficial both in terms of helping them understand cultural differences and planning and design priorities, but it also encourages them to think about the extent to which they can be applied or transferred to another context. Meeting those who live in the area is, of course, paramount to understand how local populations value their environment and what challenges they face.

6.4 Readjusting the Seminar Focus

Most of the teaching at the master's level takes place in each of the master's programs' design studios and seminars. The former is the core component of architectural training, where students are required to draw their knowledge and skills together in order to come up with design proposals. The latter is also specific to each of the school's master's programs, unlike the compulsory modules which are taken by all students regardless of the program. The seminar is therefore an arena in which each program can provide specific knowledge.

As the head of the master's program pointed out during an interview, there has always been a strong connection between research and teaching in the MArch AE&CC program. Consequently, the involvement of several members of the teaching staff in the LIFE project therefore naturally led to an integration of health in the curriculum. Yet, this was—and still is—a challenge for teaching staff involved in the master's program, particularly in terms of readjusting the content of teaching, especially that of the seminar which provides students with some of the theoretical and methodological tools that underpin work in the design studio. The head of the master's program explained that design teaching methods were not altered as such: it is the content of the seminar that was altered, in order to provide students with the knowledge required to address health in the design process.

The integration of health in the seminar was initiated in November 2017 as part of the *San-Té* conference focusing on health and the built environment, organized by LabEx AE&CC as a direct outcome of the LIFE project. The rationale underpinning this event was that research focusing on health and the built environment should involve debates and exchange of best practice among the wide range of stakeholders involved in fostering healthy cities: one of the objectives of the LIFE project is to facilitate discussions between researchers, practitioners (both in urban design and healthcare), and local elected members—therefore demonstrating the key civic role of higher education and research institutions as debate facilitators. For the 2017 academic year, the conference was fully integrated into the curriculum as a key component of the seminar. All students of the final year AE&CC master's program therefore attended the event. In order to ensure the content of the conference focused on hands-on experience, its program was deliberately centered on the experiences of two cities, Grenoble and Oxford, which have been twin towns for 30 years. The *San-Té* conference brought together over 30 speakers from Grenoble and Oxford and was organized in three sessions over 2 days. A summary of the event program is provided here, as it sheds light on some of the design issues students picked up in their final year projects.

The opening session focused on two of the many issues currently faced by most Western cities: first, the need to cater for an aging population, second, the need to think about energy in terms of its negative impacts on health due to fuel poverty. This session provided talks from leading academics in the fields, respectively, George Leeson and Brenda Boardman from the University of Oxford, whose talks were followed by responses given by Grenoble-based local elected members, namely Kheira Capdepon of Grenoble City Council and Bertrand Spindler of the metropolitan authority (Grenoble Alpes Métropole), each of whom set out the various actions taken at the city and metropolitan levels to address the challenges established in the previous talks. Students were therefore able to understand how key issues are translated into policy and action.

A second session included talks by Councillors Mondane Jactat and Ed Turned, respectively, in charge of health for Grenoble and Oxford city councils. Both focused not only on the successes of both councils in addressing some pressing issues, but also on the challenges that still need to be addressed. The speakers then took part in a round table for which they were joined by other specialists, including representatives from Grenoble and Oxford university hospitals.

Given the crucial role of transport planning in addressing health, the following session included a talk by Matthew Hardy from the Prince's Foundation for Building Community and the University of Oxford's Department for Continuing Education, who showed how active travel, in particular cycling, is gradually becoming a priority in Britain. A response was given by Gilles Novarina (LabEx AE&CC), who related the Grenoble experience, given the city's reputation as a pioneer in the promotion of active travel and public transport.

Whereas the first day of the conference provided an overview of some of the main challenges faced by cities and the ways in which specific public policy seeks to address them, the second day specifically focused on two case studies of healthy city design initiatives. By way of introduction, Daniel McDonnell of the British National Health Service outlined the key aims of the Healthy New Towns program. Councillor Alex Hollingsworth, in charge of planning at Oxford City Council, then detailed the Barton Park Healthy New Town project. The Grenoble experience was then described during two talks. The first, by Emmanuel Rouede of the Grenoble Alpes Métropole authority, explained how health issues, in particular those aiming to reduce air pollution, are being addressed at the inter-communal level. Councillor Vincent Fristot, in charge of planning, housing and energy, and Pierre Kermen, head of the publicly-owned company in charge of urban renewal in Grenoble, then focused on the regeneration of the Flaubert neighborhood which has a strong health component.

When asked to reflect upon the contribution of this conference to their training, the majority of students first said that one of the main points of interest had been the relation between energy efficiency and health, through fuel poverty. The session focusing on active travel was also quoted by four of six students, who said they gained a better understanding of the contribution urban design for mobility can make to encouraging physical activity. In other words, and unsurprisingly, they essentially recalled issues that had a direct implications for design and that could be approached in terms of their physical or spatial dimensions.

In addition to the conference, the integration of health-related issues in the seminar partly relied upon lectures given by some local and international experts who were invited to take part in a two-day workshop built around lectures focusing on designing for health. Of particular interest is the fact that the Grenoble City council has adopted a Health in All Policies (HiAP) ordinance and strategy, which require all local policies to take health into account and explicitly detail how health-related objectives will be met. Mondane Jactat, the then-local Councillor in charge of health, was thus invited to give a specific lecture to students to explain how the municipality is integrating health in urban and architectural design. International experts included Dr. Susan Parham, head of urbanism at the University of Hertfordshire and a specialist of food and urbanism, and Prof. Wendy Wills, then-head of the Centre for Research in Public Health and Community Care also at the university of Hertfordshire as well as Prof. Tim Townshend from the University of Newcastle-upon-Tyne, whose expertise in urban design and health is widely acknowledged. These meetings were beneficial to students and teachers and gave the opportunity to reflect upon ongoing policies and to gain a better understanding of the ways in which public policy contributes to providing a framework for designers.

6.4.1 Project Sites

The approach to site selection for the graduation projects at the Grenoble School of Architecture varies from one master's program to the other. Some allow students to select sites themselves, while others, in particular the MArch AE&CC program, require them to choose from a predefined portfolio of specific locations. There are several reasons for this latter approach. Firstly, site selection builds upon past and current links between research and teaching and on networks between teaching and research staff and a wide range of public sector and academic partners. As pointed out by Stickland, working on sites that involve real stakeholders means these can help set project goals and participate in project design development, thus providing help for students, particularly in terms of understanding the importance of design as a public profession (Strickland, 2017). The sites selected by the AE&CC team allow such interaction with key local stakeholders, in particular with the local council, local associations, businesses, and academics, some of whom also take part in the end-of-year panel review of student design projects. Students are offered a choice of three locations, including one in a French urban area, one in a French rural area, and one abroad. As well as offering an opportunity to interact with local stakeholders, these sites are also subject to new building or regeneration at the time they are offered. Regardless of the location of the project sites, students are given an opportunity to spend time in the local area in order to experience it themselves and meet with a range of stakeholders.

6.4.2 The Design Studio

During the second year, students work on their project over the entire academic year. Students work in pairs or in groups of three, thereby operating in a process that encourages collaboration. Teaching staff interact with students in the studio on a weekly basis. Sketching, drawing, and mapping are encouraged. As Nijhuis has stressed, these approaches are powerful vehicles of visual thinking and communication for students who deal with spatial research and design (Nijhuis et al., 2016).

The first part of the year is dedicated to the survey and analysis of the project site. Multiple site visits are organized and a special workshop runs in parallel in order to train students in cartography and geographic information systems (GIS), thus allowing them to make use of a range of statistics which are examined from a spatial perspective. Students investigate the place from different perspectives, including its history, topography, and socioeconomic environment. They also carry out a detailed study of existing building patterns and urban morphology and produce a detailed survey that aims to highlight the salient characteristics of the area. This first phase allows them to identify the area's potential and to formulate initial design proposals that could contribute to addressing local and global challenges.

6.5 Introducing Health in the Design Studio: Reflecting Upon a Pedagogical Experiment

From an early stage, the teaching staff of the MArch AE&CC program acknowledged the importance of reflecting upon the process that led to the introduction of health in the curriculum. This evolution thus became a research objective in itself and its examination was supported by a grant from the Braillard Foundation (Geneva). Semi-structured interviews were conducted with students and teaching staff of the MArch AE&CC program in the weeks following the end of the pilot 2017–18 academic year. All interviews were recorded and transcribed and each of the interviewees agreed on the material being used for publications.

The questionnaire was designed in a way that allowed all the levels of knowledge identified in Anderson's revised taxonomy to be described below. The first level deals with "remembering," in other words, recalling knowledge that has previously been gained. The second level deals with "understanding" and is related to a person's ability to make sense of material. The third level, "applying," is related to the ability to use material in a range of situations. The fourth level, "analyzing," is in regard to the use of material in a way that breaks it down in order to understand it better. The fifth level, referred to as "evaluating," is placed before "creating" in Anderson's taxonomy, and which posits that assessing a situation is required in order to be able to create or, in our case, design, something new. The final level, "creating," is understood as the most advanced and difficult function. In the design disciplines such as architecture or urbanism, this reflects the view that creation, or design, can only occur once the previous steps have fully been mastered: design is a practical answer to a set of complex issues that need to be understood and analyzed.

Through these interviews, we attempted to assess the extent to which students were able to analyze and construct links between issues related to health and other issues which should be taken into account in the design process—most importantly, in the case of this specific master's program, those related to environmental concerns. Interviewees were also asked to assess the extent to which taking health issues into account had allowed them to defend the arguments underpinning their projects. Finally, we asked whether they felt they had easily been able to keep health as a key component of the project through the design process, and how they convert it into architectural and technical solutions.

6.6 Remembering: The Place of Health in Architectural Training in Grenoble

We first sought to find out whether students remembered being taught health-related issues as part of their previous training, whether at the undergraduate or postgraduate level. Here, the objective was not so much to assess the ability of individual students to recall relevant information, but rather to assess the place of health in architectural education.

As is the case in most schools of architecture in France, the place of health in the teaching curriculum is far from central in Grenoble. When asked whether they remembered health being covered in other modules, all students paused before answering and appeared to have trouble recalling the information. Interestingly, however, they all acknowledged the fact that although no module specifically focused on health, a number of classes had touched upon health-related issues. In particular, many remembered a specific module that explored the impact of housing design on health.

The first year of the MArch AE&CC program focuses on construction and building materials, particularly on eco-friendly resources such as wood or earth.

Consequently, most students in this program acknowledged that even though the use of such materials had not been advocated in the light of health-related arguments, but rather on the merits of their possible contribution to reducing carbon footprints, for example, obvious connections between the "eco-friendly" and the "healthy" could be made. The introduction of health in the final year was thus an opportunity for them to shed new light on what they had been taught in previous years and to realize that some design solutions could contribute to simultaneously addressing a range of issues. One student, however, pointed out that it was difficult for him to come to grips with the topic, at first. From his point of view, this was due to the fact that he had no knowledge in this field: addressing health-related issues thus appeared to be a rather daunting task.

6.7 Understanding the Relation Between Health and Design: Revealing the Link Between Students' Views of Health and Personal History

Students and teachers were asked to explain how they understood and perceived the relationship between health and design, both architectural and urban. One of the aims here was to better grasp the ways in which interviewees had classified and interpreted knowledge. Many students acknowledged that until they were encouraged to address health through design, they had assumed that their understanding of health was limited to medicine and related fields. As one student put it, "I thought of health as something that was essentially about doctors curing people, I never thought architectural or urban design could actually play a major role in terms of actually preventing ill-health." In similar vein, another student explained: "I used to think that in architecture, health was related to the well-being of workers on building sites and to the types of materials one would need to be in contact with." All students acknowledged that they became aware that health involves a much wider range of issues as a result of this program.

One key point that emerged through the interviews, however, was the importance of each student's personal history. As a teacher pointed out, one of the students was involved in a number of community groups as part of her extracurricular activities. This possibly explained her concern for the elderly, an issue that she was able to look at within the context of her architectural training: her final year project included a number of solutions which allow people to live in their homes for as long as possible. Similarly, another student explained that several members of her family practiced alternative medicine, and that this context had strongly influenced her way of approaching health through design. She explained, "I am more interested in preventing than curing, our project therefore focused on health through this approach—taking care of places and people. We wanted to take care of the ground, of soils, and of buildings—so as to focus on what was already there and improve it." The student's design strategy was threefold: the ground should be decontaminated, regenerated, maintained, and cultivated; buildings should be retrofitted and built using natural materials; and raising residents' awareness of the benefits of gardening nutrition, relaxation, and other activities can contribute to improving their physical and mental health. Thus, "taking care" became an overarching objective that allowed students to think about health in a holistic way.

6.8 Applying: Identifying Key Problems to Solve

Students were subsequently asked to provide an explanation of how they applied their health-related knowledge to design. This question aimed to shed light on the way health issues had contributed to identifying key problems to solve through the survey and design process. As a member of the teaching staff pointed out, there were important variations in the ways students focused on health, and hence, interpreted their knowledge through the design process. Two main approaches can be identified in student projects. The first shows that some students decided to put health at the center of architectural design by including some key components in the program that directly addressed health. Striking examples include the transformation of an abandoned hotel into a rehabilitation and a care-center based in a mountain village or the design of a well-being center for populations suffering from exhaustion in Grenoble. The second dominant approach also highlights the central place of health in design, but its inclusion was less explicit. As an illustration, one of the projects located in a mountain village was based on the assumption that life expectancy in the area would be longer because of the mountainous environment. The project conversely suggested that this specific environment meant that it was difficult for the elderly to be independent. The student project thus sought to provide flexible living spaces for the elderly and suggested a new design for accessible public spaces, allowing people to live in their own homes for longer.

6.9 Analyzing and Interpreting Knowledge: Health as a Generator of Urban Design

We also attempted to assess the extent to which students and staff were able to analyze and construct links between issues related to health and other issues which should be taken into account in the design process. One important aspect that emerged was that the integration of health in the studio had been a particularly powerful way of raising design problems that cannot be addressed at the building scale alone. In other words, health was an important link between the various scales of design, between the architectural and the urban or regional.

One of the projects focusing on a burnout recovery center illustrates this finding. The inclusion of this specific function in the Grenoble neighborhood was, as a student explained, "an explicit response to the stress generated by cities: in an urban environment, everything is often dense and intense. Our project aimed to offer a peaceful area, both for users of the recovery center and for local residents." The design of green spaces around this center and throughout the neighborhood quickly emerged as a particularly important question. As a student put it, "focusing on green space as a key element of our design allowed us to work on voids more than on masses." The result was a design process which paid particular heed to vegetation from the point of view of physical health (possible allergies, relative contribution of certain species to fight air pollution) as well as mental health (selecting shrubs according to their foliage color to generate an appeasing yet stimulating environment). Approaching the design of green space through health allowed the students to explore challenges at a high level of detail.

In the same way, one of the groups working on the Oxford site of Barton Park knew from the start that they wanted to reflect upon food, regardless of the site they would choose: "we were really keen to focus on food production and on the integration of agriculture in the built environment." The fact that health was put forward by the teaching staff as a key issue to be addressed allowed them to focus on the same issue, but in a different way. Again, the focus on health allowed them to address the various scales of design, from the building to the city region. They suggested ways in which healthy food production and distribution could be integrated in various spaces throughout the Barton neighborhood, and beyond. As a teacher suggested, "this was an interesting example of the way garden city principles were reinterpreted, so as to make sure Barton actually incorporated local food production." In this case as with others, the time that students spent in the neighborhood during two field trips was key to raising their awareness of the issues faced by local communities, such as the lack of access to healthy food. One of the students explained that "food was a word that constantly came back in our group discussions, we thus decided to think about architecture in a way that would contribute to improving the local community's living environment and allow easier access to quality, low cost food." Their final design thus included a range of spaces to grow and sell food locally, as a response to their own field trip experience of living in a neighborhood where finding a fast-food chain was easier than walking half an hour to the closest market.

6.10 Evaluating: Can the Student Justify a Stand or a Decision? Health as an Argument

When asked whether the requirement to address health issues had helped them build the arguments that would justify the proposed design, all students replied positively. However, as is often the case, interviews generate some particularly unexpected answers.

One student explained that "the good point about health is that it easily generates a consensus: people are worried about their own health and their children's health and well-being more than about an ecosystem on the other side of the planet. When you put a health argument forward to justify your design, no one will say they disagree." In other words, and even though all students acknowledged that they had greatly benefited from the requirement to take health into account in the design process, it appears that they have already taken on board the fact that health may well become a good marketing argument in the years to come.

6.11 Conclusions

The integration of health in the design studio in the MArch AE&CC program at the Grenoble School of Architecture is a work in progress but a few preliminary conclusions can be drawn. The pilot program demonstrated that when it comes to urban design, the importance of immersion in the local context, through visits, site surveys, and interactions with stakeholders and experts is paramount. In each of the student projects used to illustrate this paper, key design issues emerged as a direct result of the time spent onsite, in the various localities and neighborhoods. The lack of access to healthy food in a neighborhood or the feeling of stress generated by the intensity of car traffic are but two examples of issues that are better understood when they have been experienced.

The integration of health in the design studio allowed students to think differently about a number of issues. For instance, although food production and consumption could be identified as a key component of student projects over the past few years, they tended to focus on the integration of agriculture in the built environment, using short supply chains as one of the main underpinning arguments to justify this approach. The social benefits of community gardens were also often central in projects. Looking at food production through health changed the way students looked at things. In Barton Park, Oxford, for example, the starting point was obesity prevention and food quality. Moreover, putting health at the center of the design studio undoubtedly contributed to engaging students positively in design at the city scale, encouraging them to think about the contributions of public space to fostering the healthy city—something with which students in architecture are not always at ease.

Interviews confirm that pedagogy has a crucial role to play in raising awareness amongst students and in encouraging them to think positively about the contributions of design to shaping the healthy city—in other words, to prevent rather than to cure. As is often the case in the studio, and as illustrated by the case of the students who deliberately decided to delve into the area of mental rather than physical health, inputs from teaching staff through suggestions rather than instructions generated unexpected yet powerful and relevant responses.

Last but not least, thinking about health and approaching it from a design perspective led students to question their own lifestyles. Several interviewees stressed that during the year, they became aware of the ways in which they could improve their own behavior. Some committed to more physical activities, such as walking or cycling to university. Others tried to better organize their time and sleep more. Some students even confessed that they managed to change their dietary behaviors, seeking to eat healthier food. Since architecture students are frequently at higher risk for illness (UNEAP, 2018), such feedback can only be welcomed. The integration of health questions in the design studio is therefore not only a way of contributing to the training of future designers who will take health on board: the MArch AE&CC experience reveals it can also help students think about their own lives.

The pilot allowed to identify and reflect upon some of the challenges for the further development of health-based approaches in urban and architectural design education. First and foremost, the complexity of health issues means that architects and other designers need to rely on the knowledge produced in other disciplines and fields in order to ground design solutions in evidence rather than intuition. Cross-disciplinary collaboration is not only desirable, it is essential. Secondly, students should be given the opportunity to experience the daily lives of those they are attempting to design for: the examples mentioned in this paper show that a full immersion over a two-week period is much more effective as an awareness raising-process than interviewing a local. Most importantly perhaps, this pilot has been a reminder that teachers too need to keep up to date. If anything, it has only confirmed the need to ensure that research contributes to lifelong learning and that the knowledge produced through research as well as they questions it raises are fed into the design studio.

Acknowledgments This research and the various research and teaching programs and activities have been supported by the French National Research Agency as part of the *Investissements d'avenir* program ANR-15-IDEX-02 (CDP LIFE) and ANR-10-LABX-0078 (LabEx AE&CC) the Braillard Architects Foundation (Eco-Century Project), Région Auvergne Rhône-Alpes (Pack Ambition Internationale and Ministère de la Culture (Actions internationales).

References

Anderson, L., & Krathwohl, D. (2001). *A taxonomy for learning, teaching, and assessing: A revision of Bloom's taxonomy of educational objectives*. Longman.

Bachman, L., & Bachman, C. (2009). Designing student learning outcomes in undergraduate architecture education: Frameworks for assessment. *The ARCC Journal for Architectural Research, 6*(1), 49–67.

Barton, H., & Grant, M. (2006). A health map for the local human habitat. *The Journal of the Royal Society for the Promotion of Health., 126*(6), 252–253.

Bloom, B., Krathwohl, D., & Masia, B. (1984). *Bloom taxonomy of educational objectives*. Longman.

Carmona, M. (2016). Urban design, a call for inter-disciplinarity. *Journal of Urban Design, 21*(5), 548–550.

Cheng, R. (2014). Designers designing design education. *Journal of Architectural Education, 68*(1), 12–14.

Coombes, E., Jones, A., & Hillsdon, M. (2010). The relationship of physical activity and overweight to objectively measured green space accessibility and use. *Social Science & Medicine, 70*(6), 816–822.

Halloran, D. (2011). Home environment, asthma, and obesity: How are they related? *The Journal of Pediatrics, 159*(1), 3–4.
Krathwohl, D. (2002). A revision of Bloom's taxonomy: An overview. *Theory Into Practice, 41*(4), 212–218.
Kuo, M., & Faber, T. A. (2004). A potential natural treatment for attention-deficit/hyperactivity disorder: Evidence from a national study. *American Journal of Public Health, 94*(9), 1580–1586.
Lara, J., & Evans-Cowley, J. (2016). Internationalizing urban design education. *Journal of Urban Design, 21*(5), 564–566.
Morelli, X., Rieux, C., Cyrys, J., et al. (2016). Air pollution, health and social deprivation: A fine-scale risk assessment. *Environmental Research, 147*, 59–70.
Nijhuis, S., Stolk, E., & Hoekstra, M. (2016). Teaching urbanism: The Delft approach. *Proceedings of the Institution of Civil Engineers - Urban Design and Planning, 170*(3), 96–106.
Papas, M., Alberg, A., Ewing, R., et al. (2007). The built environment and obesity. *Epidemiologic Reviews, 29*(1), 129–143.
Pasala, S., Rao, A., & Sridhar, G. (2010). Built environment and diabetes. *International Journal of Diabetes in Developing Countries, 30*(2), 63–68.
Sadoux, S., & Di Marco, C. (2020). The British "healthy new towns" initiative: A step towards reuniting planning and health? In J.-C. Dissart & N. Seigneuret (Eds.), *Local resources, territorial development and well-being* (pp. 180–203). Edward Elgar.
Sadoux, S., et al. (2022). La Garden City: un precedent au service de l'enseignement du projet architectural. In Association des Cités Jardins d'Ile de France (Ed.), *Des Cités-jardins pour le XXIe siècle. Valorisation, preservation, perspectives* (pp. 375–384). Editions Parenthèses.
Song, H., et al. (2019). Association between urban greenness and depressive symptoms: Evaluation of greenness using various indicators. *International Journal of Environmental Research and Public Health, 16*(2), 173–186.
Strickland, R. (2017). Editorial: Ten recommendations for enhancing urban design teaching and learning. *Proceedings of the Institution of Civil Engineers - Urban Design and Planning, 170*(3), 93–95.
Suglia, S., et al. (2011). Asthma and obesity in three-year-old urban children: Role of sex and home environment. *The Journal of Pediatrics, 159*(1), 14–20.
Townshend, T., & Lake, A. (2017). Obesogenic environments: Current evidence of the built and food environments. *Perspectives in Public Health, 137*(1), 38–44.
UNEAP. (2018). *Enquête sur la santé des étudiants en architecture.*
WHO. (1948). *Preamble to the Constitution of the World Health Organization as adopted by the International Health Conference, New York*, 19–22 June, 1946; signed on 22 July 1946 by the representatives of 61 States (Official Records of the World Health Organization, no. 2, p. 100) and entered into force on 7 April 1948, New York.
Widziewicz, K., & Rogula-Kozłowska, W. (2018). Urban environment as a factor modulating metals deposition in the respiratory track and associated cancer risk. *Atmospheric Pollution Research, 9*(3), 399–410.
Zawistowski, K., Zawistowski, M., & Joffroy, T. (2020). Evolving vernacular: Reinventing rammed earth in the context of twenty-first century seismic regulation. *Technology| Architecture+ Design, 4*(2), 158–165.

Stéphane Sadoux is a town planner and a historian. He graduated from the Universities of Oxford, Newcastle-upon-Tyne and Grenoble. He is a past Director of Unité de Recherche AE&CC at the Grenoble School of Architecture (ENSAG), Université Grenoble Alpes (UGA). He is currently leading UGA's Excellence in Architecture program (LabEx). His research mostly focuses on the history, theory, and practice of planning in Britain.

Cecilia Di Marco graduated in Architecture from the University of Naples Federico II (Italy) and holds a PhD in Planning and Urban Design. After several years as a postdoctoral researcher and lecturer in urban planning, she is now Head of the Urban Planning Department within a local authority in France. Her work explores how urban projects and spatial planning can foster healthier, more inclusive environments, with particular attention to mobility, public spaces, and environmental quality. She combines operational practice with the reflections developed over 10 years of academic research.

Part III
Health and Well-being in the Workplace

Chapter 7
Embedding the Arts into Healthcare Settings: Create+—An Arts Referral Program for NHS Staff

Kim Wiltshire and Dawn Prescott

Abstract Participatory art in healthcare is often viewed by clinicians as a distraction activity. But can participatory arts improve general well-being and mental health for healthcare professionals? If so, can we change that viewpoint and embed art into healthcare settings?

In 2022, Dawn Prescott, Director of Lime Arts at Manchester University NHS Foundation Trust (MFT), alongside British Academy Innovation Fellow Kim Wiltshire worked to set up and research the impact of the first NHS Staff Arts Referral Program in the UK, Create+.

The Create+ pilot ran across four blocks of six weekly workshops, using visual art, for staff who fell into three categories:

- Currently on long-term sick leave
- Returning to work after long-term sick leave
- Still in work but at risk of going on long-term sick leave

The WHO description of well-being encompasses "quality of life and the ability of people and societies to contribute to the world with a sense of meaning and purpose" (WHO, *Promoting well-being,* 2021, para. 1), which many of the staff referred to the program were struggling with.

A series of interviews and case studies alongside participant evaluation through the MYCaW system (by Meaningful Measures) forms a rounded view of the impact.

K. Wiltshire (✉)
Edge Hill University, Ormskirk, UK
e-mail: wiltshik@edgehill.ac.uk

D. Prescott
Manchester University NHS Foundation Trust, Manchester, UK
e-mail: dawn.prescott@mft.nhs.uk

© The Author(s), under exclusive license to Springer Nature Switzerland AG 2025

L. Dalingwater et al. (eds.), *Structural and Systemic Perspectives on Health and Well-being*, Human Well-Being Research and Policy Making,
https://doi.org/10.1007/978-3-031-99924-6_7

Keywords Arts and health · National Health Service · Lime arts · Create+ · Staff arts referral program

7.1 Introduction

In this piece, we are exploring the possibilities of embedding arts into healthcare settings by looking at the set-up and evaluative research completed on an innovative staff arts referral program in the UK, created by arts organization Lime and called Create+. This program focused on using art as a means to engender a sense of better mental well-being, considering the WHO description of well-being as encompassing "quality of life and the ability of people and societies to contribute to the world with a sense of meaning and purpose" (WHO, 2021, para.1). Therefore, we will look at how, by involving senior healthcare leaders, we ensured buy-in on the project and how time spent on choosing a multi-disciplinary evaluation method and experienced artists ensured we had evidence to provide to the senior healthcare leaders that the program improved mental well-being and allowed staff to return to work or continue in their role, enabling the project to be embedded and continued after the pilot period.

Whilst many arts and health projects concentrate, quite rightly, on patient or service user facing projects, Lime has worked with frontline healthcare staff for many years and after staff experiences following the COVID-19 pandemic, Lime wanted to set up a project that supported healthcare staff, a project that cared for the carers.

We will explore how we set up the Create+ project, the evaluation decisions we made and why, the artist decisions we made and why, and the results of the evaluation as well as looking at a specific case study. But first, we start with some context about the healthcare system in the UK and about Lime, the arts and health organization that set up Create+.

7.2 Context

The National Health Service (NHS hereafter) was set up in 1948 by the then Labour Government to provide free at the point of need healthcare to a UK population crippled by debt following World War II. In 2023 the NHS celebrated its 75th anniversary and it is still considered to be one of the main cornerstones of British society. The care and appreciation of NHS staff by the British public was clear during the many UK COVID-19 pandemic lockdowns, where people would stand on their doorstep clapping and banging pots in support of the NHS each Thursday evening.

Whilst the NHS is national, Trusts are set up in towns, cities, and municipal areas to locally manage the health needs of the community, employing healthcare staff to run the hospitals, clinics, and services it manages as well as managing its own budget. Create+, the project we focus on here, was set up by Lime as a staff referral arts program in Manchester University National Health Service Foundation Trust (MFT hereafter), which is the one of the largest healthcare trusts in the UK, with over 28,000 staff and 10 hospitals over 6 locations.[1] This project was built on previous staff arts projects designed by Lime (for more on this, see below), as the arts organization of MFT.

Lime started out as Hospital Arts, a pioneering arts project set-up by Peter Senior in 1973 and has had a continuous presence at MFT for over 50 years making it one of the oldest, continually producing, hospital-based Arts and Health teams in Europe. Over that time, Lime has gained international recognition for its commitment to diverse artistic commissioning and inclusive, process driven, modes of engagement and inclusivity in terms of arts projects working and consulting with stakeholders and participants every step of the way. We discuss Lime's work a little more, but first we will contextualize the project within the current Arts and Health landscape in the UK, considering the surprising lack of programs at that time linked to frontline NHS staff mental well-being following the pandemic.

7.3 Literature Review

Boris Groys, in his work *The Philosophy of Care* suggests that "Creativity is a symptom of great health" (Groys, 2022, p. 30). We considered that if this is the case, could we switch that assertion around? If one needs great health to create, can being creative cause better health?

Since the COVID-19 pandemic, as the *Nursing Times* has reported, "Almost two-thirds of nurses feel their mental health has deteriorated" (Ford, 2021, para.1). As Dalingwater highlights (2019) policy makers in the UK have for the past two decades linked well-being to mental health, suggesting that both objective and subjective well-being, physical well-being and good general health, are strongly linked to good mental health. However, in healthcare settings the irony is that the stigma felt by staff around mental health and anxiety leads many healthcare professionals to keep these issues hidden from more formal channels, leading to high levels of sickness in frontline staff, with mental health issues making up a large percentage of those figures.

That NHS staff were under pressure as never before, even prior to the COVID-19 pandemic, is without contention. The Royal College of Nursing's website highlighted how "Data shows NHS nurses took nearly one million days off sick with mental health problems in the first eight months of 2019 and last year [2018] the Office for National Statistics said that the suicide rate among nurses is 23% higher than the national average, with female nursing staff at particularly high risk"

[1] For more information on MFT, please visit https://mft.nhs.uk

(Farmer, 2019, Mental Health In The Workplace, para.6). The British Medical Association (BMA hereafter) released a report on *The mental health and wellbeing of the medical workforce—now and beyond COVID-19* (BMA, 2020), whilst Walton, Murray, and Christian published a paper in 2020 on "Mental health care for medical staff and affiliated healthcare workers during the COVID-19 pandemic" for the *European Heart Journal* (Walton et al., 2020) detailing the stress and psychological effects on healthcare staff when faced with infectious disease outbreaks.

Historically, participatory arts in healthcare have been viewed by clinicians and healthcare professionals as an "add-on" or distraction activity for patients, and the range of work exploring arts interventions with specific relation to frontline healthcare staff health is few and far between. In her 2017 book *Arts in Health: Designing and Researching Interventions,* Fancourt suggests a potential staff arts project template, within several types of project templates she proposes (Fancourt, 2017), whilst Norma Daykin's 2020 book *Arts, Health and Well-being: A Critical Perspective on Research, Policy and Practice* makes frequent reference to Fancourt's text yet barely touches on staff specific projects at all (Daykin, 2020). Daykin has extensive experience in arts and health, but in this text (as with many others by experts in arts and health) there is a tendency to use "health" and "well-being" interchangeably, or the phrase "arts, health, and well-being" which is used throughout the book, with no exact definition of what well-being might mean. However, Daykin does highlight projects in the UK such as social prescribing, arts interventions in institutions such as schools and youth justice settings and in mental health settings including dementia care (Daykin, 2020, p. 21) as areas where arts, health, and well-being are making significant inroads. She also suggests:

> Arts-based interventions in education and training of health professionals can contribute to enhanced well-being of staff and reduced risks to errors, enhanced teamwork and improved diagnostic observation skills in medical practitioners (Daykin, 2020, p. 21).

She cites two literature reviews, one by Perry et al. (2011) on the effectiveness of using arts in health education and the other by Acai et al. (2017) on the use of arts to develop communication skills in health professionals to support this statement. Whilst the statement above by Daykin underlines the very concept of Create+, neither of the cited literature reviews mentions "well-being", and it seems that within the arts, this inability to strongly define well-being, the links to mental health and the fact that well-being can be, as Dalingwater highlights, subjective (Dalingwater, 2019, p. 3), and therefore harder to "prove" using standard research methodologies, is part of the difficulties faced by arts and health professionals in quantifying the benefits, often relying instead on qualitative research.

There are many articles, for example "The Jameel Arts & Health Lab in collaboration with the WHO–*Lancet* Global Series on the Health Benefits of the Arts" by Nisha Sajnani and Nils Fietje (2023) and Kiely et al.'s "Effect of social prescribing link workers on health outcomes and costs for adults in primary care and community settings: a systematic review" in *BMJ Open* (2022), which cite more scoping reviews, but these rarely come to any conclusion and certainly have done little to support or embed the arts into healthcare settings.

There are a few articles that do look at specific projects and their benefits, such as Govoni et al.'s (2021) article "Adjusting to the pandemic: remote support for professionals working with asylum seekers" in *The Journal Of Applied Arts and Health* which explores the benefits of expressive arts for social workers' mental well-being. In this study, based on Barbara Fish's 2016 study of "examining supervisor-supervisee relationships from an art-based, interdisciplinary lens" (Govoni et al., 2021, p. 262) the team supervised and worked with social workers on the USA's southern border working with asylum seekers. The team suggested that the workers were suffering from compassion fatigue, highlighting "continued exposure to stories of physical violence, kidnapping and torture, sexual violence and trafficking led to debilitating conditions such as loss in quality of life, impaired functioning, family dysfunction and isolation amongst support workers" (Govoni et al., 2021, p. 261).

These findings were very similar to the information the Lime team were receiving from MFT's Employee Health and Well-being team about frontline healthcare staff following the pandemic. The project on the Mexican border used a range of art forms, but one example used writing and reflection through writing as a method to explore the worker's own understanding of compassion fatigue and burnout (Govoni et al., 2021, p. 264) alongside other art forms.

Whilst the Govoni et al. project supported our belief that the arts could be used to tackle these issues, which could come under the umbrella term of "well-being", very few projects or articles seem to have explored how a project specifically for healthcare staff might not only help improve well-being for staff, but might further embed the arts in a healthcare setting, as this project aimed to do, through showing a difference in staff well-being and attitude to well-being when engaged in a creative or cultural activity and when introducing the concept of including creativity in our everyday lives.

As the Daykin quote above shows, often the focus of research for healthcare staff will be on including creative elements in healthcare education, for example Perry et al.'s 2011 literature review on "The effectiveness of arts-based interventions in medical education". Nearly a decade and a half ago, the authors concluded "Although there are intriguing suggestions that arts-based approaches may help to foster positive attitudes towards patients, the evidence base for this is relatively weak" (Perry et al., 2011, p. 45). Alongside this is the wider recent research on healthcare professionals and the impact on mental well-being from the COVID-19 pandemic, such as McVeigh et al.'s 2021 study in *BMC Nursing* on mindfulness in nursing training and Song et al.'s 2020 paper "Mental health status of medical staff in emergency departments during the Coronavirus disease 2019 epidemic in China". Both papers, alongside the articles mentioned above, detail the toll the COVID-19 pandemic took on healthcare staff, with Song et al. concluding that "a considerable number of medical staff in the emergency department suffered from depressive symptoms and PTSD" (Song et al., 2020, p. 64).

So, there is a need to bring together research on the impact of COVID-19 on healthcare professionals with the research on the positive benefits on using participatory arts for mental and general well-being, such as that by Dragon and Madsen's

2015 article in the *Journal for Applied Arts and Health* on "Engaging in creative activity", where the authors explore the existing research on the benefits of creative interventions, the social processes, the space to make art and the creative process and suggest that "the creation of an artistically energized space stimulates creativity and a variety of materials provide choices—all influencing positive outcomes" (Dragon & Madsen, 2015, p. 332). Align this with the experienced artists at Lime and the evidence supports that a creative program purely for the mental and general well-being of the healthcare professionals (not on their ability to use creativity in the way they respond to patients or do their jobs), in a creative space with professional artists will have positive benefits on their ability to return to their work.

The aim of Create+ was to use creativity as a therapeutic tool for better mental health and general well-being and to show that creativity can be used to help staff either stay in work or come back to work after a period of long-term sick leave. Importantly, whilst there is the evidence and research explored above, the point of the project was that it built on artist experience over the many projects Lime has set up and evaluated throughout its 50-year history.[2]

7.4 Setting the Project Up

Despite Lime's solid history with MFT, the organization faced a crisis when the pandemic lockdown happened in England in March 2020; Lime came very close to being disbanded and staff redeployed into the charity section to help run the volunteers recruited for staff support. There were a difficult few weeks when the future of Lime hung in the balance, but with emergency funding from Arts Council England, the team changed direction.

It was understood that whilst all ward based and patient work had to cease, provision for staff arts courses could move online. MFT agreed, understanding that using arts as a route to better mental health and general well-being was needed at this point, perhaps more than ever. Lime Director Dawn Prescott set up an online healthcare staff project called *Create.Connect.Unwind*[3] beginning with a series of creative writing workshops run by Kim Wiltshire.

This project grew to include evening and weekend online workshops that covered not only creative writing, but also music and visual art. The workshops were accessed via the Zoom platform, so that colleagues could access them at home, and they were accessed outside of work time. The workshops were very popular, with excellent feedback, but we could not be sure that we were getting to the staff who

---

[2] For more on Lime, please visit www.limeart.org, where you can find evaluation reports on previous projects which Create+ built on.

[3] The benefits of this project have been detailed in an article by Wiltshire and Prescott (2023) in Create.Connect.Unwind: A creative response to the pandemics for NHS Staff well-being in *Journal of Applied Arts and Health,* 14:2:257–69.

needed them most, who were suffering the most. We wondered whether the staff members who were really at the frontline were in fact getting very little leisure time outside of work, and the precious time they did have was spent recuperating from the onslaught they were experiencing on the wards.

Of course, staff were suffering with poor mental health and poor general well-being even before the pandemic hit, as we show above in the literature review, and this was already being acknowledged within MFT's Employee Health and Well-being Team, who engaged in discussion with Lime. They highlighted that the stigma of mental health and anxiety issues led to many healthcare professionals keeping these issues hidden from more formal channels, meaning there were few robust preventative measures being put in place, but very high levels of sickness due to stress, burnout, and mental ill-health being recorded. A conversation began about how the therapeutic benefits of the arts workshops could be used for staff in work time.

Alongside these conversations, during 2020/2021 Lime secured a £200,000 grant from Barclays Bank in response to a visionary proposal created by Dawn Prescott to open an Arts & Well-being Centre for Lime, which would consist of a dedicated printmaking and artist studio, the first of its kind in a hospital setting. As lockdown finally ended in March 2021, the team relocated to the new Lime Arts & Well-being Centre and restarted face to face workshops.

Over time, as the whole country got back to normal, workshop participant attendance rates at Lime's new centre began to increase whilst online workshop participation began to decrease. It was at this point discussions with MFT's Employee Health and Well-being team moved forward again, considering whether trialling creative workshops during work time for staff with a specific focus on general well-being and mental health might be another tool in their well-being toolbox.

The program was named Create+ and is, as far as we are aware, the first NHS Staff Arts Referral Program in the UK. It was ratified by the Chief Nurse, the Chairman of the Trust and the Executive Director for Workforce, part of a senior leadership team whose support ensured Lime could roll out the project across MFT. We began to work on the initial planning stages in February 2022, building on the experience of the Lime team.

It was initially decided that the workshops would have three strands:

1. Preventative Workshops—for those in work but whose direct line manager believed were suffering poor mental wellness and burnout and were therefore at risk of going on sick leave;
2. Workshops for those on long-term sick leave but planning a return to work—using the program as part of their phased return to work;
3. Workshops for those on long-term sick leave and not yet returning to work—using the program as a gentle reintroduction back to the hospital site.

There had to be certain criteria set out, of course. Staff had to fall into one of the three categories, long-term sick leave was determined to be more than 12 weeks and staff had to either be referred by their line manager or refer themselves with their line manager's consent—the Trust would not accept staff referring themselves and expecting time away from work with no higher approval. This meant internal communications and advertising for Create+ had to go out to attract not just potential participants but also line managers across MFT.

We were also clear that all workshops would happen in person in Lime's new Arts & Well-being Centre, on MFT's Oxford Road Campus in central Manchester and that we would not be offering online workshops for Create+. This was because the group dynamic and artist support would be an important part of the program.

At this point, it is important to highlight that we were not suggesting art therapy, which is a system of therapy trained counsellors or practitioners use that includes creative methods; that of course has its place and can be very effective, but this program was about pure creativity and the therapeutic benefits that has. And after all, creativity is a human right, as the 2013 United Nations special report on the right of artistic freedom states, the report "includes the freedom to seek, receive and impart information and ideas of all kinds 'in the form of art', the right to 'enjoy the arts' and the creativity of others" (United Nations Special Rapporteur on Cultural Rights, 2013, para.1).

As mentioned above, using the arts for well-being is a widespread intervention, often considered a welcome distraction by some clinicians. However, our proposal was different. We were suggesting that frontline NHS staff members be referred onto a program of pure creativity, once a week, every week, for a six-week period. This suggestion was built on Lime's experience of working closely with frontline healthcare staff at MFT and the testimony after testimony from staff (as well as a range of other research projects Lime has contributed to) of the benefits of engaging with the arts in a safe environment with a group of people participants feel comfortable with, who can talk around the table whilst engaging in the arts activity (the social element in Dragon & Madsen's, 2015 article mentioned above).

During the initial discussion period with the Human Resources department, the Employee Health and Well-being Department and workers across MFT, there were suggestions that a line manager would not allow a member of frontline staff, no matter how stressed they were, two and a half hours during a shift to attend a creative workshop. However, during *Create.Connect.Unwind*, we had trialled "coffee break" workshops, with staff taking part in online workshops in the workplace. Of course, these had just been 20-min "tasters", but staff had taken the time out to attend during paid breaks, and many of whom were frontline staff attending whilst on the ward.

Discussions also included suggestions that people who were on paid sick leave would not come onto site, or indeed should not come onto site. But we highlighted that if someone was coming for regular physiotherapy sessions, for example, that would be accepted, so why not a creative workshop? And in terms of not wanting to come onto site, that indeed could be a source of anxiety, but this is where the creative and calming atmosphere of the new Arts and Well-being Centre was so important. While it is on a hospital site, it is not a clinical space. On entering the studio through the courtyard of the Peter Mount Building at the Oxford Road Campus, many staff had already commented on how it was like entering a different world.

Instead of being a source of anxiety, the workshops could act as a bridge back into the workplace itself. However, we took these points on board and initially aimed the internal advertising only at staff who were on paid sick leave but planning a return to work, as part of their phased return to work, strand 2 as laid out above. Out of the first four referrals, three were line managers saying: I know this isn't quite the remit of the Create+ program, but I've got this member of staff on the team and I really think they could do with this program to stop them going on sick leave.

The three strands were therefore reinstated and we accepted referrals for staff who fitted into any strand. We also made the decision to mix the groups, so there were workshop groups that included staff who were still on long-term sick leave, staff who were on phased return to work after long-term sick leave, and staff whose line managers considered them to be at risk of going on sick leave. We made this decision because the discussions around the craft table are often as important as the creative skills learned and the sense of artistic achievement attained during a 6-week Create+ workshop block.

We made the decision to set the workshops up on a Tuesday morning, Tuesday afternoon and a Thursday morning, so that there was flexibility for staff to be appointed to one of these sessions, but once appointed the staff member would always come to the same session for the 6 weeks, working with the same artist.

We also ran a fourth session on a Thursday afternoon which was advertised as Team Building one-off workshops. This was for two reasons:

1. With a one-off team building workshop, we could bring whole clinical teams into the Lime studio and show them directly the benefit of using the arts for well-being;
2. With a team getting to know Lime and what could be achieved in the studio, we would lessen any stigma that might be linked to Create+.

These sessions were not part of the wider evaluation, as they were one-off workshops.

We made the decision to use visual arts because we wanted an art form that could be used metaphorically for the participants; creative writing, for example, seemed too direct. But we also wanted an art form that might be out of the participants' comfort zones and would therefore give them new skills. Visual art can also encourage a group of participants to sit around a table and chat, often discussing the reasons they were referred to the program, whilst being creative with their hands—or not chat, and move to another part of the studio to work alone. Visual art is often the form of art people do at kindergarten but often stop engaging in during teenage and adult years. It is often viewed as too difficult or elite and we wanted to bust that myth and show that creativity needs time and care, but we are all creative and we all have the capability to learn new skills. As one line manager who by the end of the pilot had referred 15 members of staff said:

> I opened up this flyer [...] and thought, because I'm not an artsy person, this is some namby-pamby thing, it wasn't anything I was particularly interested in. But I could see how it would help some people and there was a member of staff who was having such a tough time and had stuff going on at home. I thought this is right up her street. She did the Create+ course and couldn't speak highly enough about it. I thought, there's going to be other people that will enjoy this. And for one of the more recent people I referred, it's as if there's a

> weight off her shoulders. She talks to me now, I'm not the enemy. [...T]his is the only thing that I can see that the staff have really actually enjoyed. It sounds like this special amazing place, they go in and they all love it and they can't really describe it but it's the one thing that's really helped people. If you can convert me, you can convert anyone and you've got to give it go, it's the one thing that people have just loved. (Wiltshire and Prescott, 2023, Interview with Clinical Manager in Endoscopy)

One of the issues with projects like this, however, is that set-up time is often underestimated. Create+ took around 8 months in all, and this timeline was built into the project planning from the start.

To begin with, we spent several months working with Human Resources to directly contact line managers across MFT. We set up internal communications to advertise Create+ through a range of newsletters and advertisements on MFT's Intranet. We met with senior front line healthcare workers such as matrons (senior nurses who often run several wards and act as line managers) and department managers, giving short presentations at larger meetings, to those line managers who could refer participants in. We set a start date of September 2022, and slowly, the referrals began to come through. And it was very slow; despite all of the meetings and the HR teams showing us the levels of sickness, the first block only saw eight referrals across the three workshop groups.

We made the decision to work with two very experienced artists, a fine artist called Lucy Burscough and a printmaker called Colette Whittington. The artists took a day each. They worked on a range of different art forms, including mask making, clay heads and printmaking. We worked with these visual art forms because they were the areas of expertise for our two artists, both of whom have worked frequently with Lime and have the workshop skills to run such sensitive sessions in an inclusive and accessible manner. Also, we needed art forms that would teach a new skill set but that participants could master to a fair extent within the 6-week period. We worked with Burscough and Whittington to set out six workshop sessions that were flexible but would ensure the participants learnt new skills and kept busy during the two-and-a-half-hour session.

Choosing the right artist is very important for all arts and health projects, because they need a specific skillset that not only includes them being an excellent and practicing artist, but also excellent people skills, alongside the ability to be intuitive and have integrity, to not make the process about them (to leave their artist ego at the door as it were) but to centre on the participant. In the same way a doctor sees a nurse or a physiotherapist as a fellow healthcare professional, we would suggest that the experienced and trained artist working in healthcare settings should be seen as a fellow professional, bringing in their own expertise, teaching their own range of skills and making their own contribution to the health and well-being of the hospital community.

7.5 Evaluation and Research Methods

There is a lot of discussion in the UK currently around what can be considered robust evidence in arts and health, indeed Lime's founder Peter Senior in his 1993 book *Helping to Heal* called for more scientific based research of arts projects in healthcare (Senior & Croall, 1993). Many different methodologies to evaluate and research arts and health projects have since been explored, including art-based, arts-informed, artistic enquiry and arts-based health research.

More recently, the idea that the only robust form of research for arts and health projects must be clinical methodologies has taken hold. The suggestion is that self-reporting, anecdotal evidence, and qualitative data are just not robust enough in the healthcare and clinical world, that this is considered nothing more than mere evaluation. That if we do not use clinical methods, the clinicians and health professionals will not take the findings seriously.

However, for this project we felt that using clinical research methodologies went against the very grain of what arts and health is there to do, of what Lime is there to do, which is to support those with issues around mental well-being through a calm, therapeutic, and creative activity, or put more simply, being human. Lime's work is about feelings, connections and giving a sense of fulfilment. For this reason, we employed a range of evaluation methodologies, but quite deliberately avoided clinical ones. We had to make an evaluation methodology decision based on our two aims:

1. Set up the first UK NHS staff arts referral program to help frontline staff at MFT.
2. Prove to the senior leadership at MFT that the therapeutic benefits of the arts can aid frontline staff in getting back into the workplace, and therefore the benefits of embedding the program into the Trust as fully funded.

We used interviews and case studies which would provide the compassion and empathy through the human stories and we contracted a company called Meaningful Measures[4] who specialize in Social Prescribing evaluation to bring in both qualitative and quantitative data. They used a range of methods, including focus groups and their employee Drivers and Drainers tool, but the most instantly useful was the Measure Your Concerns and Well-being or MYCaW tool.

MYCaW is an online tool that participants fill in on the first and last workshops. It is short, non-invasive and asks participants to cite two personal concerns or issues and rate these on a scale of 1–6, 1 being very low and 6 being the highest, and to do the same with their general well-being. The most frequent personal concern was anxiety and/or stress, followed by relaxation/time for self, workload and overwhelm, self-esteem and confidence, and depression or low mood. In the final workshop participants can write a few comments about how they have found the

[4] https://www.meaningfulmeasures.co.uk where you can find information on all the evaluation tools. The final Meaningful Measures report for the pilot program can be found here: https://www.limeart.org/wp-content/uploads/2023/08/Create-Evaluation-Report-June-2023-1.pdf

workshops and then re-rate their two concerns and general well-being. The participants are given nicknames and so the responses are entirely anonymous, with only two members of the Lime team having access to the data in its raw form, and the Meaningful Measures team having no contact with the workshops, only meeting self-selecting participants in an online focus group during the pilot.

The full evaluation report is available online (link below) but to summarize the findings, in terms of attendance, 56.4% of people attended "all of the course", with 35.9% attending most of it and only 3.39% attending "a little" of the course (Seers et al., 2023, Meaningful Measures evaluation report, p. 25). All participants worked for MFT, with over two-thirds of them still being in work at the time of attending the program, so coming to Create+ as a preventative measure. The majority of participants were female (85.7%) and were in nursing or practitioner roles (61.2%) with administrators/researchers at 16.3% and managers/doctors/unspecified at 26.5%. 87.8% of participants confirmed that they had been on paid sick leave in the past 6 months, with an average of 87.8 days of absence from work (Seers et al., 2023, p. 13). Using just the MYCaW data, over the 10-month pilot, the figures were astonishing—an 89% significant improvement in their personal concerns and a 77% significant improvement in their well-being.

To give context, in the pilot program, there were over 60 participants with around three quarters of them completing the MYCaW tool (49 in all). The figures are impressive, but the comments below (all from different participants and taken from the MYCaW raw data between 2022 and 2023) create a picture of how the participants were feeling at the end of the six-week program. Comments about reflection on how the creative activity affected health and well-being included:

- My health and well-being improving by me being able to express myself creatively and having a space and time to forget my issues.
- Spending time here has made me feel less anxious and working with a good team creating thing that I have not done before.
- This session has allowed me time for me.
- Having the time and space to just breathe and relax away from the chaos of work.
- Loved the sessions. Always felt like I had escaped work and home life for them few hours a week and felt so relieved and refreshed. Was a good feeling. Highly recommended to my colleagues. (Participant direct comments, 2023)

The highly stressed working environment meant that, anecdotally, staff were often not taking breaks and were taking work home with them, never finding time for themselves. What was also interesting was how many participants started creative activities in their own time, including one participants who stated "I have started to do some crafting at home and thinking about more activities I can do" (see also case study in box below).

What also came across clearly was the importance of their being a safe space to be creative in within their workplace, and how that made participants feel about their working environment and their employer:

- I felt with these sessions I was fully focussed in the project and any negative thoughts disappeared. It felt calming and I was fully relaxed and comfortable with the group I was with. I was really engaged and enjoyed every session I came to. I looked forward to coming each week. I also did not know how creative I really was.

- It's enabled me to find something I love doing! I never thought I would be doing anything art based at my age. If I had the opportunity I'd love to do something like this again.
- I feel like I am valued by MFT by allowing me to attend this course. As they have prioritized my well-being I have been able to prioritize myself as well. Over these 6 weeks I have not had one sick day.
- I think the most important part is the feel of freedom from anxieties and worries. The studio felt like a safe place where I can freely express myself (either alone or with the other people whom have the same struggles as me). It came to a point where every Tuesday is my most anticipated day of the week. (Participant direct comments, 2023)

What also comes across clearly is that idea of going back to something, a hobby, a creative practice, that many people associate with only being of value when a child. The fact that the program gave working people the space to "play" again is a vital aspect of the therapeutic benefits of creative interventions, along with that social aspect, the sense of purpose and achievement creating a piece of art can give someone and with that a boost to self-esteem.

In the Meaningful Measures Executive Summary, the results are summarized thus:

- 97.3% of participants rated the Create+ course as excellent or good
- A statistically significant reduction in Perceived Stress Scores and improvement in ONS4 measures of well-being. (…)
- 45% of participants at follow-up felt that the Create+ program had made them want to stay in their job and fewer people were intending to leave their role in the next 12 months
- Reasons for benefitting from the workshops included having more confidence, making it easier to return to work, having something positive to focus on, and creating a space where they could take stock and reflect on the balance of time spent at work and at home. Furthermore, participants enjoyed being able to build up friendships with other staff who could understand their situation.
- Wider benefits of Create+ were noted by several participants who took up creative activities outside of the workshops and continued to do these after the six workshops ended. Moreover, many participants also encouraged their friends and family to do creative activities with them, hence providing a health prevention element to Create+. (Seers et al., 2023, p. 3)

Out of all 49 participants who completed the MYCaW evaluation, only one participant said they felt the program had not helped with their well-being or mental health concerns at all. The 11 participants who did not complete the course left for a range of reasons, including not being able to engage at that particular time through to changes in medication that made it hard for them to come along each week.

There is no suggestion here that a program like Create+ is a cure-all, but we do contend that when we regularly engage with the arts or creative activity, our well-being improves, and if we continue to engage, for all the reasons suggested above by our participants, the benefits of embedding such a program in a Trust where there are large sickness rates linked to burnout and stress in the workforce seems to be self-evident.

As mentioned above, the full evaluation report is available on the Lime website, but the experience of many of the participants does appear to be a positive one, with far-reaching effects on those who took part, and who continue to take part.

Finally, the other way of evaluating whether the therapeutic benefits of Create+ was through the artworks created. Artist Lucy Burscough began each block with

Box 7.1 Participant Case Study

The following case study has been chosen as an example because this participant has spoken so passionately about the program at a range of meetings and symposia with Lime. It is in part due to their testimony that the senior leadership team agreed to continue the funding.

Consultant Case Study interview

I am a Consultant Anaesthetist within the trust (Manchester University NHS Foundation Trust, hereafter MFT). During the last couple of years my role changed due to the pandemic. I was re-deployed to COVID-19 ICU for the first and second waves. I then went back to elective surgical work, which I found very time pressured; I became uncharacteristically incredibly stressed. I don't think I had time to process the challenges and trauma that I had been through during COVID-19. Shortly after I hit a wall. I was very burnt-out, and I went off sick. I was on sick leave for just over a year. Human Resources (HR hereafter) suggested I attended Create+ to see if that would help with my return to work, nothing else seemed to be working.

Initially I was quite sceptical, nothing had helped so far; medication hadn't helped, conventional therapy hadn't helped, CBT hadn't helped. I also thought "I'm rubbish at art, how on earth could that possibly help me?" But because the invitation was coming from HR, I thought I better give it a go as they were paying me whilst on sick leave.

As a scientific clinician and someone who was always told that art was not my strong point, I thought it won't suit me, it doesn't suit my skill set, and I was sceptical about coming to an art program in the healthcare setting. I was, however, grateful that someone was trying to say: this may help you, why don't you give it a go? Because at that point I was close to leaving medicine all together. I thought I would never get back to work.

On the day of the first session, as I was coming on site I was absolutely petrified. I really struggled coming anywhere near the hospital and even though the Oxford Road Campus isn't my base site, it was still bringing up distressing emotions for me and triggering flashbacks just by coming on to the hospital grounds. When I walked through the courtyard to Lime it had a different feel about it; then the door opened and it just felt really welcoming, like

(continued)

Box 7.1 (continued)

a totally different environment and I almost forgot I was on the hospital site. I was still apprehensive, and I wasn't sure exactly what to expect but I was immediately put at ease by the team.

I thought collaborating with an artist was brilliant! With their guidance and support I was able to create things I never thought I'd be able to. They explained the process and taught me the skills that I needed to create; before I went to Create+ I had ideas, but had no clue how to get them on to a medium, onto paper. The artist gave me a step-by-step process to follow which I guess feels a little more scientific to me.

I've got artistic friends and I've always just been very jealous of them. I have no preconceptions about artists, I just admire and envy their talent. Even now, months on, I am surprised at what I was able to create. I am amazed that I was able to create different pieces using different techniques. The main piece that I made (the mask) I don't even know where it came from, it was from somewhere deep in my subconscious. The thoughts and feelings that came out whilst creating that piece needed to come out in some way. I hadn't managed to express those before. I know Create + is not art therapy but it was certainly very therapeutic for me.

This mask was made in the first 6-week block of Create+ I attended. On first look, it is a mask wearing Personal Protective Equipment (PPE) seen here on the table during the making process (Fig. 7.1).

Fig. 7.1 Clown mask on craft table. Photo image copyright Lime 2022

(Continued)

Box 7.1 (Continued)

Underneath the PPE, on removal of the black mask and goggles, there is a clown mask. This is the "professional" face. Clinicians often use humour as a coping mechanism during the most challenging times, like redeployment to COVID ICU. Clinicians will also hide their struggles behind a smile. Attached to the clown, sitting on its shoulders, are two rainbow masks representing my children, who got me through some of the darkest times. COVID-19 virus particles lurk at the periphery signifying their constant threat during this time (Fig. 7.2).

Fig. 7.2 Clown mask with satellite rainbow masks and COVID-19 balls. Photo image copyright Lime 2022

Underneath the clown mask lies a slightly distorted black mask with red around the eyes. This layer reflects how I was feeling underneath the professional mask. The distorted face is unrecognizable, the red, blood-stained eyes symbolize the suffering and death COVID-19 brought (Fig. 7.3).

Finally, underneath all of this is a void, the nothingness of post-pandemic burnt-out, with nothing left to give (Fig. 7.4).

I enjoyed participating in the Create+ program so much and I got so much benefit from the first block, but I still wasn't quite well enough to go back to work. I was fortunate enough to be able to re-refer myself to the second 6-week block. It was a slightly different set up as we worked collaboratively as a group which put a different spin on it. It was difficult to work together as a group when everyone's struggling with themselves.

(Continued)

Box 7.1 (Continued)

Fig. 7.3 Black mask with red eyes. Photo image copyright Lime 2022

Fig. 7.4 Void mask. Photo image copyright Lime 2022

(Continued)

Box 7.1 (Continued)

For me, it was equally enjoyable, I continued to learn new skills and I liked what we produced in the end, but I think it was a more difficult process, I don't think it flowed quite as naturally for me. The group piece was a papier-mâché octopus with words to describe personal qualities we have working in the NHS block printed onto the fabric covering it. I personally felt that some of the words chosen by the group were too corporate and didn't reflect the struggles we had faced. We wouldn't all have been on a well-being return to work program if we were all feeling so positive. For me, the octopus didn't feel authentic. I felt that as a group, we were holding back, and we weren't represented by the art piece that we'd made. I thought it should be honest, maybe I am too honest, but I made a list of words that resonated with my journey. I suggested that the octopus could be caught up in a fishing net of burnout and bureaucracy, with the alternative words spread across the net. I was happy that the finished piece was more indicative of the struggles that we had faced. Perhaps in future projects I should try to reign in my dark side! (Fig. 7.5)

What would I say about Create+ to anyone working in the NHS? Just try it. Try to put your preconceptions of what may be helpful to you to one side. It's

Fig. 7.5 Octopus. Photo image copyright Lime 2022

(Continued)

Box 7.1 (Continued)

a brilliant space to have some time to yourself and not be distracted by anything else going on in your life. You'll be amazed at what you create and hopefully you'll have at least some of the benefits I've felt from the program.

I think it's really important to have a separate space where you feel safe and can communicate with the artist and the other people in the group. I think trying to do that in a clinical area or an area that's associated more with the hospital might make that a little more challenging. I think that the way that the Lime studio is a creative space, it just feels very relaxed. I think the space that the sessions happen in is really important. It wouldn't be the same in a seminar room, for example. I think you'd have to work on the seminar room before it was even suitable to try it. But there are these secret spaces around the hospital that would be good for the workshops; they just need to be sought out and re-purposed but there definitely should be a dedicated space for well-being.

I've worked in hospitals for 25 years as a doctor and they're generally quite bleak places to work, not just experience wise but decor wise. It's all whites, creams, and beiges and not very pleasant. I have always enjoyed working in places like the children's hospital which are brighter and have art installations, maybe it lifts my mood. I haven't really ever put those two things together until I took part in the Create+ program. On my return to work, I found myself walking through the Wythenshawe corridor from the car park and through theatre corridors looking at the walls and it really stood out to me that the spaces are really important. They really do contribute to how you're feeling. Brighter spaces with artwork on the walls, not so many corporate messages and pictures from the 1950s of children that have obviously been separated from their parents for a long time aren't the right messages to be giving to our staff on a daily basis.

I'd like to emphasize about Create+—well, just the massive benefits that it's brought me. I know now that if I'm not doing art myself weekly it feels like something is missing and I do really miss that time doing something mindful and creative and creating something. I changed what happens at home as well as using it to get back to work. It's an ongoing process and I've really enjoyed it. It brought back a hobby into my life which I'd really neglected before.

I've just had my yearly appraisal and I've discussed being involved with Lime projects as one of my objectives for next year. My clinical director and HR are supportive, and we are meeting to discuss how we can help move forward with bringing Create + to the Wythenshawe site.[5]

---

[5]This interview was carried out by Kim Wiltshire in June 2023, via phone, with full ethical approval and with the participant editing the transcribed response.

Fig. 7.6 Clay heads. Photo image copyright Lime 2022/2023

some clay making, with participants creating small clay heads that represented themselves and then adding on top of these heads all the things they cared about in their lives (Fig. 7.6).

These clay heads then formed the basis of creating their mask, which was modelled on their own face. The mask as a creative concept has several meanings, including of course reference to the PPE staff had to wear during the pandemic, the masks that we all show the world, as the above case study highlights, and the masks that hide our true feelings. Some people chose to just make a beautiful thing whilst others (as the case study below shows) used the masks to explore and sometimes to make a statement about how they were feeling and what had brought them to Create+ (Fig. 7.7).

The printmaking workshops run by Colette Whittington also produced beautiful artworks but concentrated on the specific skills element, so allowed people to work in a quieter atmosphere. Where the masks felt craft-based, the printmaking workshops enabled staff to work on a technical skill set they would not encounter within their own role, producing work from simple screen-printed tote bags through to complex etching techniques, such as those in Fig. 7.8.

7.6 Discussion

Considering the Groys statement we began with "Creativity is a symptom of great health" (Groys, 2022, p. 30) as mentioned above, did the participants' practice of creativity help them reach for great health? The aim of the program is to foster a lifelong engagement with culture and the arts to improve mental health and

Fig. 7.7 Participant's mask and painted clay head. Photo image copyright Lime 2022/2023

Fig. 7.8 Etching techniques. Photo image copyright Lime 2022/2023

well-being alongside an investment in that engagement from healthcare organizations, to encourage creative well-being in their staff.

The MYCaW data and the anonymized comments suggest that during that time of creative engagement, greater health was reached and often led participants towards making space for their own creativity outside of work, with one participant setting up a craft shed in their garden and another participant seeking out art classes. Many participants continued their relationship with Lime, indeed Lime set up a series of Masterclasses for the Create+ alumni.

Of course, staff members may not need an intensive six-week course such as Create+; team building and creative away days, gallery tours or even one-off workshops have all been successful interventions for NHS staff members at Lime in terms of improving mental well-being. As discussed above in the literature review, there has been a range of research over the years, from Peter Senior and Jonathan Croall's 1993 book *Helping to Heal* through to Daisy Fancourt's vast body of work over the past decade or so that shows how the arts impact on patient well-being and mental health in both healthcare and community settings. It is not much of an extrapolation to show that these same interventions with frontline healthcare staff can and will have the same impact on both general well-being and mental well-being. However, the aim of the pilot was to show MFT that Create+ needed to be embedded within the hospitals and healthcare settings, through the case studies, the interviews, the artwork, and the Meaningful Measures evaluation. Did the research help with that decision? The Executive Director of Workforce at MFT said:

> The next questions, therefore, is how do I embed [Create+] strategically? It's through the evidence of Create+, through the positivity, the participant feedback. [...]
>
> If you can't draw the correlation between staff well-being and patient care you're not reading the right documents, you're not seeing the right evidence, you're not seeing the sickness levels, you're not seeing staff turnover levels, because that's all telling you there's a cost you are choosing to ignore.
>
> Of course, in the current climate all NHS Trusts are worried about that Daily Mail headline aren't they? That says, "hard up Trust that can't treat patients in A&E spends £10,000 on Papier Mache" or something like that. The reality of the media agenda for me is, you can't do anything about that, that doesn't mean to say you shouldn't do the right thing and [Create+] is the right thing.
>
> (Wiltshire, 2023, Interview with Director of Workforce, Unpublished)

Of course, there are always the questions of finance raised, as the Director of Workforce himself highlights in the quote above. Whilst the finances were not in any way a major driving force of the research carried out, we did work with the MFT Human Resources team to consider this and the figures they gave us suggested that a consultant who has been on paid sick leave for 6 months or more can cost an NHS Healthcare Trust somewhere in the region of £150,000. The cost for one participant on one block of Create+ is under £400. Whilst this is not an exact economic comparison, if you extrapolate those costs across the 60 participants on the pilot, the value for money in terms of participants returning to work or not being on paid sick leave is very clear.

7.7 Conclusions and Recommendations

After working on such an innovative project, we are still assessing our full recommendations, but we would suggest it is self-evident that hospital trusts need to recognize the benefits of the arts, not just for environment and patients, but for staff as well. Caring for the carers. By embedding the arts into healthcare settings, by engaging staff in creative activity as part of their daily working lives, mental health and general well-being can be improved.

But more importantly, using evaluation and research methods that suit the purpose of the project, are persuasive and can make the argument for embedding arts into healthcare settings, is also vital.

At the time of writing (2024), Create+ continues, is funded and goes from strength to strength, has won two awards and Lime has set up the Create+ Alumni program.

References

Acai, A., McQueen, S. A., McKinnon, V., & Sonnadara, R. R. (2017). Using art for the development of teamwork and communication skills among health professionals: A literature review. *Arts and Health, 9*(1), 60–72. https://doi.org/10.1080/17533015.2016.1182565

British Medical Association. (2020). *The mental health and well-being of the medical workforce – Now and beyond COVID-19*. https://www.bma.org.uk/media/2475/bma-covid-19-and-nhs-staff-mental-health-wellbeing-report-may-2020.pdf

Dalingwater, L. (2019). Linking health and wellbeing in public discourse and policy: The case of the UK. *Revue Interventions Economiques, 62* (2019), Online. http://journals.openedition.org/interventionseconomiques/6243. https://doi.org/10.4000/interventionseconomiques.6243

Daykin, N. (2020). *Arts, health and well-being: A critical perspective on research, policy and practice*. Routledge.

Dragon, S., & Madsen, W. (2015). Engaging in creative activity. *Journal of Applied Arts and Health, 6*(3), 323–338.

Fancourt, D. (2017). *Arts in health: Designing and researching interventions*. Oxford University Press.

Farmer, P. (2019). Mental health in the workplace. *RCN Magazines*. https://www.rcn.org.uk/magazines/Activists/2019/Oct/Mental-health-and-the-workplace

Ford, M. (2021). Survey reveals state of nurses' mental health one year into pandemic. *Nursing Times*. https://www.nursingtimes.net/news/mental-health/nursing-times-survey-reveals-state-of-nurses-mental-health-one-year-into-pandemic-31-03-2021/

Govoni, D., Ramirez, K., & Rubesin, H. (2021). Adjusting to the pandemic: Remote support for professionals working with asylum seekers. *Journal of Applied Arts and Health, 12*(3), 259–269.

Groys, B. (2022). *Philosophy of care*. Verso.

Kiely, B., Croke, A., O'Shea, M., Boland, F., O'Shea, E., Connolly, D., & Smith, S. M. (2022). Effect of social prescribing link workers on health outcomes and costs for adults in primary care and community settings: A systematic review. *BMJ Open*, *12*, Article e062951. https://doi.org/10.1136/bmjopen-2022-062951

McVeigh, C., Reid, J., Carswell, C., Ace, L., Walsh, I., Graham-Wisener, L., Soham, R., Potes, A., Atkinson, K., Edginton, T., & Noble, H. (2021). Mindfulness as a well-being initiative for future nurses: A survey with undergraduate nursing students. *BMC Nursing, 20*(253), 1–9.
Perry, M., Maffully, N., Willson, S., & Morrissey, D. (2011). The effectiveness of arts-based interventions in medical education: A literature review. *Medical Education, 45*(2), 141–148.
Sajnani, N., & Fietje, N. (2023). The Jameel Arts & Health Lab in collaboration with the WHO–*Lancet* global series on the health benefits of the arts. *The Lancet, 402*(10414), 1732–1734.
Seers, H., Sabey, A., & Polley, M. (2023). *Meaningful measures evaluation of Create+*. https://www.limeart.org/wp-content/uploads/2023/08/Create-Evaluation-Report-June-2023-1.pdfeate-Evaluation-Report-June-2023-1.pdf
Senior, P., & Croall, J. (1993). *Helping to heal: The arts in healthcare*. Calouste Gulbenkian Foundation.
Song, X., Wenning, F., Xiaoran, L., Zhiqian, L., Rixing, W., Ning, Z., Shijiao, Y., & Chuanzhu, L. (2020). Mental health status of medical staff in emergency departments during the coronavirus disease 2019 epidemic in China. *Brain, Behaviour, and Immunity, 88*, 60–65.
United Nations. (2013). *Artistic freedom report of the special rapporteur in the field of cultural rights*. https://digitallibrary.un.org/record/755488?v=pdf
Walton, M., Murray, E., & Christian, M. D. (2020). Mental health care for medical staff and affiliated healthcare workers during the COVID-19 pandemic. *European Heart Journal: Acute Cardiovascular Care, 9*(3), 241–247.
WHO. (2021). *Promoting well-being*. https://www.who.int/activities/promoting-well-being
Wiltshire, K. (2023). *Interview with Executive Director of MFT Workforce*. Unpublished.
Wiltshire, K., & Prescott, D. (2023). *Interview with Manager of Endoscopy at MFT*. Unpublished.

Kim Wiltshire is Reader and Programme Leader for Creative Writing at Edge Hill University. During 2022 and 2023 she was a British Academy Innovation Fellow working with Lime to explore ways of embedding the arts into healthcare settings. She is a playwright and short fiction writer; her plays *Project XXX* and *The Value of Nothing* were both published by Aurora Metro Books and, alongside a range of academic articles and chapters, she co-wrote *Scenes from the Revolution* with Billy Cowan, published by Pluto Books in 2018. Between 2004 and 2011 she was a lead artist and project manager for Lime Arts.

Dawn Prescott is a visionary innovator within Arts and Health, with a professional portfolio spanning 20 years as lead artist, arts and health practitioner and consultant and arts programme director. Currently leading Lime, based at Manchester NHS Foundation Trust, she garnered international recognition for pioneering approaches to integrating art and music into patient care and recovery. In 2021, she spearheaded a groundbreaking arts programme dedicated to supporting NHS staff, including a unique hospital-based Arts + Wellbeing Centre and the award winning Create+ Art Referral Service. Dawn continues to push boundaries in healthcare, inspiring others through the dedicated creation of inclusive healing environments where art thrives.

Chapter 8
Women's Well-being in the Workplace Across the Lifespan: Comparative Perspectives on Menopause Workplace Policy and Practices in the United Kingdom, France, and the United States

Louise Dalingwater, Liana B. Winett, and Laurence Peru-Pirotte

Abstract Women play an increasingly important role in the workplace, yet legislation and policy in companies do not necessarily take into account significant health and societal challenges encountered by 50% of the population. While the menopause transition is a natural process, which can last as long as 15 years, it tends to be experienced when women are playing the most significant roles in the workplace. Women aged 45–55 years are often at the height of their careers which requires devoting more time and energy to their jobs. Menopause symptoms (such as hot flashes, headaches, memory issues, sleep impairment…) can cause significant issues for women to complete their daily tasks in the workforce if the work environment does not have policies and practices in place that allow for management of symptoms while on the job such as ventilation, flexibility in wardrobe, and ability to adjust schedules if needed. Added to these are the societal taboos surrounding menstruation and the menopause. The current chapter focuses on a cross-country comparison of workplace legislation, policy and discourse surrounding the menopause drawing on corpora in the three countries. This includes Hansard debates in the UK, Congressional records in the US and governmental debates in the France, legal reviews and legislative discourse as well as union and menopause advocacy group documentation. Finally, the paper draws on secondary literature collected on

L. Dalingwater (✉)
Faculty of Arts and Humanities, Sorbonne University, Paris, France
e-mail: louise.dalingwater@sorbonne-universite.fr

L. B. Winett
Faculty of School of Public Health, Oregon Health & Science University-Portland State University, Portland, OR, USA
e-mail: lwinett@pdx.edu

L. Peru-Pirotte
Université de Lille III, Villeneuve-d'Ascq, France
e-mail: laurence.peru-pirotte@univ-lille.fr

© The Author(s), under exclusive license to Springer Nature Switzerland AG 2025

L. Dalingwater et al. (eds.), *Structural and Systemic Perspectives on Health and Well-being*, Human Well-Being Research and Policy Making,
https://doi.org/10.1007/978-3-031-99924-6_8

workers' views on policy processes and legislation on the issue. Analysis of the three corpora highlights four major themes regarding menopause in the workplace, policy and legislation and its impact on women's well-being: (1) women's health and well-being in the workplace, (2) economic incentives and imperatives of improving women's health, (3) questions of equality and equity and (4) protection against discrimination and harassment.

Keywords Menopause · Workplace · Well-being · Women · Policy · Legislation

8.1 Introduction

Women[1] represent a significant portion of the global workforce, yet employment legislation and policy do not necessarily consider the significant health and societal challenges encountered by what is approximately 50% of the population. The menopause transition, commonly beginning around age 45 and continuing through the sixth decade of life, is a natural process that tends to occur when women also have amassed significant skillsets and have greatest potential for advancement in their work roles. Menopause is the period following cessation of menses for at least 12 consecutive months, marking the end of a woman's reproductive years (NICE, 2015). The transition period towards menopause, often termed perimenopause, can last as long as 15 years. Importantly, the experience of menopause[2] and whether any symptoms are problematic varies by individual and may even vary over time for a single person. For example, working women may experience heightened and unpredictable bleeding, hot flashes, headaches, and even sleep impairment—the latter bringing attendant symptoms of its own. These can be problematic if the workplace does not have policies and practices in place that allow for management of symptoms while on the job, such as access to ventilation, flexibility in wardrobe, and ability to adjust schedules or working format, if needed. Added to these challenges are the societal taboos surrounding menstruation and menopause that make it difficult for employees to discuss their circumstances with supervisors and teammates.

In this chapter we ask, in three well-resourced western nations with significant proportions of female employees in this predictable stage of life, what is the status of the issue and how is it being described in policy, employment, and labor circles? In particular, we wished to know whether and how menopause at work is addressed at a policy level (public or private) in three western national contexts, including the existence of any current applicable law, proposed legislation, legislative debates, and corporate or other contributions from extra-governmental entities. Specifically,

[1] We use the term "women" throughout this work as is consistent with much of the corpora we reviewed and for brevity, and yet we acknowledge the limitations in this language and that this gendered identity does not represent all persons who experience menopause in the workplace.

[2] For brevity, we will use the term "menopause" to refer to the entire experience, including the perimenopausal period, menopausal transition, and the years following.

we asked where, in addition to any potential legislative efforts, other interventions to support women experiencing menopause in the workplace may also be underway.

To respond to these questions, we conducted a cross-country comparison of national policy discourse, proposed legislation, and assessments of employment policy surrounding menopause, drawing on corpora in the United Kingdom (UK), France, and the United States (US).[3] We explored parliamentary debates in the UK and France and congressional records in the US, as well as legislative committee hearings, legal reviews, organized labor messaging and initiatives, and corporate and menopause advocacy group websites in the three countries. While none of the three nations, at the time of writing, has yet enacted overarching legislation explicitly governing approaches to menopause in the workplace, analysis of the three corpora highlights a number of relevant policies and/or initiatives which have at least been discussed. Such discourse, in turn, reflects the potential impacts that the absence of workplace structures and policies can have on quality of life for midlife and older female workers. We sought both similarities and differences across these three nations for purposes of exploring where progress has been made, and to help identify where ongoing opportunities may lie.

8.2 Women's Well-being and Quality of Life in the Workplace

In order to discuss the well-being of working women and the impact of menopause, it is important to reflect on the more general literature on well-being at work. Drawing on a literature review of well-being in the workplace, Devi Aryanti et al. (2020) define workplace well-being as the intrinsic and extrinsic value of work (or work values). The literature on well-being at work has focused on impacts, which include level of income, satisfaction, health risks, hazardous working conditions, and work-related stress. However, while the literature is abundant on well-being at work more generally, the specific case of working women is an under-researched area (Connerley & Wu, 2016). Even less present is a reflection on menopause and its impact on well-being in the workplace. Public attention in all three countries is increasingly acknowledging that the workplace, in general, is not yet adapted to these needs. This is an area requiring attention to ensure both the economic security and general well-being of women in the workplace.

Menopause symptoms may be worsened by specific workplace conditions. For example, working through inadequate ventilation, high temperatures, and/or excessive humidity and dryness (Griffiths et al., 2006; Healthtalk.org, n.d; Kopenhager & Guidozzi, 2015). Also problematic are lack of adequate and accessible sanitary

[3]This project expands upon our prior analysis of U.K. and U.S. national policy discourse surrounding menopause, partially reproduced here in illustrative comparison with France (See Dalingwater and Winett, 2025).

toilet facilities, and work uniforms in fabrics or constructions that trap body heat or otherwise make it difficult to manage symptoms during the workday. Some workers also are reticent to disclose symptoms to managers due to privacy concerns or fear that they will not be well received (Griffiths et al., 2006). Such concerns are not unfounded, as there have been examples of menopause-related workplace discrimination and harassment brought to court in the UK and the US (Healthtalk.org, n.d; Irni, 2009; Moloney et al., 2006; Crawford et al., 2022).

Workplaces that are not structured for employees across the lifespan can challenge good functioning in the workplace, which in turn can affect engagement and even longevity in employment. A Fawcett Society report, for example, found that 77% of UK women surveyed had experienced one or more symptoms which they described as difficult to manage in their work contexts, and 44% felt such unaddressed symptoms affected their ability to work. Further, one in ten women surveyed said they had left employment because menopausal symptoms were too difficult to address in the workplace (Fawcett Society, 2022). In France, a study carried out in 2021 for the group Alan by Harris interactive which polled 2140 women managing menopause at work revealed significant issues: 51% of women reported negative effects in the workplace, 16% reported it had a direct impact on their productivity, 8% suffered from stigma, and 21% were obliged to take time off from work (up to a few days at a time) because of menopause symptoms (Harris interactive, 2021). Others switched to part-time work and 10% felt that menopause had put a brake on career progression. Respondents in the study felt the need for more flexibility and accommodative measures, including access to windows, ventilation, temperature-controlled rooms in which to rest, and easier access to toilets and showers. Moreover, 20% of those polled believed that sanctions should be taken against companies who do not employ or assist midlife and older women in career progression, and 19% were in favor of legislation to protect menopausal women at work (Harris interactive, 2021).

The literature has thus explored women's experiences of menopause and the need for more action to be taken to combat symptoms. Yet, a deeper analysis of legislation and other workplace strategies is needed to fully understand the issue and the status of efforts on this issue. It is also particularly valuable to explore three quite different contexts of Western labor markets where stakeholders have raised the question of menopause in the workplace in varying ways.

8.3 National Policy Governing the Workplace in the UK, France, and US

From the outset, we should note that these three nations' governments stand in somewhat different relationships to workplace policies but none of these so far are sufficient to fully cover the needs of women experiencing the menopausal transition. In the UK, for example, all employers, workers, and unions are bound by the labor law which regulates relations between the former actors. It also sets forth a number of employment rights which apply across the four nations of the UK and stem from Acts of Parliament, Regulations, common law, and equity. Such employment rights include a minimum wage (National Minimum Wage Act), 28 days paid holiday, breaks from work and limited working times (Working Time Regulations 1998), the right to childcare leave and flexible working patterns (Employment Rights Act 1996), and pension rights (Pensions Act of 2008). There are also collective agreements to ensure the right to strike. Fair treatment of employees is upheld by the 2010 Equality Act.

In France, article 34 of the Constitution gives the Assemblée Nationale and Sénat the power to draw up laws concerning labor law, trade union rights, and social security. Labor law regulates many areas such as the employment contract, remuneration, working hours, leave, discipline, dismissal, employment, training, safety and health at work, collective bargaining, strikes, and staff representation. These rules are supplemented by implementing decrees taken by the government which is also responsible for taking all the rules which do not fall within the scope of the law, for example the rules of procedure. Collective negotiation, meaning production of agreements between worker representatives and the employer party, and the employment contract, comprise the suite of rights and protections. In principle, the preemptive rule known as "social public order" applies, which makes the collective agreement superior to the law and the contract if its provisions are more favorable for employees.

Both France and the UK provide for health insurance and related terms via nationalized health and social care systems. In the US, by contrast, the federal government has only partial control over workplace and employment policies, sharing responsibility with the states and local municipalities. Federal law is, however, preemptive of any state or local legislation that is less stringent or otherwise conflicting. For example, the 1970 Occupational Safety and Health Act currently sets health and safety standards that apply to both public and private workplaces. Congress also has a role in specifying the categorical basic and/or preventive services that must be included in qualifying employer-provided health insurance programs, which in the decentralized healthcare model of the US is one of the primary sources of health services payment. Such authority exists in policies including the 1974 Employee Retirement Income Security Act and 2010 Patient Protection and Affordable Care Act, with relative applications depending upon factors such as size of employer and its insurance structure and minimum requirements for employer-sponsored health insurance. US Congress also has direct influence over conditions affecting federal civilian employees (who totaled 2.9 million as of 2022) and active-duty military (who totaled 1.3 million that same year). This includes requirements for publicly owned facilities in which these employees serve, via Federal Acquisition Regulations and Department of Defense budgeting (Statista, 2023, 2024a, 2024b).

None of these three countries has yet introduced targeted legislation at national level to provide for workplace conditions that specifically address menopause-related needs, although the Employment Rights Bill which is currently going through Parliament in the UK would enforce certain rights for menopausal women in the UK, if enacted. In addition, at the time of writing, law does exist in all three countries to ensure aspects of worker well-being, more generally.

Specifically, there are laws intended to uphold gender equality at work and prohibit discrimination in employment. For example, in France, articles L1132-1 et seq. of L1225-1 (C. Trav) prevent discrimination in the workplace according to sex, pregnancy, health, and disability. Moreover, Articles L4121-1 et seq. provide that the employer must assess the risks and, where necessary, implement preventive measures, which may relate to work organization, working conditions, sexual and moral harassment, and sexism. In the UK, the Employment Rights Act 1996 covers all employment rights including contracts, unfair dismissal, parental leave, and lay-off compensation. Moreover, the UK Equality Act of 2010 prevents discrimination in the workplace and the recruitment process. In the US, the 1970 Occupational Safety and Health Act provides standards to assure safe working conditions across employment facilities, resources, and practices, although it does not specify terms related to menopause. Federal anti-discrimination laws pertaining to sex, ability, and age (e.g., Title VII of the Civil Rights Act of 1964; Americans with Disabilities Act of 1990 (ADA); Age Discrimination in Employment Act of 1967) all could be interpreted to have bearing on this intersectional issue, even though they, too, lack mention of menopause (see Cahn et al., 2024 for a full review). Instead, this lack of menopause-specificity has historically left workers without clear paths for redress. For example, findings for disability protections have been applied to "early" or "abnormal" menopause (i.e., that caused by illness or medical intervention) but have not historically been considered applicable to symptoms of "normal" age-related menopause (Cahn et al., 2024; Crawford et al., 2022). Legal scholars of this issue have suggested that the 2008 Amendment to the ADA may offer limited protections (Crawford et al., 2022), provided accommodations are not determined to pose "undue hardship" to the employer. Further, scholars suggest that the 2023 Pregnant Workers Fairness Act, including provisions for menstruation, may also have unstated implications for menopause (Karin, 2022; Mullins, 2022).

Thus, in all three countries under study, employers are bound by obligations to protect the health and safety of their employees which could, feasibly, be clarified and/or extended to address menopause needs even though menopause is not currently mentioned. In France, for example, it is sufficient to demonstrate that the health of employees has been compromised for the employer to be held liable for corrective action; it is not necessary to prove fault (C. Trav. L4121-1; Cass. Soc., 25 Nov. 2015, n°14-24.444). In the UK, the Health and Safety at Work Act 1974 provides for safe working conditions. This protection could be extended to employees experiencing menopause whose health concerns are not being appropriately managed by their employer. Recent guidance from the US Department of Labor recommends that employers incorporate menopause needs in their policies, including employees' increased access to toilet and sanitary facilities, ability to control ventilation and temperature, and flexible uniform guidelines and codes that enable better management of symptoms during the workday (Women's Bureau, 2024). These agency guidelines are important, and yet also indicate that they exist in the absence of explicit policy: US "federal law currently does not explicitly protect against discrimination based on menstruation or menopause" (Women's Bureau, 2024, p. 3).

8.4 Methods and Analysis

8.4.1 The Corpora

In order to survey the country-specific situations and to draw comparisons, documentation and discourse from influential political, economic, and social groups or individuals were reviewed. The British corpus includes records of parliamentary debates and menopause-related hearings from 2016 when menopause workplace issues started to become central to debate in the two houses of Parliament, policy documents from the UK's two biggest trade unions (Trade Union Congress (TUC) and Unison), charities and Civil Society Organizations (CSO) website review. The French corpus includes legal texts and regulations, administrative and judicial case law, parliamentary documents (committee reports, public sessions, draft laws), and company agreements retrieved from the "legifrance.gouv.fr" database. These documents were supplemented by searching various legal databases (lexis 360, Dalloz, doctrinal+) and the cairn.info database to find other references. The US Congressional corpus includes all electronically available introduced bills, congressional hearings, and other remarks available via Congress.gov, as well as via commercial legal database, HeinOnline and ProQuest Congressional. We further searched published US legal reviews available via HeinOnline and GoogleScholar and conducted a snowball-search of current efforts in news coverage, industry reports, union documentation, and advocacy group websites (e.g., North American Menopause Society, Let's Talk Menopause, The Menopause Society). For all three countries the primary search term was "menopause" and its cognates as was related to work (including workplace, employment); for the US, we added the term "menstruation" and its cognates to also capture policy debate related to managing bleeding—a known symptom of perimenopause—at the workplace. This added term did not yield additional records in the UK and France.

Identified relevant documents date from 2016 in the UK and France and 1980 in the US (the earliest records found in each) to 2024. For each country we reviewed the breadth of themes and examples to assemble a survey of the current policy landscape, from the biggest public (national) platforms to individual corporate and organizational engagement, each with important levers that can help advance the issue of workplaces designed for employees across the lifespan.

We describe each corpus in turn, below, beginning with a scan of discourse among national legislators, followed by examples of efforts outside these legislative bodies including organized labor, individual employers, and community-based and municipal entities.

8.5 National Legislative Discourses Regarding Menopause and the Workplace

Significant debate has taken place since 2016 on the question of menopause in UK Parliament. The UK Labour Government's Employment Rights Bill proposes legislation to ensure that workplaces do not discriminate on the basis of menopause. Yet, UK parliamentary discourse on menopause is dominated by attention to the economic imperative to make accommodations for women, which is a narrow driver toward ensuring women's well-being in the workplace. Nevertheless, health and equality issues are also dominant in the UK corpus, similar to issues raised in France, where equality is of major concern. The US case stands out in contrast, where we could expect economic drivers to be at the forefront given that the US is equally a flexible and profit-driven labor market. However, analysis of US legislative discourse shows that emphasis on terms for employer-sponsored health insurance, health service provisions for active-duty military, and attempts to assure sanitary toilet facilities and supplies in workplaces were more dominant.

In the *UK* debates, we identify occupational health, the economic drive, equality to ensure women stay in the workplace, and preventing discrimination against older women to be at the forefront of debates. In the UK, recent Parliament debates have underlined the importance of menopause as an *employee health concern*: "The menopause is an occupational health issue that rests on the desks of managers—male as well as female managers, and managers who are frequently younger than the person" (Hansard, 2018). Carolyn Harris (Labour MP for Swansea) argues during the same debate that all employers can be called to introduce a menopause policy owing to a statutory duty of care: "Employers have a duty of care to all their employees. While no respectable company would even consider running their business without a maternity policy, very few will have given any thought to the introduction of a menopause policy" (Hansard, 2018). In English tort law, a "duty of care" refers to an obligation to ensure that an individual does not suffer any unreasonable harm or loss, in this case, in the workplace. The policies that the speaker recommends under the duty of care are allowing appropriate clothing, more flexible working conditions, and site temperature controls.

This specific debate also indicated that as many as one quarter of women consider leaving the workplace because of severe menopausal symptoms:

> One woman's symptoms were so severe that she thought she had early-onset dementia. It was only when she left her job as a result of her fear of not being in control and her GP [General Practitioner] diagnosed her symptoms and prescribed [Hormone Replacement Therapy] that she realised that she was not suffering from dementia. She had experienced an early menopause, which was not picked up because she was on the contraceptive pill (Hansard, 2020).

Debates in the UK Parliament focus on *the economic imperative* for the nation of supporting menopausal women in the workplace. For example, a parliamentary debate on July 2, 2022, entitled "Women Leaving the Workplace" underlines that perimenopausal and menopausal women are often at the height of their careers and therefore, without support, may depart creating a vacuum of skills and expertise:

> There is no policy in place to protect and retain the huge skills and experience bank that these women offer. Other Members have referred to the point in people's lives and careers when they are particularly valuable for the workplace, so the menopause is also an economic issue (Claire Hanna, Belfast South, SDLP; Hansard, 2022a).

Debates in the UK also highlight that when there is *workplace discrimination* on grounds of menopause, it is very hard for employees to bring forward claims. On 8 September 2022 in a parliamentary debate entitled "Women and Equalities Committee," Caroline Nokes, Conservative MP for Romsey and Southampton North noted that, under current legislation, it is very difficult for women to bring discrimination claims to employment tribunals: "Members will immediately see the problem with a menopausal woman having to compare herself to a sick man in order to get redress" (Hansard, 2022b). Indeed, in the UK under the 2010 Equality Act, it is extremely difficult for women to bring sex discrimination claims because it requires male-experience comparators to be made and there are no truly comparable male experiences. Bringing a disability discrimination claim is also complicated because menopause is considered a "natural" stage of life. It is thus debatable whether women with severe menopause symptoms are "disabled" (or whether there is a desire to label them as such). However, recent guidance from the Equality and Human Rights Commission (EHRC) is encouraging employers to consider severe conditions as a disability in order for employers to provide more support for women experiencing debilitating symptoms. The Commission is also currently supporting an alleged case of menopause discrimination on disability grounds, which, if successful, will represent a precedent for women to use the Disability clause in the 2010 Equality Act (EHRC, 2024). Moreover, the Employment Rights Bill, introduced to Parliament on October 10, 2024, and currently making its way through Parliament, contains a new statutory obligation for companies of 250+ to produce Equality Plans, including menopause. As the Secretary of State for Business and Trade Jonathan Reynolds and initiator of the bill commented:

> Despite existing protections, we know it is not always a level playing field, and too many women are being held back at work. By expanding gender pay gap reporting requirements, requiring large employers to produce action plans on how to address their gender pay gaps and support employees through the menopause (...) this Bill will put gender equality front and centre of our employment legislation (Hansard, 2024).

Nevertheless, this bill is not as far reaching as the failed 2021 Menopause Support and Services Bill. The latter aimed to include more components which affected women's well-being across the lifespan, including exemption of HRT from NHS prescription charges and menopause support and services (UK Parliament, 2022). The aborted bill drew on hearings from the Menopause and the Workplace inquiry in 2021, which raised issues on treatment, workplace discrimination, and the importance of destigmatizing menopause. The need for an intersectional approach to women's well-being at work was also noticeable from a number of witnesses to the enquiry. As Professor Joanna Brewis, head of the department of People and

Organizations at the Open University Business School, commented in oral evidence submitted to the inquiry:

> We know nothing about how women of different racial or ethnic origins might experience the conjunction between menopause and work. We know nothing about trans women. We know nothing about women who identify as anything other than heterosexual. We know nothing about women in the gig economy. Really, the majority of the research that focuses on the workplace is about professional or managerial white, middle-class, able-bodied women (House of Commons, 2021).

Notwithstanding this, the Employment Bill if successful could lead to a sizeable and overdue cultural change. As Caroline Nokes, Conservative MP and chair of the UK Women and Equalities Committee which drew together the evidence from the inquiry in an extensive report, lamented: "For too long women have faced stigma, shame, and dismissive attitudes when it comes to menopause" (UK Parliament, 2022). As we shall see, this rooting of attitudes toward menopause in pervasive and overarching myths about the life stage is a theme that is reiterated by legislators in France and the US, as well.

In *France*, the debates put much emphasis on equality between women and men. Taking measures to reduce the negative interactions of menstrual health and menopause makes it possible to get closer to real equality between women and men (formal equality already being ensured by anti-discrimination laws). It is also about no longer making suffering invisible but, on the contrary, taking it into account in order to reduce this other aspect of inequality between women and men. On March 8, 2023, Elisabeth Borne's government announced the implementation of a "Toutes et tous égaux" (All Equal) plan, the aim of which is to make equality between women and men a reality in professional, economic, and social terms by adopting an inter-ministerial plan to cover the period 2023–2027 (Dumeau, 2023). This action plan is built around four pillars: action to combat violence against women, women's health, professional and economic equality and the culture of equality. Among the measures planned under the "women's health" pillar is the creation of a prevention consultation at the age of 45, which would address concerns related to menopause. An annual "Women's Health Week" has also been introduced on a given theme (national campaign and actions in the field), and menopause is one of the themes mentioned by way of example, alongside cardiovascular risks, physical activity, body image, sexual health, health at work, and the role of midwives. The other three pillars are silent on the issue. This shortcoming was acknowledged by Isabelle Rome (Minister attaché to the Prime Minister, responsible for equality between women and men, diversity, and equal opportunities) at her hearing on the plan before the Assemblée Nationale (National Assembly)'s Social Affairs Committee on July 11, 2023:

> Another subject has not really been addressed. After the taboos surrounding miscarriage and menstruation, there's another one that needs to be raised: that of menopause. In our society, women are often invisible; after the age of 50, they are even more so. This health issue deserves to be taken into account in the workplace, and it's clear that we need to work together on this (Assemblée nationale, Compte rendu de reunion n°100, July 11 2023).

Linked closely to equality between women and men is occupational health. The Information Report no. 780 (June 27, 2023) on "Women's Health at Work" was presented to the Sénat by its Delegation for Women's Rights (Cohen et al., 2023). This 141-page report addressing women's occupational health issues highlights that working conditions, work-related risks, and health at work are still viewed through the prism of the average man, leaving aside issues that only affect women or that concern the majority of them. In particular, "the persistent lack of a gendered approach to health in the workplace has resulted in a lack of preventive measures to promote women's health in the workplace" (Cohen et al., 2023). Companies are reluctant to differentiate, for fear of the costs this could entail and of being accused of discrimination, to which the authors counter that "differentiation is not discrimination" (Cohen et al., 2023, p. 20) and that improvements in women's health could well benefit everyone. The authors of the report also note that women's health is not sufficiently considered within the current Occupational Health Plan: "only one action, Action 3.3, provides for 'making Quality of Life and Working conditions approaches genuine levers for gender equality'" (Cohen et al., 2023, p. 73). This involves "designing tools dedicated to women's occupational health, in conjunction with the occupational health and prevention services to support companies in preventing sexist and sexual violence at work and in dealing with domestic violence" (Cohen et al., 2023, p. 73). For the authors of the report, despite the Ministry of Labor's assertion at its hearing before the Delegation for Women's Rights that "women's occupational health is an important issue that mobilizes us in an interministerial context," the delegation doubts whether this issue is visible at a national level and whether it is being taken into consideration by public authorities (Cohen et al., 2023).

The fourth part of the aforementioned Information Report, "Sexual and reproductive health: a new field of social conquest for women?" addresses endometriosis, pregnancy, assisted procreation and, on the final six pages, menopause. The latter is presented as the "last of the female taboos" and as a major inequality between women and men. According to the authors of the report, work can have harmful consequences for women during menopause, and menopausal symptoms can also have a negative impact on work. They draw on the hearing comments made by gynecologist Doctor Brigitte Letombe, including the joint pain caused by estrogen deficiency, which can make it difficult to do physical work and increase the risk of musculoskeletal disorders (MSDs). Moreover, it is underlined that "menopause can also alter the work done and the performance of intellectual work" (Cohen et al., 2023, p. 138). The authors of the report add, "In fact, for women doing essentially intellectual work, tiredness and problems with concentration and memorization can have serious consequences for their work." Finally, they note that menopause can lead to retraining into different positions thus losing seniority and potentially compromising previously amassed skills or even early retirement, owing to a lack of support for women and inevitable self-deprecation (Cohen et al., 2023).

As in the UK and France, the earliest *US* Congressional discourse also highlighted *discriminatory myths* surrounding menopause-aged women and the workplace. In an early hearing entitled "Work After 65, Options for the '80s," for example, invited witness Janet Roberts of the Women's Survival Center recommended:

> [...] that industries have advisory committees of their older workers to give valuable input based on their life experiences. I also believe that we should address the whole belief system of top management people who hire and promote who believe that aging is indeed deterioration. I don't believe that is so" (US Senate Special Committee on Aging, 1980).

Four years later during a hearing entitled "The Role of Older Women in the Workforce," academic social scientist Elizabeth Markson (who also provided the only mention "menopause" in the transcript) also spoke to the harmful myths surrounding this time of life:

> Another area that I think could stand some attention in terms of education is the broad area of myths about the aging worker and myths about the woman worker. For example, there are still many, many myths that women are going to be sick all the time on the job, all the women are going to be particularly sick, they are going to go through menopausal blues, et cetera. I think some simple straightforward education, just comparing some of the available Federal data and national health survey data, showing illness and disability rates might be rather useful just to publicize (US Joint Economic Committee, 1984).

Whereas in these two 1980s records we find the theme of the *general experience, and perceptions* of, menopause as a working person, when the dialogue again resumes in the 1990s and continuing to present, the foci of congressional discourse and policy proposals related to menopause and work shift. They later include emphasis on insurance coverage requirements (treatment and screening) for employer-sponsored health plans, health care provision for active-duty military and other federal employees, and workplace sanitary facilities and supplies requirements for managing menstrual bleeding, including during the menopausal transition.

On the issue of employer-sponsored health insurance, for example, the proposed Hormone Replacement Therapies and Alternative Treatments and Fairness Act, introduced in 2001, and followed by similar proposals in 2005, 2007, 2009, and 2011, would have required all group plans (including employer-sponsored insurance) to cover "hormone replacement therapy for menopausal symptoms and alternative treatments for such therapy on the same basis as outpatient prescription drugs" (US House of Representatives, 2002, 2005, 2007, 2009, 2011). These bills did not pass.

Coming at the issue of employer authority in determining employee insurance coverage, lawmakers and witnesses during 2001 and 2014 hearings expressed concern that oral contraceptives—often used for symptoms such as irregular bleeding, a symptom of perimenopause—can be excluded from employee plans on the basis of their employers' religious opposition. As one gynecologist testifying in 2001 observed of the added roadblocks:

> I have patients who are using forms of birth control pills in menopause. [....] and they cannot get that prescription unless I indicate on there that it is not for contraception, and then I still have to write little letters to try to support that (US Senate Committee on Health, Education, Labor, and Pensions, 2001).

Thirteen years later, Senator Carl Levin [Democrat-Michigan] cautioned during a hearing for the proposed 2014 Protect Women's Health from Corporate Interference Act, again addressed oral contraceptive therapies in employee health insurance plans, this time following a Supreme Court decision upholding employers' prerogative to exclude it:

> [C]orporations don't have faiths. People do. That includes the women who have now lost their ability to make the most important and personal decisions about their health care (US Congressional Record, 2014).

Terms governing employment conditions and benefits for members of the US military and the broader federal workforce are more directly under the purview of Congress than other work contexts and thus provide examples of some of the ways legislators conceptualize the roles of employment and workplaces in the experience of menopause. The 1994 National Defense Authorization Act, for example, specified that female active-duty members should be entitled to preventive care that incorporates "Menopause, including hormone replacement therapy and counseling regarding the benefits and risks of hormone replacement therapy" (US National Defense Reauthorization Act, 1993). Thirty years later, Representative Chrissy Houlahan's [Democrat-Pennsylvania] proposed Servicewomen and Veterans Menopause Research Act, specifically considers military work environments, exposures, and roles in members' menopause experiences and outcomes. This bill, which did not make it to a vote, would have required that research be conducted into:

> [T]he relation to and impact of military service to perimenopause and menopause; [...] the effect of combat roles on perimenopause and menopause-related symptoms, including exposure to burn pits, toxic chemicals, and perfluoroalkyl and polyfluoroalkyl substances (commonly known as "PFAS"); and [...] the impact perimenopause and menopause has on the mental health of women who are members of the Armed Forces or veterans (US House of Representatives, 2024).

In addition to provisions surrounding health insurance coverage for federal employees, a specific topic of discussion has been workplace facilities, and specifically access to sanitary toilet areas and supplies for the management of menstrual bleeding which also, notably, often increases and becomes unpredictable during the menopausal transition. In a 2010 hearing addressing "Potty Parity" via the Restroom Gender Parity in Federal Buildings Act, for example, witnesses addressed the insufficiency of women's toilet areas both for the very large federal workforce and all those who come to federal buildings in the conduct of business. Karen Anthony, an academic architect, professor of Gender Studies, and invited witness, noted in her expert testimony:

> We may laugh, and we may joke, but for millions of people around the world, boys and girls, men and women of all ages, especially pregnant and menstruating women, using the restroom is no laughing matter. [...] Public restrooms are a fundamental part of our Nation's infrastructure, just as important as our roads and bridges. [...] Public restrooms are a health and safety issue (US House of Representatives, 2010).

Representative Grace Meng (Democrat-New York) has been a particular champion of this issue, introducing since at least 2019 several bills to address the insufficiency of available sanitary and physical resources for menstrual bleeding at the workplace. These include her 2019 introduction and 2021 reintroduction of the Menstrual Products in Federal Buildings Act, requiring that "sanitary napkins and tampons that conform to applicable industry standards" be made available free of charge in all covered buildings under federal authority (US House of Representatives, 2019b, 2021). In a 2019 testimony, she argued:

> The U.S. government is the largest employer in the country. It is time that our government finally walks the walk and sets an example by providing free menstrual hygiene products in all federal buildings, just as they do toilet paper, paper towels, and hand soap. Doing so will help alleviate the real-life barriers in accessing and affording these everyday products, while normalizing this monthly necessity and basic human right (US House of Representatives Committee on Transportation and Infrastructure, 2019).

Neither introduction of this bill resulted in law.

Similarly, and again considering the US military, Representative Deborah K Ross [Democrat—North Carolina] introduced an amendment to the *2022 National Defense Authorization Act* intended to require study and report on "the availability of menstrual hygiene products on military bases, and accommodations related to menstrual hygiene available to members of the Armed Forces" (US House of Representatives, 2022a). This bill passed the House but was not adopted in compromise with the Senate.

The need for access to menstrual hygiene supplies at the workplace for female employees across the working lifespan was also part of Representative Meng's 2016 *Menstrual Products for Employees Act*, which then preceded the *Menstrual Equity for All Act* introduced (and reintroduced) in 2017, 2019, 2021, and still pending as of this writing in 2024 (US House of Representatives, 2016, 2017, 2019a, 2022b, 2023a). Among the bill's requirements, it would direct that employers with 100 or more employees make available, at no-cost, onsite menstrual supplies for their workforce. Arguing the importance of the then-proposed 2021 bill in a letter to President Biden, Representative Meng asserts: "It is long overdue for the United States to implement a national, whole-of-government strategy to address menstrual equity, and ensure that everyone who requires menstrual products have access to this basic health care right" (Meng, 2021).

Perhaps in an echo of 1980s testimony, in 2023 Representative Meng along with Senators Amy Klobuchar [Democrat-Minnesota] and Tammy Duckworth [Democrat-Illinois] introduced into both the House and Senate a resolution entitled, *Recognizing That the United States Needs to Support and Strengthen Mothers in the Workforce by Investing in the Mom Economy*. The following represents a wide-view acknowledgment of the breadth of reproductive responsibilities shouldered by female workers across their careers, and the potential financial impacts these roles and responsibilities have both on the workers, themselves (and on women overall), and on their families and more broadly, the country as a whole. Among its policy directions the Resolution asserts:

> [T]he United States should invest in its mothers by expanding and developing the social safety net in order to secure meaningful and sustainable economic growth by investing, at a minimum, in programs including [...] [P]aid menstrual leave and remote work

accommodations for workers experiencing debilitating menstrual or menopause symptoms..." (US House of Representatives, 2023b; US Senate, 2023).

While it is not policy unto itself, in providing a map of policies and practices needed to support female workers in the US across their working lifetimes, the resolution importantly places menopause within the broader continuum of a woman's reproductive life to approach as a coherent whole. In other words, the *Mom Economy* reassembles the female lifespan rather than addressing this sizeable percentage of the workforce only within discrete age groups. The resolution also makes the case, as in the UK, that investing in women's reproductive and parenting well-being also is an economic imperative, first at the level of women's financial independence, and secondarily on a national scale. The resolution did not receive a vote in either chamber.

8.5.1 Frustrated Efforts Toward Menopause-Specific Legislation

Despite these debates in the three nations, each raising important issues with policy implications for female employees, the majority of proposals to create menopause-specific law have not yet advanced with the exception of the Employment Rights Bill in the UK.

In the *UK*, recommendations made to the government in 2022 by the Women's and Equalities Committee to produce a model of menopause policies for companies, including paid menopause leave to allow for the management of symptoms, were rejected (UK Parliament, 2022). The 2021 Menopause Support and Services Bill failed to get through the two houses. In particular, the government rejected calls to legislate arguing that it could call into question the existing 2010 Equalities Act by discriminating against male employees, in favor of women. However, the Employment Rights Bill introduced to Parliament under the current Labour government does contain a clause to support menopausal women even though it does not cover the breadth of the Menopause Support and Services Bill.

In *France,* five Bills (four in front of the Assemblée Nationale; and one in front of the Sénat) were presented in 2023 and the first half of 2024 (Bouloux 2023, Bouloux 2024, Conweay-Mouret 2023; Peytavie 2023; Peytavie, 2024). All were about the subject of leave during painful menstrual periods and in case of endometriosis. But menopause was not taken into consideration, only the pre-menopausal period was considered. None of these bills passed. The arguments that were advanced mainly raised questions of medical privacy, fear of discrimination (with regard to men and to women's careers). The negative impact on the presence of workers in female dominated-sectors was also highlighted.

In the *US*, the repeated introductions of nearly identical bills over the course of years suggests that—despite the repeated efforts of a dedicated group of legislators across these decades—menopause is an issue that has been unable to gain traction, despite its ultimate universality for half the country's population. In the US, as opposed to France and the UK, proposals have by and large been more granular (e.g., insurance coverage requirements and workplace sanitary supplies) than overarching (e.g., paid leave and flexible work arrangements for symptom management, and requirements for workplace adaptations). However, it seems unlikely, given that proposals for sanitary pads in public bathrooms and non-binding resolutions expressing the value of female employees have (yet) been unsuccessful, that broader protections and adaptations of the type proposed in the UK and France would have progressed across the Atlantic.

Importantly, none of the three countries yet has requirements that workplaces be designed a priori for workers during this expected stage of life. In this context of frustrated policy efforts, we turned to sources outside national legislatures to see where efforts to shape the workplace environment for midlife and older workers in each country also may lie. These include organized labor, as well as corporate, institutional, and municipal efforts.

8.6 Efforts from Other Key Workplace and Labor Actors

UK trade unions stands out as an example for measures to be taken in the workplace with key recommendations to ensure that menopause matters. We did not find evidence that organized labor is yet taking on the issue of menopause in France. In the US, as described below, there have been efforts among some labor groups to move the issue of menopause to the forefront with recommendations resembling those in the UK; however, such steps appear to be less than universal.

8.6.1 Organized Labor

In the *UK*, trade unions are very active in calling for specific attention to the question of women's health even if the economic imperative is also evident in trade union documentation. The Trade Unions Congress (TUC), for example, underscores the importance of the health of menopausal women. It reported that in Wales 9 in every 10 women experienced noticeable symptoms (TUC Wales, 2017). As way of comparison, the Fawcett Society reported 8 in 10 women suffer noticeable symptoms across the UK in their survey (Fawcett Society, 2022). TUC also use such findings in their documentation and their own reporting to underline that conditions at the workplace can exacerbate symptoms (TUC, 2021). Further, the TUC also argues that women have reported that menopause makes other underlying health issues worse.

As such, TUC UK asserts that employers have a health and safety responsibility to make accommodations for employees managing menopause: "Risk assessments should consider the specific needs of menopausal women and ensure that the working environment will not make their symptoms worse" (TUC, 2021). In addition to needs related to regulating temperature, ventilation, toilet facilities, and access to cold water, they also note "It is important that workplace stress is also considered and addressed properly using the Health and Safety Executive (HSE) stress management standards" (TUC, 2017). Likewise, UNISON—a public service union with a 70% proportion of female members—reiterates that menopausal symptoms are an occupational health issue and therefore also a trade union issue. They call for flexible working conditions and schedules as well as line management support to help employees manage symptoms at the workplace. One example provided is addressing unsuitable manufacturing uniforms and equipment. As one union representative recounted:

> I successfully negotiated gender specific protective personal equipment (PPE), t-shirts, trousers and most importantly footwear, and a good selection and choice of safety glasses (lightweight frames, lenses specific to needs i.e. varifocal, bifocal and thinned as much as acceptable for safety glasses). This meant not having to wear standard safety glasses over our own" […] "A few of my women members also had problems with feet or legs so they were sent to have shoes specific to their needs made to measure (UNISON, 2021).

For UNISON, dealing with menopause is also about supporting equality: "it's an issue for everyone who cares about fairness in the workplace" (UNISON, 2021, p. 10).

Much of the literature provided by trade unions also focuses on the question of menopause-related discrimination. The TUC Toolkit, for example, explains why menopause is an organized labor issue: "Union reps have a key role in supporting members and helping to challenge workplace discrimination and harassment of all kinds, including that linked to the menopause" (TUC, 2021). The fact that women have reported to the TUC that employers do not recognize the issue, or that menopause was not given the same weight as other health issues, is significant. TUC also underlines corporate obligation in another regard: "Employers have a duty to prevent workplace discrimination and to make adjustments to ensure women can work safely through the menopause" (TUC, 2021). The union describes bullying, age, harassment, and inappropriate and discriminatory attributions of employee reactions to menstrual cycles or menopausal symptoms. Similarly, UNISON also raises the issue of discrimination by referring to the 2017 Government Equalities Office report which found that discrimination in terms of gendered ageism was quite significant and that, unsympathetic responses to those suffering from menopausal discomfort at work had been reported (UNISON, 2021).

Both trade unions also point to the unique problems experienced by trans men, trans women, and non-binary persons who may suffer the effects of menopause but do not necessarily wish to expose gender issues (TUC, 2021; UNISON, 2021). UNISON further argues that physical and psychological symptoms may worsen because of discrimination, in turn compounding challenges in the workplace (UNISON, 2021).

Both unions' perspectives are that menopause should be taken into consideration when establishing performance criteria in case it has bearing on an individual's work experience. UNISON underlines, for example, how women undergoing menopause can be penalized via the Bradford Factor, which is a performance monitor used in the UK to assess the impact of employee absenteeism and which indicates that short, frequent, and unplanned absences are disruptive to organizations. UNISON suggests that the use of this factor thus discriminates against women experiencing episodes of more profound menopause symptoms and who may need to be periodically absent to address them. UNISON further recommends contextualizing menopause in this process, because otherwise-inflexible performance management could well lead to the implementation of capability and disciplinary procedures or dismissal (UNISON, 2021).

Overall, both large UK labor unions recommend a tailored approach to menopause, each recognizing the full dimensions of menopause and women's well-being throughout this life stage. Yet, implementation of these recommendations in the workplace has been uneven, as we further describe, below.

In *France* we were unable to find discussion of menopause on the websites of the four representative unions. It is noteworthy that on March 8, 2024, a Confédération Générale du Travail (CGT) (one of the leading trade unions) leaflet mentions menopause as a taboo to be lifted in the workplace (CGT Tract, 2024), and that an open letter from Forces-Ouvrières Aéroports de Paris (Forces Ouvrières Aéroports de Paris, 2024) calls for, among other things, the establishment of a perimenopause–menopause leave. Although they do not seem to be making this issue a national cause, unions are, as we will see below, increasingly active in bringing issues related to menopause through collective bargaining.

Organized labor in the *US* is also making moves in support of employees experiencing menopause at work. For example, the American Federation of Labor-Congress of Industrial Organizations (AFL-CIO), one of the two "voluntary federations" of labor unions in the US, has adopted Resolution 8: Promote Gender Equity. Although lacking specific mention of menopause, it does specify commitment to menopause-relevant concerns including the right to reproductive health care, gender justice, and protection against gender-based harassment (AFL-CIO, 2022). More directly leading the way on menopause and working conditions is AFL-CIO Affiliate union, the United Steelworkers, which has explicitly identified menopause as a priority area requiring unique assessment and assurances. In their guidelines entitled, "Raising the Bar on Women's Health and Safety," which includes a chapter on menopause, they specify both the symptoms that can be made worse by the conditions in the workplace (e.g., hot flashes, headaches, musculoskeletal pains), and the policy and environmental design strategies that may be needed to address them. Such actions can include adjustable ventilation and ambient temperature control; adaptations to workstation layout, structure, or lighting; modifications to uniforms and personal protective equipment (PPE); and accessibility, sufficiency, and availability of toilet facilities (United Steelworkers, 2024). Further, United Steelworkers' guidelines acknowledge the potential for harassment from colleagues and/or supervisors and the pressing need to prevent it. As such, the "Women of Steel" have developed a "Menopause Hazard Checklist and an Inspection Checklist," with which union representatives, employees, and supervisors can systematically assess menopause supports across workplace domains including policy, information, infrastructure, and applied considerations (United Steelworkers, 2024; United Steelworkers, n.d.)

8.6.2 *Corporate, Institutional, and Municipal Actions*

In the UK, some organizations have been quick to adopt accommodative practices. West Midlands Police, for example, organizes menopause awareness workshops for officers and staff. Some examples of corporate workplace support for women experiencing menopause include: Pricewaterhouse Coopers, Boeing, Network Rail, Bristol Myers Squibb, Tesco, John Lewis, Timpson, Bupa (a private healthcare provider), ASOS, and the media giant ITV, who all have policies in place that provide for flexible working time, more comfortable uniforms, desk fans, and other possible adaptations.

Many of these companies have also signed a menopause workplace pledge to be a "Menopause Friendly Workplace," established by the UK charity Well-being of Women, which funds research and treatment for women's reproductive and gynecological health. On signing the pledge, employers commit to supporting employees experiencing menopause, and the charity advises these companies on how they can help women going through the menopausal transition through adaptations to working conditions. More than 2500 employers have signed the pledge, including the BBC, Tesco, and Royal Mail. Such initiatives are also backed by high-profile UK personalities including HRH The Duchess of Edinburgh, and media personalities Baroness Karren Brady, Carol Vorderman, and Dr. Nighat Arif, as well as MPs Caroline Nokes and Carolyn Harris. The pledge has also been signed by the House of Commons (Well-being of Women, 2024). Others in high-profile roles also have called for menopause-friendly policies in the workplace and in the public space, including Dorothy Byrne, head of news and current affairs at Channel Four, and Diane Danzebrink, founder of Menopause Support (Hansard, 2021).

In the public sector, Devons and Cornwall Police have set up a Single Point of Contact (SPOC) phone line for menopausal women. Employees in distress due to menopause or unfair treatment can contact this number to receive help for the issue. Meanwhile, Norfolk and Suffolk Police have created a Menopause Passport whereby staff can identify symptoms to request adjustments or inform line managers of symptoms. The National Health Service (NHS) also has menopause policies in place for its employees and is currently developing a menopause workplace support package informed by the National Institute for Health and Clinical Excellence (NICE) guidelines. This institution, the UK's largest employer, notably has a workforce that is 77% female. In addition, in 2022 London City Hall announced a "world-leading" menopause policy which included practical steps to provide better support for colleagues going through the menopause transition. Its aim was to change negative perceptions and stigma surrounding menopause in the workplace (London Assembly, 2022).

Despite these initiatives, as one MP and a strong advocate of legislation to support menopause policies at work noted, whether or not an employee receives needed support remains very uneven and a question of chance: "Support in the workplace is still a lottery, with some employers excelling but others letting their employees down at a really difficult time" (Carolyn Harris, Labour MP, Swansea East) (Hansard, 2021). Indeed, despite these initiatives in the workplace, most Charities, Civil Society Organizations (CSOs), and Non-Governmental Organizations (NGOs) also point to the low level of uptake for these policies in the workplace. For example, a British Menopause Society survey reported that less than 1% of those surveyed reported that their employers have a policy in place but 90% of women polled would welcome menopause policies in the workplace (British Menopause Society, 2022).

At the local level in *France* there are recent examples of menopause having been taken into account in both the public and private sectors, potentially with a promising "snowball" effect.

Since 2023, municipalities have enacted measures for women who suffer from endometriosis or painful and/or disabling periods. Menopausal women suffering from these ailments therefore benefit even if they are not the "targets" of these measures. In March 2023, the City of Saint Ouen sur Seine was the first to have implemented workplace adaptations (e.g., adjustments to workstation, flexible schedule, teleworking) and/or paid leave of up to 2 days per month for municipal agents with medical authorization (Bouamrane, 2023). Similar measures also were enacted in 2023 and 2024 by the department of Seine Saint-Denis (Département de Seine-Saint-Denis, 2023), the Lyon metropolitan area (Métropole Grand Lyon, 2023), the cities of Abbeville (EL Asraoui Mara, 2023), and Sceaux (Lenhardt, 2024). This is also the case for certain public establishments or those responsible for public service missions, such as the national drama center in Aubervilliers (Théâtre national La commune CDN Aubervilliers, 2023). Since September 1, 2024, Strasbourg has explored a series of measures including changes to workplace environments, contexts, duties, and access to medically authorized paid leave. This model also provides for an awareness campaign on the subject of gynecological health (Eurométropole de Strasbourg, 2024).

Over the past decade, some companies in the French private sector have taken up the issue of menopause at work during collective bargaining. For example, in companies with fewer than 300 employees with representative trade union sections, the employer undertakes negotiations on professional equality between women and men every 4 years. Such negotiations focus, in particular, on pay differentials, on quality of life and working conditions (C. Trav. Art. L22242-1), and on forward-looking job management (C. Trav. Art. L22242-2). They are required to negotiate on the subject of wages every year (C. Trav. Art. L12241-8).

We located 20 company agreements containing provisions addressing menopause and the transition. The framework of these agreements is varied since it can be a negotiation intended to address equality between men and women (e.g., in Kellogg's: accord, 2022), diversity (e.g., in Eurotunnel Services GIE: accord, 2024), quality of life at work (e.g., in ASS Diffusion Services: accord, 2023; in TV studio

France: accord, 2023, in SFIL: accord, 2022), teleworking (e.g., in AIDES: accord, 2021, in Plan International: accord, 2022), women's health at work (e.g., in DCI Environnement: accord, 2023, in Eurotunnel Services GIE: accord, 2024), pay (e.g., in Centrale de Logistique L'Oréal: accord, 2022; in FAPROREAL: accord, 2022), health and social protection costs (e.g., in Audiens: accord, 2017, in Baie de Somme Habitat: accord, 2021), or the management of jobs and career paths (e.g., in Sodexo: accord, 2022).

The stated objectives are either general, and thus with *potential* application to menopause, such as equality between men and women and quality of life at work (e.g., in Kellogg's: accord, 2022), women's health at work (e.g., in DCI Environnement: accord, 2023), or more specific to particular health "situations" (such as menopause) allowances for teleworking (e.g.,in AIDES: accord, 2021, in Plan International: accord, 2022). Objectives also may address age and career management for older employees (ages 50 or 55 and older; e.g., in SFIL: accord, 2022, in L'Oréal produits de luxe international: accord, 2022, in Centrale de Logistique L'Oréal: accord, 2022, in FAPROREAL: accord, 2022; in Sodexo: accord, 2022). The perimenopausal stage, although never mentioned as such, is considered in these agreements through approaches designed for the population suffering from dysmenorrhea (e.g., in AIDES: accord, 2021, in DCI Environnement: accord, 2023). Menopause is in all instances approached with nuance, depending on the company, which will have within its scope people "affected by" "temporarily disabling symptoms" (e.g., in AIDES: accord, 2021) of menopause or "suffering" either from "menopausal disorders" (e.g., in SASU BALKIS Développement: accord, 2018), "menopause" (e.g., in Kellogg's: accord, 2022), "disorders" related to menopause (e.g., in DCI Environnement: accord, 2023), or "disabling symptoms of the menopause" (e.g., in Plan International: accord, 2022). Such symptoms must be deemed work-incapacitating and temporary, in order to benefit from such provisions.

Corporate initiatives also may consist of simple declarations of intent (e.g., in ASS Diffusion Services: accord, 2023) or awareness-raising actions (e.g., in Eurotunnel Services GIE: accord, 2024, in SFIL: accord, 2022). But they mainly involve guarantees of health check-ups, payment for care and treatment, exceptional leave and teleworking days. Some agreements provide for health check-ups (e.g., in SFIL: accord, 2022), psychological support (e.g., ASS Diffusion Services: accord, 2023); other agreements cover treatment which is not refunded by social security, up to a ceiling (e.g., in BTP group: pro BTP, BTP Vacances, BTP RMS: accords, 2019, in Audiens: accord, 2017, in Baie de Somme Habitat: accord, 2021) or with no ceiling (e.g., in SASU Balkis Développement: accord, 2018). Thus, some companies are leading the way with an employee-centered/responsive approach. Many more will need to follow to become the norm rather than the exception, but these examples represent an important start.

In the *US,* some enterprise also is entering the menopause dialogue. For example, a 2023 Bank of America/National Menopause Foundation report reported survey data from more than 2000 full-time female employees aged 45–60 and 500 male or female human resource "decision makers" at employers of more than 1000 workers. The report's authors identified "a number of disconnects" between employer- and employee-perceived corporate culture surrounding menopause. Notably, both groups identified a majority perception that menopause is a life stage rather than medical concern (89% employees and 67% employers). And 38% of employers reported policies supportive of menopause at their companies, such as paid time off or flexible scheduling, among other benefits (e.g., access to specialized health professionals, health insurance coverage that includes Hormone Replacement Therapy). However, fewer than 1 in 3 women reported that they were aware of these benefits (Bank of America, 2023).

A small number of corporations also have publicly announced steps toward providing menopause benefits to employees. At present, the trend appears to be toward contracts with external providers that help female workers cope with symptoms, rather than changes to workplace design and policies that may be triggering or exacerbating those symptoms (Butler, 2023). We also found that some US-based businesses that tout their menopause services and designations for employees in the UK or France do not yet mention on their website the same or similar services for US employees.

In late 2024, The Menopause Society' launched the "Making Menopause Work" guide and toolkit, each designed to support employees and workplaces in considering the impact of the work environment on workers experiencing menopause (The Menopause Society, 2024). This effort, including a planned voluntary employer designation program, may bring similar visibility to the issue of menopause workplace design and policy as has the "Menopause-Friendly Workplaces" designation in the UK, even if neither program is binding.

We were unable to find US state governments or municipalities that had publicly announced menopause-related programs or services for employees. We were able to find that the Mayor of New York City (NYC) has promised an expert committee to assess programmatic options for workers within existing wellness services, as well as a designation program for menopause-supportive workplaces that would be a "first in the nation" framework (Office of the Mayor, 2023). Further, the NYC Commission on Gender Equity published its "Menopause in the Workplace" guide to help workplaces determine how they may better be designed for workers across the lifespan (New York City Commission on Gender Equality, 2023).

8.7 Discussions and Conclusions

Our survey of these corpora explores policy and programmatic efforts across multiple domains, which are shaping thought—if not always policy—about workplaces designed for workers experiencing menopause in these three countries. Overall, we find that despite the repeated efforts of some legislators, labor unions, and even corporations, efforts toward menopause-specific workplace policies remain uneven.

In France, there is some concern that such legislation may add to already existing discrimination against women in finding work or progressing in their careers

(Kantar Public, 2023, p. 34; Rapport Sénat n°780, p. 31). In the UK, the Conservative government in 2021 also voiced the same concerns but equally that it could result in other forms of discrimination, notably against men. However, the UK's current employment bill shows a changing perspective at state level under the Labor government. Previous attempts to pass legislation failed here because, as the UK trade union TUC explains, menopause is often seen as a private, taboo subject not to be addressed at work. Menopause is therefore generally not recognized by managers and related adjustments not made for workers will span age, disability, and sex; in some cases, thus, some women have felt forced to leave the workplace altogether. In the US, pressure to acknowledge the realities of menopause is also coming from organized labor, as it is from a small and dedicated group of Congressmembers who have introduced—and, indeed, reintroduced—efforts to make facilities for at least federal workers more adapted to female physiology. They also have struggled without success to ensure that all workers with employer-sponsored health insurance will have access to the hormonal treatments they may need through this stage of life.

Overall, we identify a common concern across all three nations: the need to dispel myths and effect systematic cultural and attitudinal change so that the well-being of midlife and older female employees may be assured. Within this, we find that targeted corporate activities are more numerous in the UK and France, whereas organized labor has stepped forward on menopause-targeted efforts in the UK and US. We also see that "menopause-friendly" workplace designation programs, established over several years in the UK and now developing in the US, seek to establish resources and frameworks with which workplaces can support their employees through midlife and beyond. And, we find a small minority of exemplar municipalities in each of the three countries who are taking a vocal lead on establishing employee menopause supports, each implicitly inviting others to do the same.

More difficult to directly compare from these corpora are the depths and extents of existing national policy with respect to menopause protections. Inadequacies in the nations' current laws are, however, revealed in other legal scholarship exploring cases brought by workers who have charged wrongful action. Some have observed, for example, that the tendency of US courts to find in favor of women experiencing harms related to "abnormal" menopause (e.g., that which is deemed caused by illness or medical intervention), but not for women experiencing harms related to "normal" (i.e., age-related) menopause, leaves the majority of US female workers in this life stage without clear direction or recourse (Waldman et al., 2022). At the same time, legal scholars reviewing cases brought in the UK observe that the current inactivation of the Equality Act's Section 14, which would permit workers to charge intersectional discrimination, forces legal claims that insufficiently capture the extent of menopause-related harms spanning age, disability, and sex (Myhill & Sang, 2023).

Still, other work comparing US and UK laws' applicability to menopause find that even in its lack of specificity, the UK Equality Act has features that US law lacks (Cahn et al., 2024). In particular, UK law allows for a more expansive definition of "disability" that includes any limitation of "normal day-to-day activities," whereas the US requires a higher (and less applicable to the vicissitudes of menopause symptoms) standard of compromised "major life activities." Also in the UK, disabling symptoms related to "normal" menopause can be recognized as "disability," as it historically has not been in the US (Crawford et al., 2022). Still, notwithstanding the US' even greater insufficiency in protecting menopause-aged workers, the UK law has not guaranteed all female workers the protections they need (Myhill & Sang, 2023). This is precisely the work that the UK Women and Equalities Committee has undertaken in seeking to close such gaps and make protections specific and proactive rather than those that workers need to individually pursue in legal tribunals. The enactment of the Employment Rights Bill should also help to remedy this. In France, at least strong health policy can cover some of the health needs of women going through the menopausal transition even though more robust policy is needed to achieve true equality.

We also must acknowledge that, across all three countries, menopause has lacked the same level of dedicated and organized advocacy as has been seen with menstruation and pregnancy (e.g., Crawford et al., 2022; Mullins, 2022; Waldman et al., 2022). This may be due to a range of factors, including social and conceptual separation of the stages of a woman's life into reproductive quartiles (premenarchal, reproductive, perimenopausal, menopausal); the greater valuing of reproduction over the reproductive person; and the pervasive, intersectional social stigmas surrounding aging, gender, sex, race/ethnicity, identity, and ability (among other menopause-affecting factors) rendering reluctant those experiencing menopause and others to speak to this issue.

As always, there are limitations in this study including the possibility that some efforts were missed in our collection of documents and related records. However, the consistency of our findings both over time and across these three countries suggests that anything overlooked would have been unlikely to significantly change the status of discourse surrounding menopause and work, nor the potential opportunities for national change described. Rather, what we find are consistent missing pieces in the puzzle of creating workplaces *designed* for all employees, across their working lifespans. Nothing less will be required to help assure women's well-being at the workplace.

References

National Corpora

France

Accord Contrat supplémentaire frais de santé du groupe Audiens. (2017, December 8). art. 2.4, https://www.legifrance.gouv.fr/acco/id/ACCOTEXT000036579453

Accord d'entreprise au sein de SASU Balkis Développement. (2018, April 26). *CH5 et annexes* (pp. 36, 52–53). https://www.legifrance.gouv.fr/acco/id/ACCOTEXT000037000453

Accord relatif à la diversité et au bien vivre au travail chez SFIL. (2022, June 20). IIB. https://www.legifrance.gouv.fr/acco/id/ACCOTEXT000046050762

Accord relative à l'égalité professionnelle entre les femmes et les hommes et la diversité au sein d'Eurotunnel services GIE (2024, September 11). Article 3.6. https://www.legifrance.gouv.fr/acco/id/ACCOTEXT000048167960

Accord relatif aux frais de santé du personnel, au sein de Pro BTP (2019, June 26). Article 1. https://www.legifrance.gouv.fr/acco/id/ACCOTEXT000038981701

Accord relatif aux frais de santé du personnel, au sein de BTP vacances. (2019, June 28). Article 1. https://www.legifrance.gouv.fr/acco/id/ACCOTEXT000039399064

Accord relatif aux frais de santé du personnel, au sein de BTP RMS. (2019, June 28). Article 1. https://www.legifrance.gouv.fr/acco/id/ACCOTEXT000038981703

Accord relatif à la Gestion des Emplois et des Parcours Professionnels au sein de SODEXO (2022, July 12). Article 7.2.1. https://www.legifrance.gouv.fr/acco/id/ACCOTEXT000047694743

Accord relatif à la Qualité de Vie et des Conditions de Travail, à la santé et à l'égalité professionnelle au sein de ASS Diffusion Services, (2023, october, 18) https://www.legifrance.gouv.fr/acco/id/ACCOTEXT000048502739

Accord d'entreprise relatif à la mise en œuvre du télétravail au sein de AIDES (2021, November 15). Articles 26 and 27. https://www.legifrance.gouv.fr/acco/id/ACCOTEXT000044320122

Accord relatif aux négociations annuelles obligatoires au sein de L'Oréal produits de luxe international. (2022, November 10). Articles 5 and 6. https://www.legifrance.gouv.fr/acco/id/ACCOTEXT000046620323

Accord relatif aux négociations annuelles obligatoires au sein de Centrale Logistique de L'Oréal (2022, November 14). Articles 5 and 6. https://www.legifrance.gouv.fr/acco/id/ACCOTEXT000046620323

Accord relatif aux négociations annuelles obligatoires au sein de FAPROREAL. (2022, December 20). Articles 6 and 7. https://www.legifrance.gouv.fr/acco/id/ACCOTEXT000047018783

Accord relatif à la prise en compte de la santé des femmes au travail, au sein de DCI Environnement. (2023, May 5). Articles 1.2.3, 1.2.4, 2 and 4. https://www.legifrance.gouv.fr/acco/id/ACCOTEXT000047598365

Accord sur l'égalité Femme-Homme au sein de Kellogg's produits Alimentaires. (2022, May 12). Article 3.2. https://www.legifrance.gouv.fr/acco/id/ACCOTEXT000046007496

Accord sur l'égalité professionnelle et la qualité de vie au travail 24/25/26 au sein de France TV Studio. (2023, December 15). Article 5. https://www.legifrance.gouv.fr/acco/id/ACCOTEXT000048900198

Accord sur le régime de protection sociale complémentaire santé, avenant n°1. (2021, December 6). Baie de Somme Habitat. Annexe 1 (p. 15). https://www.legifrance.gouv.fr/acco/id/ACCOTEXT000045342564

Accord de télétravail au sein de Plan International France. (2022, September 1). Articles 3.1.3 and 3.1.4. https://www.legifrance.gouv.fr/acco/id/ACCOTEXT000047320054

Accord d'entreprise théâtre La commune CDN Aubervilliers: accord expérimental sur la mise en place d'un congé menstrual. (2023, September 27). Accessed November 11, 2024, from https://www.maitredata.com/app/accords-entreprise/theatre-d-aubervilliers/264991

Assemblée Nationale. (2023, July 11). Compte rendu de Réunion n° 100 (p. 11). Commission des Affaires Sociales. https://www.assemblee-nationale.fr/dyn/16/comptes-rendus/cion-soc/l16cion-soc2223100_compte-rendu

CGT. Tract. (2024, March 8). *Pour une meilleure prise en charge de la santé des femmes.* https://www.cgt.fr/sites/default/files/2024-02/TRACT_8mars2024_SANTE.pdf

Cohen, L., Jacquemet, A., Richer, M. P., & Rossignol, L. (2023). Information faite au nom de la délégation aux droits des femmes et à l'égalité des chances entre les hommes et les femmes: Santé au travail, *des maux invisibles.* Rapport Sénat n°780. June. https://www.senat.fr/rap/r22-780-1/r22-780-1.html

Bouamrane, K (2023). *Le Congé Menstruel: un droit fundamental.* Saint-Ouen sur-Seine. https://www.saint-ouen.fr/actualites/13-actualites/1740-le-conge-menstruel-un-droit-fondamental.html
Bouloux, M. (2023, May 10). *Proposition de loi relative à la prise en compte de la santé menstruelle, n°1219.* https://www.assemblee-nationale.fr/dyn/16/textes/l16b1219_proposition-loi
Bouloux, M. (2024). *Proposition de loi du 16 janvier 2024 visant à créer un arrêt de travail indemnisé pour menstruations incapacitantes, n° 2059.* https://www.assemblee-nationale.fr/dyn/16/textes/l16b2059_proposition-loi
Conweay-Mouret, H. (2023). *Proposition du 18 avril 2023 visant à améliorer et garantir le bien-être des femmes au travail, n°537.* https://www.senat.fr/dossier-legislatif/ppl22-537.html
Dumeau, S. (2023, May 31). Congé menstruel, PMA : quand l'entreprise s'invite dans l'intimité. *Les Echos.* https://www.lesechos.fr/idees-debats/editos-analyses/conge-menstruel-pma-quand-lentreprise-sinvite-dans-lintimite-1947763#
Département de Seine-Saint Denis. (2023, May 25). Communiqué de presse. https://seinesaintdenis.fr/Sante-menstruelle-et-reproductive-le-Departement-de-la-Seine-Saint-Denis
Eurométropole de Strasbourg. (2024, September 19). La ville et l'Eurométropole de Strasbourg expérimentent un congé gynécologique. https://www.strasbourg.eu/-/bloc-notes-conge-sante-gynecologique
El Asraoui Mara, Narjis. (2023, July 17). Congé mentruel: Abbeville est la deuxième ville de France à lancer l'expérimentation pour les femmes qui souffrent de règles douloureuses. *France 3 Hauts de France.* https://france3-regions.francetvinfo.fr/hauts-de-france/somme/abbeville/conge-menstruel-abbeville-est-la-deuxieme-ville-de-france-a-lancer-l-experimentation-pour-les-femmes-qui-souffrent-de-regles-douloureuses-2813648.html
Force Ouvrière Aéroport de Paris. (2024, March 8). *Lettre ouverte à la DRH.* https://www.cgt.fr/sites/default/files/2024-02/TRACT_8mars2024_SANTE.pdf
Kantar Public for MEGEN et la Fondation de France. (2023, October 4). *Regard des Français sur l'avancée en âge et la ménopause.* https://fondationdesfemmes.org/fdf-content/uploads/2023/10/71DD90_MGEN_Ménopause_2023-Rapport-final-du-4-octobre-2023-1.pdf
Lenhardt, M. (2024, June 3). Sceaux, première ville des Hauts-de-Seine à mettre en place le congé menstruel. *Le Parisien.* https://www.leparisien.fr/hauts-de-seine-92/sceaux-premiere-ville-des-hauts-de-seine-a-mettre-en-place-le-conge-menstruel-03-06-2024-MLDOGYSOWVBS5IOJFPN4TVM36A.php
Métropole Grand Lyon (2023, September 29). *Mise en place du congé menstrual.* https://met.grandlyon.com/la-metropole-de-lyon-met-en-place-le-conge-menstruel
Peytavie, S. (2023). *Proposition de loi du 15 juin 2023 portant diverses mesures relatives à la reconnaissance de la santé menstruelle et gynécologique dans le monde travail, n°1386.* https://www.assemblee-nationale.fr/dyn/16/textes/l16b1386_proposition-loi
Peytavie, S. (2024). *Proposition de loi du 20 février 2024 visant à reconnaître et protéger la santé menstruelle et gynécologique dans le monde du travail, n°2227.* https://www.assemblee--nationale.fr/dyn/16/dossiers/reconnaitre_sante_menstruelle_gynecologique_travail#

United Kingdom

British Menopause Society. (2022). *National Survey: The results.* https://thebms.org.uk/wp-content/uploads/2023/01/BMS-Infographics-JANUARY-2023-NationalSurveyResults.pdf
Equality and Human Rights Commission. (2024). *Regulator provides advice for employers on menopause and the Equality Act.* February. https://www.equalityhumanrights.com/media-centre/news/regulator-provides-advice-employers-menopause-and-equality-act
Hansard. (2018, 18 October). HC Deb. vol. 647, col. 846. https://hansard.parliament.uk/
Hansard. (2020, March 10). *HL*, Deb. vol. 802. https://hansard.parliament.uk/

Hansard. (2021, October 21). HC Deb. vol. 701. https://hansard.parliament.uk/
Hansard. (2022a, June 9). HC Deb. vol. 715, col. 421WH. https://hansard.parliament.uk/
Hansard. (2022b, September 8). HC Deb. vol. 719, col. 153WH. https://hansard.parliament.uk/
Hansard. (2024, October 10). HC Deb. *vol.* 754, col. 24WS. https://hansard.parliament.uk/
House of Commons. (2021). *Women and equalities committee, oral evidence*. Menopause and the Workplace, HC 602. https://committees.parliament.uk/oralevidence/9793/html/
London Assembly. 2022. Mayor announces world-leading menopause policy. March 8. https://www.london.gov.uk/media-centre/mayors-press-releases/mayor-announces-world-leading-menopause-policy
Trade Union Congress (TUC). (2021, December 21). *Menopause and the workplace: TUC response to the Women and Equalities Select Committee inquiry*. https://www.tuc.org.uk/research-analysis/reports/menopause-and-workplace
Trade Union Congress (TUC). (2017, January 26). *Tackling workplace stress using the HSE Stress Management Standards*. https://www.tuc.org.uk/resource/tackling-workplace-stress-using-hse-stress-management-standards
Trade Union Congress Wales. (2017). *The menopause: A workplace issue*. Wales Trade Unions Congress. https://www.tuc.org.uk/sites/default/files/Menopause%20survey%20report%20FINAL_0.pdf
UK Parliament. (2022, July 28). *Menopause and the workplace*. https://publications.parliament.uk/pa/cm5803/cmselect/cmwomeq/91/report.html
UNISON. (2021). *The menopause is a workplace issue: Guidance and model policy*. https://www.unison.org.uk/content/uploads/2019/10/25831.pdf
Well-being of Women. (2024). *Menopause workplace pledge*. https://www.well-beingofwomen.org.uk/menopause-workplace-pledge/

United States

Bank of America. (2023, April). *Break through the stigma: Menopause in the workplace*. https://business.bofa.com/content/dam/flagship/workplace-benefits/id20_0905/documents/BofA_Lifestage-Report.pdf
Butler, K. (2023, October 25). Microsoft is offering menopause benefits to keep women in workforce. *Seattle Times*. https://www.seattletimes.com/business/microsoft/microsoft-is-offering-menopause-benefits-to-keep-women-in-workforce/
AFL-CIO Committee on Women Workers and Executive Council. (2022, June 14). *Resolution 8: Promote gender equity*. https://aflcio.org/resolutions/resolution-8-promote-gender-equity
Meng, G. (2021, March 25). *Letter to the Honorable Joseph R. Biden Jr.* https://meng.house.gov/sites/evo-subsites/meng.house.gov/files/Letter%20to%20Biden.pdf
New York City Commission on Gender Equity. (2023, December 14). *Menopause in the workplace*. https://www.nyc.gov/content/genderequity/pages/menopause-at-work
Office of the Mayor. (2023, January 17). *Mayor Adams Commits to Making New York City Future of Women's Health*. https://www.nyc.gov/office-of-the-mayor/news/037-23/mayor-adams-commits-making-new-york-city-future-women-s-health#/0
The Menopause Society. (2024, September). *Making Menopause Work*. https://menopause.org/workplace
US Congressional Record. (2014, July 16). *Protect Women's Health from Corporate Interference Act*. https://www.congress.gov/congressional-record/volume-160/issue-111/senate-section/article/S4534-1
US Joint Economic Committee. (1984, June 6). *Testimony of Elizabeth W. Markson, The role of older women in the work force*. Hearing, Congress of the United States, ninety-eighth

Congress, second session. U.S. Government Printing Office. https://www.google.com/books/edition/The_Role_of_Older_Women_in_the_Work_Forc/_hvG2-2KstsC?hl=en
US House of Representatives. (2002, November 14). *H.R.5204 - 107th Congress (*2001-2002*): Hormone Replacement Therapy Alternative Treatment Fairness Act.* https://www.congress.gov/bill/107th-congress/house-bill/5204
US House of Representatives. (2005, April 18). *H.R.1410 - 109th Congress (*2005-2006*): Menopausal Hormone Replacement Therapies and Alternative Treatments and Fairness Act.* https://www.congress.gov/bill/109th-congress/house-bill/1410
US House of Representatives. (2007, July 9). *H.R.1812 - 110th Congress (2007-2008):* Menopausal Hormone Replacement Therapies and Alternative Treatments and Fairness Act of 2007. https://www.congress.gov/bill/110th-congress/house-bill/1812
US House of Representatives. (2009, January 16). *H.R.584 - 111th Congress (2009-2010):* Menopausal Hormone Replacement Therapies and Alternative Treatments and Fairness Act of 2009. https://www.congress.gov/bill/111th-congress/house-bill/584
US House of Representatives. (2010, May 12). *H.R.4869 - 111th Congress (*2009–2010*): Restroom Gender Parity in Federal Buildings Act.* https://www.congress.gov/bill/111th-congress/house-bill/4869
U.S. House of Representatives. (2011, February 25). *H.R.383 - 112th Congress (2011-2012):* Menopausal Hormone Replacement Therapies and Alternative Treatments and Fairness Act of 2011. https://www.congress.gov/bill/112th-congress/house-bill/383
US House of Representatives. (2016, September 19). *H.R.5929 - 114th Congress (*2015-2016*): Menstrual Products for Employees Act.* https://www.congress.gov/bill/114th-congress/house-bill/5929
US House of Representatives. (2017, March 2). *H.R.972 - 115th Congress (2017-2018):* Menstrual Equity for All Act of 2017. https://www.congress.gov/bill/115th-congress/house-bill/972
US House of Representatives. (2019a, May 3). *H.R.1882 - 116th Congress (2019-2020):* Menstrual Equity for All Act of 2019. https://www.congress.gov/bill/116th-congress/house-bill/1882
US House of Representatives. (2019b, May 1). *H.R.2403 - 116th Congress (*2019-2020*): Menstrual Hygiene Products in Federal Buildings Act.* https://www.congress.gov/bill/116th-congress/house-bill/2403
US House of Representatives. (2021, April 14). *H.R.2478 - 117th Congress (*2021–2022*): Menstrual Products in Federal Buildings Act.* https://www.congress.gov/bill/117th-congress/house-bill/2478/text
US House of Representatives. (2022a, March 1). *H.R.4350 - 117th Congress (2021-2022):* National Defense Authorization Act for Fiscal Year 2022. https://www.congress.gov/bill/117th-congress/house-bill/4350/all-actions
US House of Representatives. (2022b, November 1). *H.R.3614 - 117th Congress (2021-2022):* Menstrual Equity for All Act of 2021. https://www.congress.gov/bill/117th-congress/house-bill/3614
US House of Representatives. (2023a, May 26). *H.R.3646 - 118th Congress (2023-2024):* Menstrual Equity for All Act of 2023. https://www.congress.gov/bill/118th-congress/house-bill/3646/text
US House of Representatives. (2023b, July 20). *H.Res.605 - 118th Congress (*2023–2024*): Recognizing that the United States needs to support and strengthen mothers in the workforce by investing in the Mom Economy.* https://www.congress.gov/bill/118th-congress/house-resolution/605/text
US House of Representatives. (2024, March 8). *H.R.7596 - 118th Congress (*2023-2024*): Servicewomen and Veterans Menopause Research Act.* https://www.congress.gov/bill/118th-congress/house-bill/7596/text
US House of Representatives Committee on Transportation and Infrastructure. (2019, May 1). *Testimony of Hon. Grace Meng, A Representative in Congress from The State Of New York, CHRG-116hhrg43103.* https://www.govinfo.gov/content/pkg/CHRG-116hhrg43103/pdf/CHRG-116hhrg43103.pdf
US National Defense Reauthorization Act of 1994. Pub.L.No.103-160. (1993).

US Senate. (2023, July 20). *S.Res.306 - 118th Congress (2023-2024): A resolution recognizing that the United States needs to support and empower mothers in the workforce by investing in the Mom Economy.* https://www.congress.gov/bill/118th-congress/senate-resolution/306

US Senate Committee on Health, Education, Labor, and Pensions. (2001). *Improving Women's Health: Why Contraceptive Insurance Coverage Matters. S.Hrg.107–391.* https://www.congress.gov/event/107th-congress/senate-event/LC16421

US Senate Special Committee on Aging. (1980, July 9). *Work after 65, options for the '80s. S.Hrg. 96. Hearing before the Special Committee on Aging, United States Senate, Ninety-sixth Congress, second session. 2.* https://www.HeinOnline.org

United Steelworkers. (n.d.). *Inspection checklist for raising the bar on women's health & safety.* Accessed December 23, 2024, from https://m.usw.org/get-involved/wos/resources/Raising-the-Bar-Inspection-Checklist20.pdf

United Steelworkers. (2024, April 15). *Raising the Bar on Women's Health and Safety.* https://m.usw.org/get-involved/wos/resources/Raising_the_Bar_rev_aa_4-15_web.pdf

Review of Literature

Cahn, N., Crawford, B. J., & Waldman, E. G. (2024). Menopause discrimination at work: Comparing the law in the United States and United Kingdom. In S. Westwood (Ed.), *Research handbook on law, society and ageing* (pp. 281–297). Edward Elgar Publishing.

Connerley, M. L., & Wu, J. (2016). *Handbook on well-being of working women.* Springer.

Crawford, B. J., Waldman, E. G., & Cahn, N. R. (2022). Working through menopause. *Washington University Law Review, 99*(5), 1531–1592.

Dalingwater, L., & Winett, L.B. (2025). A Duty of Care: National Policy Discourse Regarding Menopause, Well-Being, and the Workplace. *The Journal of Aging and Social Change, 15*(1): 53–76.

Devi Aryanti, R., Diah Sari, E., & Siwi Widiana, H. (2020). A literature review of workplace well-being. In *Proceedings of the international conference on community development (ICCD), Advances in social science, education and humanities research* (Vol. 77, pp. 605–609).

Fawcett Society. (2022, April). *Menopause and the workplace.* https://www.fawcettsociety.org.uk/Handlers/Download.ashx?IDMF=9672cf45-5f13-4b69-8882-1e5e643ac8a6

Griffiths, A. Cox, S., Griffiths, R., & Wong, V. (2006). *Women police officers: Ageing, work & health.* Institute of Work, Health and Organisations. The University of Nottingham. https://www.bawp.org/wp-content/uploads/2019/06/Ageing-Police-Officers.pdf

Harris Interactive for Allan. (2021). *Ménopause en entreprise, lever le tabou.* https://alan.com/lp/menopause-en-entreprise-un-tabou

Healthtalk.org. (n.d.). *Work and the menopause.* The Dipex Charity. https://healthtalk.org/experiences/menopause/work-and-menopause/

Irni, S. (2009). Cranky old women? Irritation, resistance and gendering practices in organizations. *Gender, Work and Organization, 16*(6), 667–683.

Karin, M. L. (2022). Addressing periods at work. *Harvard Law & Policy Review, 16*(2), 449–518.

Kopenhager, T., & Guidozzi, F. (2015). Working women and the menopause. *Climacteric, 18*(3), 372–375.

Moloney, M. F., Strickland, O. L., DeRossett, S. E., Melby, M. K., & Dietrich, A. S. (2006). The experiences of midlife women with migraines. *Journal of Nursing Scholarship, 38*(3), 278–285.

Mullins, L. (2022). Is it hot in here or is it just me? Call for menopause equity in the workplace. *UDC/DCSL Law Review, 25*, 1–31.

Myhill, K., & Sang, K. (2023). Menopause at work: An analysis of the current law and proposals for reform. *Industrial Law Journal, 52*(1), 214–229.

National Institute for Health and Care Excellence (NICE). (2015). *Menopause: Diagnosis and management*. www.nice.org.uk/guidance/ng23

Statista. (2023, November). *Total Active-Duty United States Department of Defense Personnel Numbers from 1995 to 2022*. Accessed November 4, 2024, from https://www.statista.com/statistics/232350/us-department-of-defense-personnel-numbers/

Statista. (2024a, October). *Population of the United Kingdom from 1937 to 2023, by gender.* Accessed November 4, 2024, from https://www.statista.com/statistics/281240/population-of-the-united-kingdom-uk-by-gender/

Statista. (2024b, July). *Total number of government employees in the United States from 1982 to 2022*. Accessed November 4, 2024, from https://www.statista.com/statistics/204535/number-of-governmental-employees-in-the-us/

US Department of Labor. (2024, September). Let's talk about it: Menstruation and menopause at work. *Women's Bureau*. https://www.dol.gov/sites/dolgov/files/OPA/MenstruationAndMenopauseAtWork.pdf

Waldman, E. G., Cahn, N. R., & Crawford, B. J. (2022). Contextualizing menopause in the law. *Harvard Journal of Law and Gender, 45*(1), 1–62.

Louise Dalingwater is full professor of British politics and health policy at Sorbonne Université. Her current research focuses on health policy, healthcare delivery and well-being in the United Kingdom, with comparative research on European health systems and global health policy research. She has also co-edited several publications on well-being in Europe. She is Principal Investigator (PI) for the *Digital Health Systems* IITD Delhi-Sorbonne Multi-Institutional Faculty Interdisciplinary Research Project, a member of the steering group for the 4EU+ global outreach project Meta-UN and Chair of the Health Wellness and Society research network based in Illinois, United States.

Liana B. Winett is Associate Professor in the Oregon Health & Science University-Portland State University School of Public Health (Portland, Oregon, USA). She explores how we, as communities and as societies, discuss the complex and controversial social and political problems that affect the public's health, and how framing of these problems can help support broad public participation in these important debates. In 2022–23 she was an invited researcher at le Centre d'Études Politiques et Sociales (CEPEL), l'Université de Montpellier, France, where this work began.

Laurence Péru-Pirotte is Associate Professor in private law at the University of Lille (France). Her research focuses on the fight against discrimination. She is the author of articles including "La lutte contre les discriminations: loi n°2008-496 du 27 mai 2008" (JCP S, 2008, n°23, étude n°1314, pp. 12–17) and "Discours du législateur et critères de discrimination interdits: ce qui n'est pas bien énoncé ne peut être bien qualifié" (in Galstyan, Garik, Sargsyan, Gayane and Blbulyan, Taguhi, "Lectures croisées des Discours," Translation studies: Theory and practice, special Issue, Erevan, 2023.

Chapter 9
Cross-Border Workers' Well-being on the Island of Ireland: A Blind Spot of Cross-Border Cooperation?

Vanessa Boullet and Julien Guillaumond

Abstract The chapter considers cross-border labor mobility between Northern Ireland and the Republic of Ireland after Brexit and COVID-19. It highlights the importance of cross-border workers' well-being and explores how their well-being is both linked with their visibility in the public sphere and their presence in official discourse. Our case study of three websites (BorderPeople, CBPES, Citizens Information), which provide online information to cross-border workers in Ireland, shows the commonly positive correlation between well-being and easily accessible and available information. Notwithstanding, any improvement of their well-being would require both jurisdictions to further address workers' specific issues in the wake of Brexit and COVID-19 such as taxation and social benefits. This study is part of a wider and acute questioning on well-being, labor mobility, and cross-border cooperation. Additional research would be needed to better understand and address the daily challenges cross-border workers face in a north–south/east–west Ireland perspective, as well as in an all-Ireland and EU/UK perspective.

Keywords Ireland · Northern Ireland · Well-being · Cross-border workers · Mobility

V. Boullet (✉)
Université de Lorraine, Nancy, France
e-mail: vanessa.boullet@univ-lorraine.fr

J. Guillaumond
Université Clermont Auvergne, Clermont-Ferrand, France
e-mail: julien.guillaumond@uca.fr

© The Author(s), under exclusive license to Springer Nature Switzerland AG 2025

L. Dalingwater et al. (eds.), *Structural and Systemic Perspectives on Health and Well-being*, Human Well-Being Research and Policy Making,
https://doi.org/10.1007/978-3-031-99924-6_9

9.1 Introduction

Over the last decade, two shocks have had important effects on the island of Ireland: Brexit and COVID-19.[1] The decision of the British voters to leave the EU following the referendum on 24 June 2016 opened a period of deep uncertainty, leading many to wonder what would happen if Brexit led to a hard border. By then, the border separating the two jurisdictions, Northern Ireland (NI) and the Republic of Ireland (RoI), was hardly visible.[2] Walking along the border, author Garrett Carr (2017) was unable to locate it most of the time as it meanders across the land, its most obvious manifestation, in the end, being of road-signs difference as one drives across the border. Considering the impacts of Brexit on the island of Ireland in the months that followed the referendum, Anthony Soares (2016), director of the Centre for Cross-Border Cooperation (CCBC) wrote with foresight: "What had become to all intents and purposes an invisible and open border as a result of its de-securitization following the cessation of paramilitary violence and the removal of customs posts with the establishment of the EU's Internal Market, now risks regaining some of its 'hardness'."

A hard border was feared by many among border communities as possibly leading to the end of cross-border mobility and North-South cooperation, and posing a direct challenge to the Good Friday/Belfast Agreement and to peace in Northern Ireland (Coakley & O'Dowd, 2007). It was also expected that the return of a border between the two parts of the island would have an impact on economic activities through border controls, on labor markets (notably on access to jobs), as well as various other issues around cross-border mobility, including taxation, social welfare and, possibly, shopping (Soares, 2016). The situation was even more complex as the Irish border would then draw an international line between two now completely foreign jurisdictions on the same island, one still being an EU State, the other a non-EU State. As the withdrawal negotiations between the UK and the EU unfolded, the border question and its status soon came to dominate and complicate the process (Murphy, 2021, 405), all the more so as the negotiation brief of Michel Barnier identified the numerous existing areas of cooperation between both parts of the island (European Commission, 2019, 63; Coakley et al., 2007).

In that respect, health is a significant example of cooperation developed between the two entities since the Good Friday/Belfast Agreement of 1998. As one of the six areas of cooperation supervised by the North South Ministerial Council (NSMC) and implemented separately in each jurisdiction, it has since allowed both Irish and British citizens access to some specialized services (especially for those living along the border where health services could be less accessible), and also allowed, for both sides, to reach "economies of scale" due to their respective sizes (European

[1] The financial crisis and Brexit have been considered as two external crises in particular on Irish foreign policy (Rees & O'Brennan, 2019). We follow suit adding COVID-19 to the equation.

[2] Both terms Northern Ireland and the Republic of Ireland will be used throughout the chapter to avoid ambiguity. In other instances, the chapter will refer to the south and the north of Ireland.

Commission, 2019). Patients can access medical services on both sides of the border (O'Rourke, 2019, 228–229), for example "an all-Ireland paediatric cardiac surgery service in Dublin and cross-border radiotherapy and emergency cardiology services for the whole north-west in Derry" (Pollak, 2020, 63; Northern Ireland Audit Office, 2018). To some extent, such cross-border services have helped improve people's lives and overall well-being. However, recent studies have underlined the negative impacts of COVID-19 on cross-border cooperation in health (Heenan, 2021; Centre for Cross-Border Studies, 2020; O'Connor et al., 2021; Guillaumond & Boullet, 2023). Indeed, cooperation was made more difficult between the two parts of the island due to a lack of communication, a delayed response to the crisis and the setting up of distinct lock-down periods on both sides of the border. De Mars and O'Brien (2022) have referred lately to the impact of Brexit, and to cross-border workers' post-Brexit lives, in terms of health cover and family rights, identifying a much larger impact on EU and other frontier workers than on British or Irish cross-border workers. This situation has become even more difficult after 2020 with COVID-19.

As the island of Ireland celebrates the 25th anniversary of the Good Friday Agreement marking the end of three decades of violence in the North, as the Irish government has set up a task force on a Shared Island and with the potential union between the two parts becoming an increasingly debated issue, it seems appropriate to consider cross-border mobility, and more specifically, the life situation of cross-border workers in those challenging times when an EU internal border has become an international border.[3] The promotion of cross-border movements, cooperation and cordial relationships, has been at the core of the European construction, and the Irish case offers an opportunity to consider what happens when the EU influence on a border is somewhat losing its impetus. As mentioned previously, the COVID-19 pandemic has already shown the difficulties with such a shift in international relations since the former does not recognize borders even though States are adamant they exist.

In the wake of the pandemic, various studies have looked at the impact of border closing on cross-border workers' mobility and life outcomes in a European perspective (Nonnenmacher et al., 2021). Haist and Novotný (2022) have considered the work life experiences of Czech workers crossing the border with Germany and examined the effects of COVID-19 on their lives. Conversely, although Brexit has led to a wave of studies on the reasons behind the Leave vote as well as its political, economic, and social consequences,[4] there is hardly any publication on cross-border

[3] In passing, it should be noted that at a recent OECD conference on international borders held in Paris in November 2024, one researcher estimated that "COVID-19 led to an increased awareness of cross-border development challenges" at a time when re-bordering territories have returned on international agendas across the world (OECD, 2024).

[4] In the run-up to the final Brexit negotiations, various organizations intervened in the process to show how damaging the border was. Professor K. Hayward and colleagues, for instance, published a series of reports for the Centre for Cross Border Studies on the perceived impacts of the border for the island of Ireland. The Irish government itself addressed the issue of the border, turning it

work across the island of Ireland, more specifically on cross-border workers' mobility, and the transformation of the contemporary workplace in the wake of Brexit and COVID-19 as instanced with the shift to new ways of working, among them hybrid and remote work practices.[5] With the notable exception of a study on cross-border workers published by the Economic and Social Research Institute (ESRI) in June (McGuinness et al., 2024) and one released in November 2024 by the Centre for Cross Border Cooperation (O'Reilly et al., 2024), it is possible to obtain some elements on who cross-border workers are, and some reasons for cross-border movement. However, both publications remain quite factual, based on figures and surveys. Both consider the day-to-day impact of cross-border movement across the island of Ireland with some issues cross-border workers face, namely fiscal issues associated with remote working, and the advantages of cross-border recruitment for companies. They do not consider the well-being determinants of people moving across the border. Some reasons could account for this: namely, the Irish border now separating an EU state from a non-EU state is a relatively new phenomenon and the amount of cross-border workers (around 18,000) is much smaller than other cross-border workers' movement in the rest of the EU with around two million in 2019 (Eurostat, 2020); secondly, and as a consequence of Brexit, the Irish border is no longer part of the European border network which brings together every cross-border region, meaning it no longer has the same EU visibility. A third element that explains that the well-being drivers of people moving across the border are not considered is that the border has a specific status on the island of Ireland due to the definition and extent of cross-border movement across the British Isles with the Common Travel Area.

Well-being is a much debated and much contested notion, often equated with happiness, and often used in relation to life satisfaction or quality of life (Dalingwater et al., 2019). The distinction becomes more complex as social sciences can regard the notion of well-being as falling into two research directions, considering either people's opinions on their own lives and feelings, i.e. subjective well-being, as opposed to objective well-being which is much more related to real-life conditions

---

into a prerequisite for all negotiations with the support of other EU members. A succession of officials for instance toured the border, and the Irish authorities made sure people were familiar with the Northern Irish border, its significance as well as its history. However, nothing, it appears, was done on cross-border workers' well-being. The situation of the border region was central to many publications, but the more long-term implications of this decision as well as the impact of COVID on the current situation have not been dealt with. See Hayward (2017, 2018, 2021), Hayward and Komarova (2019) or Connelly (2017).

[5] In the report *Making Remote Work: National Remote Work Strategy*, it was explained that many expressions are used to refer to remote work such as "telework, e-Work, mobile work, smart working, telecommuting, flexible working, hub-work, locationless work, co-working, home office, virtual office and platform work, ICT-based mobile work (TICTM)". As remote working and work from home are the broadest concepts encompassing all of these terms, we will use those two terms in this paper (Government of Ireland, Department of Enterprise, 2021, 8). Today, the number of people working full time from home tends to run out of steam, most workers now practice hybrid working, alternating between the office and home, or even on the go (Wigert et al., 2023).

and specific indicators (Dalingwater, 2019). It is often in the health domain that the overlap between objective and subjective well-being is the most obvious, as the equation between physical and mental health can attest in policy papers on health in the UK (Dalingwater, 2019). To some extent, a similar case could be made on the link between well-being and work, in particular on the correlation between life satisfaction and job satisfaction (Bialowolski & Weziak-Bialowolska, 2021). Indeed, the current literature on life satisfaction and job satisfaction often emphasizes the reciprocal influence life satisfaction might have on job satisfaction and vice versa. Life and work spheres are thus "interrelated not only in the area of satisfaction but also meaning, purpose, mental health and social connectedness," stressing the strength of the "life–job link" (Bialowolski & Weziak-Bialowolska, 2021, 1288). And other factors (age, gender, family roles, the importance of work or personality, among others) can also have a strong influence. In that respect, companies and professional organizations, through specific policies, can have an influence on both workers' life and job satisfaction, creating better working environments which are conducive to improved working conditions and, eventually, growing productivity. In the realm of industrial relations, the state also has the possibility to influence and set up policies designed to improve the life–job link and, henceforth, the overall well-being of its citizens.

It is beyond the scope of the present chapter to study the evolution of cross-border workers' well-being across the island of Ireland as such. Nor does it account for workers' testimonies, or offer an analysis resting on various professional categories' opinions. A wide and indeed long-term study on the Irish experience of cross-border mobility would be required, and would, undoubtedly, encounter the caveat identified with overall studies on subjective well-being. Considering companies' workplace policies designed to help staff and encourage their professional mobility across the border, and/or accommodate firms' policies with new work trends such as remote work, would allow fruitful comparisons of both jurisdictions and address a more objective dimension of workers' well-being. This would call for many specifications, but it would again retain too large a scope, unless limited to some specific sectors of the economy. This chapter however will rather concentrate on external drivers which impact on cross-border workers' well-being in particular such as relevant information on social benefits and taxation issues. As the border and the existence of two jurisdictions limit the extent of comparative work on policy documents on cross-border work, two research directions could provide some preliminary answers, namely whether both jurisdictions consider the case of cross-border workers and make them visible as a result and the information they get, and the way the information provided interacts with the improvement of their general well-being.

We argue that cross-border workers' well-being is closely associated with their visibility in the public sphere and their issues being addressed through different media. In other words, pending the existence of more precise and detailed data on their actual well-being, their existence in the public sphere is paramount. But the information delivered to them is also important. Some studies consider the link between the use of ICT and life satisfaction. Lissitsa and Chachashvili-Bolotin (2016) have shown, for instance, that "internet adoption and digital uses can constitute an important channel for increasing life satisfaction" and well-being. Indeed, the use of the Internet and social networks have been seen as factors strengthening social cohesion as well as online communities of users with more information delivered, even though the long-term impact of internet adoption and use on individual well-being in general and life satisfaction in particular has received limited attention from scholars (Lissitsa & Chachashvili-Bolotin, 2016).

This chapter will start by reviewing some initiatives defining and furthering well-being in Ireland, North and South. It will then turn to the question of the visibility of cross-border workers in terms of data. The research will concentrate on Irish/Northern Irish workers working across the border in the other jurisdiction. It will not study the case of workers living in other parts of the UK, or residents from another EU country and working on the island as those non-Irish/Northern Irish workers could be seen as a specific group with even more challenging work conditions. Finally, the chapter will address the situation of cross-border workers in terms of information delivered to them to increase their well-being through a case study approach. A succinct survey of tools on display, websites and other elements available to cross-border workers complemented by interviews will close this analysis.[6] This section will determine to what extent these tools are conducive to an increased form of well-being as they provide information about what being a cross-border worker entails.

9.2 Well-being Indicators, North and South of the Border

In the Republic of Ireland, research often tends to associate well-being with happiness or life satisfaction (Madden, 2010; Walsh, 2011). Before the COVID pandemic, the National Economic and Social Council (NESC), which advises the Irish government on policy issues, brought together work and well-being in its framework in its 2009 report entitled *Well-being Matters: A Social Report for Ireland.* During the COVID pandemic, the Department of the Taoiseach (Prime Minister's Office) called for a rethinking of Ireland's policy on well-being with a series of publications to review and assess international best practices in measuring well-being and imagine an Irish well-being indicator (Government of Ireland, 2021; NESC, 2021; Government of Ireland, 2020). Since then, the concept of well-being, and especially citizens' well-being, appears to have become central to all policies in Ireland with the creation of a well-being dashboard and an associated web portal in October 2021.[7] In this framework, work is well represented in several categories such as work–life balance, work and job quality, income and wealth.

[6] Four interviews were conducted in 2023 with representatives from the Republic and Northern Ireland working in different organizations that help cross-border workers (CBPES, CCBS, Dundalk Chamber of Commerce).

[7] In June 2022, a *Second Report - A Well-being Framework for Ireland / Understanding Life in Ireland: the Well-being Framework, second report,* was published. In this report there was a stron-

In Northern Ireland, a dashboard was also set up in 2023, a delayed creation due to the absence of an Executive (2017–2020 and 2022–2024).[8] In this dashboard, work and well-being are not mentioned but are implicit in the "healthier lives" and "stronger economy" categories.[9] As for the Republic, its dashboard was created following a series of publications post-COVID which emphasized life satisfaction and personal well-being. While they both implemented a dashboard on well-being in line with OECD recommendations, the two jurisdictions differed on their approaches due to the specificities of each area. In the well-being dashboard set up in the Republic of Ireland for example, work is more present than in its Northern counterpart.

Well-being is not just the preserve of government policies. The Irish Business Employers Confederation (IBEC), an Irish business representative lobbying organization, also focuses on well-being in the workplace. As early as 2017, it sold well-being accreditation to firms to ensure "the highest standards of good workplace health, well-being, and safety practices." ((IBEC, 2024). This accreditation checks whether there is a working environment that is conducive to well-being and if a company protects the mental well-being of its staff. In Northern Ireland, the Confederation of British Industry does not propose such an accreditation, but a survey on well-being in the workplace was commissioned in 2023 (CBI). In its report, the CBI also insists on the need to invest in well-being in the workplace, synonymous with returns on investment:

> [the] return on caring for employee health and well-being is both financially beneficial but also the right thing to do. Research shows that for every £1 invested in mental health by employers, businesses get £5 back, raising employee productivity by around 12%. (CBI, 2023, 4)

As those publications demonstrate, there is a link between the workplace and job and life satisfaction. In the wake of the 2016 United Kingdom European Union membership referendum (Brexit referendum) and through the negotiation phase, a series of reports were published by the Centre for Cross-Border Studies on Brexit and its consequences on the border (Hayward, 2017, 2018; Hayward & Komarova, 2019). Although they insisted on the various impacts of Brexit on border communities and people themselves using personal testimonies (for instance on the consequences on border trade or on people's mobility), there was no, or hardly any, mention of cross-border workers as if they were invisible or they were too few to be mentioned. If the two dashboards implemented by both jurisdictions refer to two different exercises, where do cross-border workers fit in the equation, and to what extent is their situation taken into consideration?

---

ger focus on sustainability and a well-being approach into the policy-making system. Finally, two reports were published, *Understanding Life in Ireland: The Well-being Framework 2023* and *Ireland: The Well-being Framework 2024*.

[8] An interesting comparison would be to assess whether there are similarities throughout the UK as regards this well-being dashboard, and what the extent of regional disparities is, if any.

[9] The Executive Office and NISRA, *Wellbeing in Northern Ireland*, yearly publication starting in 2020/21.

9.3 Border-Crossing Across the EU and on the Island of Ireland

The EU commission defines "a frontier worker [as] someone who is employed in a Member State but resides in another, where he/she returns at least once a week" (O'Kane, 2015, 2). In terms of labor mobility, the Common Travel Area, the Good Friday Agreement of 1998 and the Celtic Tiger are milestones in the political and economic development of the island. The Common Travel Area (CTA) set up in the early 1920s created the basis for an all-island integrated market:

> Under the Common Travel Area (CTA), Irish and British citizens move freely and reside in either jurisdiction and enjoy associated rights and entitlements including access to employment, healthcare, education, social benefits, and the right to vote in certain elections (Government of Ireland, 2022).

In the European Union, since the creation of the single market in 1992 with the free movement of labor, the movement of workers across national borders has increased significantly. The creation of the single market coincided with the initial development of the Celtic Tiger in the Republic. Shuttleworth (2007, 969) mentions that "the impact of state borders on local labor markets in Northern Ireland started to receive official attention in Northern Ireland in the 1990s when the phenomenon of the Celtic Tiger emerged." Workers in Northern Ireland started looking to the Republic of Ireland to work as the economic situation was far better in the South because of the economic boom.[10] Finally, the Good Friday Agreement of 1998 encouraged cross-border cooperation between the two parts in a number of domains, amongst them the economy through the implementation of all-island bodies (Coakley & O'Dowd, 2005). There were business calls for an "all-island economy" for Ireland to achieve economies of scale and there were instances of North–South contacts between officials (Anderson, 1994). Nevertheless, it took time to set up clear goals and efficient bodies in a political context where the national question weighed tremendously on relationships. As Shuttleworth explains:

> Yet, there were also clear limitations to cooperation and cross-border interaction. Differences about the "national question" in the North meant that political opinion was divided on the benefits of cross-border cooperation and all-Ireland initiatives; and in practice mutual suspicion and competition between the two jurisdictions sometimes hindered or otherwise limited the degree of cross-border cooperation that was considered necessary or desirable. One area of greater ambiguity concerned official thinking about the importance of the border for labour markets and economic development. (2007, 974)

Following the Common Travel Area, the Good Friday Agreement and the Celtic Tiger, the island, and more specifically the border area could be seen as one "local labor market" (Shuttleworth, 2007, 969). The EU has for decades published documents on cross-border relationships, promoting a better integration of border regions and making sure that cross-border circulation is as easy as possible. The four

---

[10] To some extent, the RoI is still an attractive place for Northern Irish workers as one interviewee told us.

objectives of the EU being free movement of goods, services, capital and people, one might expect that the situation across the Irish border is broadly similar to other EU border regions. The EU has also encouraged the creation of a network of European cross-border agencies. The creation of the Cross-border Partnership Employment Services (CBPES), which belonged to the European Employment Services network (EURES), has shown how people could work together under EU influence, so much so that when Brexit happened, although the Northern Ireland counterpart had to exit the European partnership, a new structure was set up to promote cooperation between the two parts of Ireland along existing lines.[11]

This cross-border mobility could improve the well-being of cross-border workers through better job satisfaction and better pay. In the literature and reports, cross-border labor mobility is often seen as an advantage for both national labor markets and the economy of both countries which share a border, and consequently for the whole border region specifically. Indeed, it allows regions and countries to promote sustainable growth and "adjust in the face of economic fluctuations and asymmetric shocks" by allowing "more efficient matching of worker skills with job vacancies," particularly in a time of tight labor markets as both jurisdictions are experimenting at the moment "and facilitating the general up-skilling of European workforces" (Heinz & Ward-Warmedinger, 2006). Economically, cross-border workers also make Ireland a more attractive all-island proposition for investments given the scale effects on the labor market.

Moreover, policy-makers have also generally recognized the benefits of increased cross-border labor mobility to individuals within Europe in the form of offering new opportunities and, perhaps, better career prospects. In that respect, transport can be one element of cross-border workers' life satisfaction. As Medeiros states, "from a strictly policy guideline point of view, the EU transport policy expresses the rationale that a well-functioning transport system connecting the EU and neighboring countries is crucial for sustainable economic growth and the well-being of EU citizens" (Medeiros, 2019). If mobility can be presented as an asset to increase life satisfaction, the lack of transport infrastructure can therefore act as a real impediment to cross-border mobility. So are other elements regarding social and economic rights. The literature and the EU reports list the obstacles to cross-border mobility, which are quite numerous, despite the free movement of people and labor. The most common ones are the existence of legal and administrative barriers such as the limited portability of pension rights, social rights, and tax issues. In the Irish case, Shuttleworth has identified "differences in exchange rates, taxation, health, and banking systems" which can act as "either major disincentives that prevent some individuals from crossing the border or significant problems that have to be overcome for those who cross the border to work" (2007, 969).

Although moving across the border has been made easier, and cross-border life and mobility has been promoted across the EU, it is striking to see that a dearth of

[11] Interview with the authors. The CCBS became in early 2025 the Centre for Cross Border Cooperation (CCBC).

data exists about cross-border workers in Ireland. Through our interviews, we have been struck by the lack of information or imprecise available data on cross-border traffic. The numbers vary but over the last 15 years, publications estimated that the number of people crossing the border for different purposes ranged from 23,000 to 30,000, including people shopping, studying, and working. As early as 2007, Ian Shuttleworth wrote about the lack and limitations of data on Irish/Northern Irish cross-border workers. He particularly insisted on the limitations of the censuses carried out both North and South referring to different units to measure distances, different incompatible distance bands or information on workers in workplace only collected in Northern Ireland (2007, 971).

In previous work, censuses reported 12,740 cross-border workers in 2011. The Department for the Economy in Northern Ireland then estimated in 2018 that there were 25,000 cross-border trips daily for work or study. Finally, following the COVID-19 pandemic and Brexit, new studies were released in 2024 as cross-border workers became more vocal (Boullet & Guillaumond, 2023). First, in mid-2024, an ESRI report on cross-border traffic and workers (from the South) used previous figures provided by the Centre for Cross-Border Studies together with estimates from census reports of both jurisdictions (McGuinness et al., 2024). Another study was launched on Twitter by the Cross-border Partnership Employment Services but data has not yet been made available. In November 2024, the Shared Ireland unit and the Labour Employer Economic Forum (LEEF) published another survey based on new detailed estimates. Though they highlighted that there is "no single data source that records the definitive number of people crossing the border" (LEEF, 2024, 25), using figures from 2021 and 2022, findings showed that the stronger flow of cross-border workers were those commuting from North to South with 10,541 workers living in Northern Ireland—accounting for 1.3% of people living in the Northern Irish border area (818,500) compared to 7777 workers living in the Republic (1.4% of people living in the Irish border area, or 556,000 persons). Consequently, cross-border workers are estimated at 18,318.[12] Moreover, the ESRI report explains that "almost 50% (over 40%) of workers traveling North to South (South to North) live within ten miles from the border. Approximately two-thirds of cross-border workers, irrespective of the direction of travel, live within 20 miles from the border" (McGuinness et al., 2024, 13). The report also gave some details on job types and sectors. Most cross-border workers, traveling from North to South are professionals, particularly in senior management and executive roles. Those traveling from south to north are generally employed in ICT, health, and education. There are also many cross-border workers in the construction industry but as it is a very volatile market and the workers are highly mobile, it is very difficult to assess the extent of that movement.

Though there are now clearer figures, it is widely recognized that these statistics are unlikely to fully capture the extent of cross-border work as cross-border workers do not always declare their job situations (due mainly to tax issues). Moreover, the

[12] Corresponding to the figures stated in McGuinness et al., 2024.

latest figures are based on census and online surveys. Even though they may give a global picture of cross-border work, these figures may lack precise information or some categories may be more represented as they have been better informed of the existence of online surveys (for example professionals vs construction workers).

These new surveys in 2024, especially the one by the ESRI, allow us to have a clearer and more global vision of the determinants of cross-border work. When asked "Why do you work in the other jurisdiction?", well-being and life satisfaction always seemed present in their choice even though the reasons and benefits for cross-border workers differed significantly between those working in the North from those in the South. First, two-thirds of Northern-Irish workers working in the Republic ranked higher earnings as their main motivation and over 40% ranked better career opportunities second. Indeed the wage differential between the two jurisdictions is quite important: "the difference in earnings with approximately 30% of Northern Irish workers, working in Ireland, earning over €75,000, in contrast to 12% of workers moving in the other direction" (McGuinness et al., 2024, 7). For example, one cross-border worker employed in the Republic of Ireland stated: "Industry in the Republic of Ireland is more professional, less nepotistic, better paid, (and has) better prospects" (NI to RoI) (McGuinness et al., 2024, 19).

The situation for workers commuting from the Republic to Northern Ireland is very different, as among the determinants cited, not one seems to stand out. Moreover, the respondents mentioned other determinants which are not salary-related. What is pointed out is the proximity of the job, the career progression, the type of job, the work–life balance and the company's reputation (McGuinness et al., 2024, 14). Child benefit top-up and access to healthcare (free NHS in the UK versus paying national insurance in the Republic) and better pensions were also mentioned (McGuinness et al., 2024, 23). The survey concluded: "the results suggest that workers travelling RoI to NI may, at least to some extent, be compensated for lower earnings by higher levels of job satisfaction" (McGuinness et al., 2024, 18).

The latest reports published in 2024 also dealt with existing concerns to cross-border work and an integrated labor market. In the survey, respondents stated the barriers that they experienced as a direct result of being a cross-border worker. The main obstacles are mainly financial: the cost of commuting (train or fuel), fluctuating exchange rate, increasing costs of insurance, as well as tax issues. Those living in the Republic and working in the North felt unhappy and disadvantaged regarding remote working and the extra-cost it implied due to double taxation when they worked from home:

> As a cross-border worker living in the Republic of Ireland, I can't work from home/work remotely therefore I have more travel expenses than other employees who live in Northern Ireland and I can't avail of the flexibility that the company offers their employees *e.g.* leaving/picking up children from school etc. [one person from the Republic of Ireland to Northern Ireland] (McGuinness et al., 2024, 24)

This point, indicating that workers cannot work from home, is erroneous. Workers from the Republic working in Northern Ireland can work from home, but in this case, they will pay taxes in Northern Ireland and in the Republic. But this opinion was shared by many cross-border workers and it may indicate a lack of information, which clearly has an impact on their life satisfaction and ultimately their general well-being. In terms of information, what can cross-border workers find, and to what extent does it help?

9.4 Case Study: An Analysis of Three Informational Websites

If a lack of data is one aspect that contributes to cross-border workers being made rather invisible, the contention that a well-informed individual is more likely to adapt and enjoy his/her professional situation needs to be studied. As seen previously, access to information through social networks and internet websites can act on people's life satisfaction.[13] Do specific websites for cross-border workers exist and what type of information do they provide? And to what extent does it provide some clues as to how well-being is understood?

The Good Friday Agreement has allowed for the setting up of several cross-border institutions. Although not specifically targeting cross-border workers, some institutions have tried to promote trade between Northern Ireland and the Republic of Ireland. InterTradeIreland is but one example.[14] On the Internet, three websites provide general and, sometimes, specific information for people living and/or working along the border, whether they are in the North or the South of the island. These information websites are BorderPeople information service, the Cross-Border Partnership Employment Services (CBPES) website and Citizens Information.[15] The first two websites are specifically managed by cross-border organizations while the third one is managed by the Citizens Information Board, an Irish state organization providing Irish citizens with information on their rights and entitlements.[16]

After a short presentation of each website, this section will touch upon the way each information website has been designed to provide information to cross-border people. In that sense, the focus will rest on the information provided and whether the information enlightens cross-border people and/or provides valuable insights for people who are crossing the border.[17] When possible, some remarks will be added

---

[13] A specific analysis on social networks (Twitter feeds and LinkedIn in particular) could be useful together with a more general survey of web-users' profile and interactions with the platforms.

[14] See website https://intertradeireland.com/

[15] The three websites can be found respectively at www.borderpeople.info, https://www.cbpes.com/ and https://www.citizensinformation.ie/

[16] It was included in the study as it presents the view from the RoI. Its equivalent, Northern Ireland Direct (NIDirect), redirects users to the CBPES's website (https://www.nidirect.gov.uk/articles/find-job-republic-ireland).

[17] An analysis from web users' own perspective does not enter the realm of this study.

on the evolution of the different websites in time.[18] Wayback Machine (WM) offers the "ability to retrieve historical website content" and has become quite useful in the realm of social sciences (Arora et al., 2016, 1904). In this case study, the focus on three websites corresponds to what Arora et al. have identified when considering company practices, i.e. the possibility to get access to "both a breadth of information" and have the "capability to present this information from prior periods" (1905). Such an approach has obviously some limitations, and it will only be used with the view to illustrate the points already made.[19] Scanning those websites throughout their existence will, to some extent, help to draw some conclusions as to what each website considers to be well-being drivers of cross-border workers.

Borderpeople information service (www.borderpeople.info) provides cross-border information for people in the Republic and in Northern Ireland. It is managed by the Centre for Cross Border Studies in partnership with the North/South Ministerial Council (Joint Secretariat). Two bodies also work behind the scenes: Citizens Information Board (for the Republic) and Citizens Advice Bureaux (for Northern Ireland). In November 2001, a study on obstacles to mobility between the two parts of Ireland was commissioned by the North/South Ministerial Council (NSMC) to look at the different obstacles which hinder or constrain people from moving across the border in either direction to live, to work or to study. This was the first time cross-border mobility issues on the island had been studied systematically. The "complexity and difficulty in accessing information on the range of issues affecting North/South labor mobility" was clearly identified.[20] The report noted that cross-border people lacked "accurate or up-to-date data about the extent of cross-border mobility to work, use services or retire" (O'Kane, 2015, 6). During a North South Ministerial Council Plenary Meeting held on 28 June 2002, it was decided that "the development of both a physical and a virtual service to highlight information on the range of issues affecting North-South mobility" should be set up. A one-stop cross-border mobility information website was then established to provide comprehensive and easily accessible information on key aspects of jobs, learning opportunities and living conditions on both sides of the border. It was also decided that the website would provide linkages to websites for government departments as well as representative agencies and voluntary groups (O'Kane, 2015, 6). The website was launched in October 2007. It has expanded in response to "an ever-growing demand for information from citizens and from the Advice Sectors in both jurisdictions."[21] It is a portal to a range of information for people crossing the border

---

[18] To study the evolution of these websites, Wayback Machine (WM) will be used through its web archives depository. Wayback Machine (WM) is a web-based tool that archives websites. More on https://web.archive.org/

[19] Some limitations with the use of this methodology include the inability to choose the date when the data is stored. It does not seem to be a real limit as the website does not change daily or monthly. But the archives may not date back to the creation of the website. Secondly, the uploading of the website may be fragmented and may entail some lack of information.

[20] http://www.northsouthministerialcouncil.org/obstacles_to_cross_border_mobility

[21] https://web.archive.org/web/20170102114008/http://borderpeople.info/feature/2160.html

to live, study, work, or retire on topics such as banking, education, health, housing, social security, taxation, and telecommunications.

Using WM and comparing web pages over a number of years, some important points were retrieved from this website. On 20 January 2010, the website mentioned a survey by the Centre for Cross Border Studies on people who crossed the border to work.[22] A new website was launched in 2014, and a special section on Brexit came up in 2016. It appears that the two peaks of activity were in 2017 and 2022, following the two shocks previously mentioned. The first mention of well-being as an issue came on 9 March 2017 referring to EU fundings for a cross-border project on mental health.[23] Overall, the website provides online information but also proposed direct support to the public and to firms, even podcasts in 2019 and 2020.[24] In the following years, the WM analysis returned no specific addition to the website, and the same articles on Brexit remained unchanged.

In 1994, the European Employment Services (EURES) was set up by the European Commission to facilitate the free movement of workers within the European Union. The goal was to provide information, advice, and job-matching services. In Ireland, the service was coordinated by the Department of Social Protection for the Republic and the Department for Communities for Northern Ireland. Following Brexit, EURES Cross-Border Partnership Ireland—Northern Ireland became the Cross Border Partnership Employment Services (CBPES). It covers all the border counties of the Republic and all Northern Ireland, and works with the chambers of commerce, Unite (a trade union) and the two employer bodies previously mentioned (CBI and IBEC). As Lorraine O'Malley, CBPES coordinator, explains:

> CBPES was established to facilitate the free movement of those who commute across the border in order to find work. We provide information to workers and job seekers, unemployment-related issues on both sides of the border. We also assist employers by providing them with access to a larger pool of labour and advice on a range of cross-border recruitment matters, so we support the cross-border job seeker, worker and employer.[25]

CBPES also provides support regarding tax and welfare issues. To do so, documentation is made available and events are organized such as job fairs, online meetings on different topics, very often linked to taxation, healthcare, benefits, and remote

[22] https://web.archive.org/web/20100118143323/http://www.borderpeople.info/bp2-ug1

[23] *Western Health and Social Care Trust*. 2017. 9 March. "A €7.6 million EU INTERREG VA funded cross-border project has been launched in response to the increase in numbers of people with mental health problems. Over the next four years, the large-scale, cross border Innovation Recovery project offers an unprecedented opportunity to empower and enable people and communities to take greater control over their own mental and emotional wellbeing." https://web.archive.org/web/20180319111046/http://borderpeople.info/feature/cross-border-recovery-college-networks-to-be-set-up.html

[24] https://web.archive.org/web/20201210204431/https://borderpeople.info/a-z/podcasts.html

[25] Video presenting CPBES, available at https://www.cbpes.com/about-us, last accessed 3 December 2024.

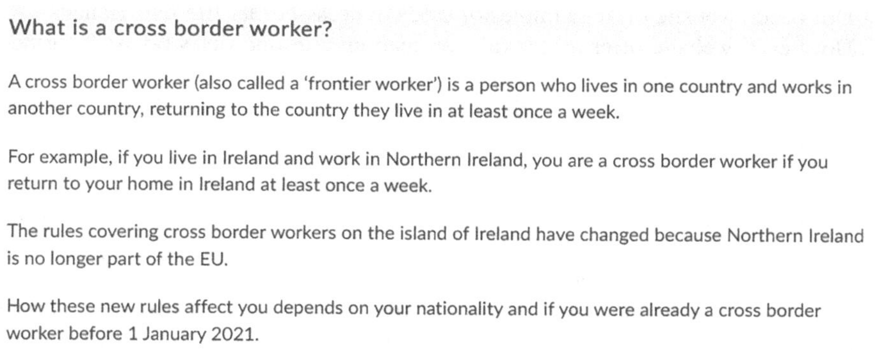
What is a cross border worker?

A cross border worker (also called a 'frontier worker') is a person who lives in one country and works in another country, returning to the country they live in at least once a week.

For example, if you live in Ireland and work in Northern Ireland, you are a cross border worker if you return to your home in Ireland at least once a week.

The rules covering cross border workers on the island of Ireland have changed because Northern Ireland is no longer part of the EU.

How these new rules affect you depends on your nationality and if you were already a cross border worker before 1 January 2021.

Fig. 9.1 Screenshot; definition of a cross-border worker (Citizens Information website, https://www.citizensinformation.ie/en/government-in-ireland/ireland-and-the-uk/cross-border-workers/#l8edb6.

working.[26] CBPES is also present on social media. Again, the WM analysis returned no specific changes. The FAQ section was the most interesting one regarding the current study, but again, there seems to be no change over a period.

The third website, Citizens Information, is wider in scope since it covers citizens' rights and entitlements in the Republic of Ireland. However, it does not contain much information on cross-border work or cross-border workers. On a specific web page devoted to cross-border workers[27] of this website operated by the Irish government, there does not seem to be much information as the following snapshot can attest (Fig. 9.1):

The page offers two external links, pointing web users to Borderpeople and gov.uk. It is also worth mentioning that the page was edited on 25 August 2022, the same date as the current webpage. That may mean that no information was added or updated since it was first created.[28]

If those three websites display different information, is it possible to identify some formulation of well-being drivers? To do so, a series of questions will be used to provide a tentative answer:[29]

- Does each website provide web users with a definition of what a cross-border worker is?
- Does each website display specific sections for cross-border workers?

[26] On their websites, the *FAQs Cross-Border Workers Employers and Jobseekers* booklet lists a series of 26 questions about tax, social rights and wages. See https://www.cbpes.com/media/uploads/cbpes_faqs_booklet_a5_proof(1).pdf last accessed 3 December 2024.

[27] https://www.citizensinformation.ie/en/government-in-ireland/ireland-and-the-uk/cross-border-workers/

[28] The only data available goes back to 24 May 2023. According to WM data, the website was saved 6 times between May 24, 2023 and October 8, 2024.

[29] Due to its exploratory nature, this study presents some limits. The two authors would like to follow up this analysis with interviews of representatives from each organization.

- Does each website offer examples or cases of cross-border life-experiences?
- Does each website offer other ways of keeping cross-border workers informed such as online meetings or in-house training, etc.?
- Does each website allow likely interaction with the online platform to find out more?

The Borderpeople website opens on two questions on its main page: "Crossing the border regularly? Need cross-border information? We're here to help."[30] Contrary to the more general definition offered by Citizens Information, Borderpeople is even less precise as it aims at people living along the border and so defines cross-border workers in the following way: "A cross-border worker lives in one EU Member State and works in another. They usually return home daily, but at least once per week."[31] Being a website dedicated to cross-border workers, CBPES does not find it useful to have a clear definition of what a cross-border worker is. Nevertheless, its homepage clearly indicates what it does "Cross Border Partnership for the provision of free information and recruitment services to job seekers, workers, and employers."[32] The contents of the homepages of Borderpeople and CBPES show that both websites are better able to provide answers than Citizens Information. Citizens Information only has one page dedicated to cross-border workers. On this page, there are several sections: what is a cross-border worker, who can live in Ireland and work in Northern Ireland, Non-EEA family members, Tax, Social welfare and a further information section with two external links: one to BorderPeople and one to Gov.uk. The information provided is very factual on the rights and entitlements of cross-border workers with links to other websites such as nidirect.gov.uk or other pages of Citizens information.

Borderpeople presents information based on web users' profiles: "I'm crossing the border to… live, work, study, and retire." Then on the "work" page, there are 74 A-Z categories devoted to queries from cross-border workers. The website is therefore very detailed, going from "bank accounts" to "illness Benefits" or "trans-border Workers Relief." Nonetheless, there is no specific section dedicated to well-being. The CBPES website displays information articulated around a series of entries relating to work, taxation and social security, education, health and rights. The "work" page offers links to other pages such as taxation, social security, medical care, redundancy, etc. It seems as detailed as Borderpeople. Both websites offer the possibility to subscribe/sign up to a mailing list. Nevertheless, the CBPES is the only website with a contact page offering web users the possibility to contact advisers for queries on both sides of the border.[33] CPBES does not have pages linked to the well-being of cross-border workers. It does, however, offer specific examples of cross-border life-experiences in its FAQ and also in a PDF documentation entitled

[30] https://borderpeople.info/—last accessed 15 January 2025.

[31] https://borderpeople.info/crossing-the-border-to-work

[32] https://www.cbpes.com/

[33] https://www.cbpes.com/contact-us

"FAQ Cross Border Workers Employers & Jobseekers."[34] It answers specific questions such as "Q1 I am resident of Ireland and about to start a new job in Northern Ireland, what taxes do I have to pay?". Borderpeople has the same type of FAQ, using specific questions asked by cross-border workers such as: "My partner works as a public servant in Ireland. She lives in Newry. Does she have to summit a NI Tax Return or is she exempt as she is a Civil Servant? Is there any document to confirm this exemption?".[35] Nonetheless at the end of this section, there is a warning sentence: "Please use this information as general guidance only. Cross-border tax issues can be complex and every situation is different. A quick conversation with a trained tax expert or accountant can keep you on the right path."[36] Job fairs and meetings are regularly organized, addressed to both employers and cross-border workers, with 3 out of 8 events planned for 2025 devoted to tax issues (for instance "Cross Border Webinar—Tax Implications for Cross Border Employers & Workers—August 2025").

This concise survey of three websites shows that web users, be they ordinary citizens or more especially cross-border workers, can find free information which may answer their queries. However, without statistics on the number of monthly visits or the most often viewed pages, it remains difficult to assess whether those websites represent valuable channels of communication to cross-border workers. Moreover, if the information is freely available, does it mean that it is easy to understand for cross-border workers? As we have seen, cross-border workers in Ireland are not representative of one socio-professional group and if an executive may easily get access to the information he/she seeks and understand it, will it be the case for a construction worker, commuting everyday between Belfast and Dublin? BorderPeople recently suggested that "an overwhelming majority of respondents (98%) did not believe they had access to clear and concise advice from government sources."[37] Our survey also tends to show that prospective well-being drivers of cross-border workers, as identified by these information websites, amount to issues pertaining to rights and entitlements on both sides of the border, together with taxation. The insistence on the latter, in particular, seems to indicate that taxation truly is an issue people are feeling strongly about as the numerous information sessions or seminars attest. In our interview with CBPES, it is clear that the team tries to help cross-border workers as much as they can. But is it enough? Are a website, a social media presence and some fairs enough to improve cross-border workers' well-being? During our interviews with practitioners and cross-border workers, the focus was on the tax issues linked to working from home in the Republic as cross-border workers felt disadvantaged compared to their Northern-Irish colleagues. But the only thing that those agencies can do is to inform citizens, not change policies. Only

---

[34] https://www.cbpes.com/media/uploads/cbpes_faqs_booklet_2022(2).pdf

[35] https://borderpeople.info/faqs/taxation.html

[36] https://borderpeople.info/faqs/taxation.html

[37] Border People. 2024. Cross-border worker survey 2023–24. https://www.youtube.com/watch?v=zPf9hsLCQ3k

the Irish Government can, but is it willing to act for 7777 cross-border workers which represent a minority of the Irish labor force (0.003%) in the Republic of Ireland? And, are Northern Irish authorities also willing to act for 1.2% of its labor force (10.541 workers)[38]?

9.5 Conclusion

One tenet of the EU project has been the mobility of its citizens. Cross-border mobility still exists on the island of Ireland, but Brexit and COVID-19 have shown some of the limits to cross-border cooperation and cross-border relationships. The EU influence is still present, but cross-border workers on the island of Ireland do not seem to be much visible. Although it would appear that they could recover some visibility in the coming years, following the reports previously mentioned, they do not currently represent a large group able to influence politics at the national level on both sides of the border. The present chapter has indeed identified a lack of data together with a vision of cross-border workers' lives centered on rights and taxation as the main drivers of their well-being through communication websites, in particular with the transformation of new working practices. The unresolved issue on taxation reveals to some extent the marginalization of cross-border concerns. The Shared Island unit set up by the previous Irish Minister for Foreign Affairs has done much work to bring border issues to the fore over recent years, although this initiative remains limited to the Republic. If the "All-island economy" project takes some momentum (co-led by Dublin City University and Ulster University),[39] it will become a necessity for both governments to take care of those specific workers, important for the economy of the island. With such a project, their visibility and well-being might improve. One final note on that chapter would be to set up a larger study on cross-border workers' well-being, and a worthwhile supplement would be to engage with other EU border areas to further question the determinants of cross-border workers' life satisfaction.

References

Anderson, J. (1994). Problems of interstate economic integration: Northern Ireland and the Irish Republic in the European Community. *Political Geography, 13*, 53–72.

Arora, S. K., Li, Y., Youtie, J., & Shapira, P. (2016). Using the wayback machine to mine websites in the social sciences: A methodological resource. *Journal of the Association for Information Science and Technology, 67*, 1904–1915. https://doi.org/10.1002/asi.23503

[38] For cross-border figures, see McGuinness et al., 2024; for the Republic of Ireland, see CSO, 2023 and for Northern Ireland, see NISRA, 2024.

[39] https://all-islandeconomy.com/

Bialowolski, P., & Weziak-Bialowolska, D. (2021). Longitudinal evidence for reciprocal effects between life satisfaction and job satisfaction. *Journal of Happiness Studies, 22*, 1287–1312. https://doi.org/10.1007/s10902-020-00273-1

Boullet, V., & Guillaumond, J. (2023). *Voicing the concerns of cross-border workers in a post-Brexit/Covid Ireland: the example of the Cross-Border Workers' Coalition*. Conference paper given at GIS EIRE. Available at https://ubicast.visio.univ-rennes2.fr/permalink/v126666f2aba44wfkzuj/iframe/

Carr, G. (2017). *The rule of the land. Walking Ireland's border*. Faber and Faber Ltd.

CBI Economics. (2023, February 7). *Employee wellbeing in a changing working world*. https://www.cbi.org.uk/articles/employee-wellbeing-in-a-changing-working-world/

Centre for Cross-Border Studies. (2020). *Briefing paper: Approaches to the COVID-19 pandemic: Bordering on (non-) cooperation*. https://crossborder.ie/reports/briefing-paper-approaches-to-the-covid-19-pandemic-bordering-on-non-cooperation/

Coakley, J., & O'Dowd, L. (2005). *The Irish border and North-South cooperation: An overview*. University College Dublin, Institute for British-Irish Studies, IBIS Working Papers 47. http://www.ucd.ie/ibis/filestore/wp2005/47/47_jclod.pdf

Coakley, J., & O'Dowd, L. (2007). The 'new' Irish border: Changing political, economic and social dimensions. In J. Coakley & L. O'Dowd (Eds.), *Crossing the border. New relationships between Northern Ireland and the Republic of Ireland* (pp. 3–28). Irish Academic Press.

Coakley, J., Caoindealbháin, Ó., & B., & Wilson, R. (2007). Institutional cooperation: The North-South implementation bodies. In J. Coakley & L. O'Dowd (Eds.), *Crossing the border. New relationships between Northern Ireland and the Republic of Ireland* (pp. 31–60). Irish Academic Press.

Connelly, S. (2017). *Brexit and Ireland. The dangers, the opportunities and the inside story of the Irish response*. Penguin.

CPBES. Video. Retrieved December 5, 2024., from https://www.cbpes.com/about-us

CSO. (2023). *Census of Population 2022 - Summary results*. https://www.cso.ie/en/releasesandpublications/ep/p-cpsr/censusofpopulation2022-summaryresults/employmentoccupationindustryandcommuting/

Dalingwater, L. (2019). Linking health and wellbeing in public discourse and policy: The case of the UK. *Revue Interventions économiques, 62*. https://doi.org/10.4000/interventionseconomiques.6243

Dalingwater, L., Costantini, I., & Champroux, N. (2019). Wellbeing: Political discourse and policy in the anglosphere. Introduction. *Revue Interventions économiques, 62*. https://doi.org/10.4000/interventionseconomiques.6492

De Mars, S., & O'Brien, C. (2022). Inevitably diminished: Rights of frontier workers in Northern Ireland after Brexit. *Northern Ireland Legal Quarterly, 73*(2), 119–147. https://doi.org/10.53386/nilq.v73iS2.1061

European Commission. (2019, June 21). *Task force for the preparation and conduct of the negotiations with the United Kingdom under Article 50 TEU*, 63 – Commission to EU 27.

Eurostat. (2020). *People on the move, the 2020 edition*, "2.3 Crossing borders". https://ec.europa.eu/eurostat/cache/digpub/eumove/bloc-2c.html?lang=en

Government of Ireland, Department of Enterprise. (2021). *Trade and employment, making remote work: National remote work strategy*.

Government of Ireland, Department of Finance. (2020, October). *Budget 2021 - Wellbeing and the measurement of broader living standards in Ireland*.

Government of Ireland, Department of Finance. (2023). *Budget 2024: Beyond GDP—quality of life assessment*.

Government of Ireland, Department of Foreign Affairs. (2022). *The common travel area 2022*. https://www.gov.ie/en/publication/a3498-the-common-travel-area/

Government of Ireland, Department of Taoiseach. (2021, July). *First report on a well-being framework for Ireland*.

Government of Ireland, Department of Taoiseach. (2023, June). *Understanding life in Ireland: The well-being framework 2023*.

Guillaumond, J., & Boullet, V. (2023). COVID-19 and the Irish border: A preliminary analysis of cross-border cooperation considering health and work issues. *Revue Française de Civilisation Britannique, 28*(2). https://doi.org/10.4000/rfcb.11048

Haist, J., & Novotný, L. (2022). Moving across borders: The work-life experiences of Czech cross-border workers during the COVID-19 pandemic. *Journal of Common Market Studies, 61*(1), 124–142. https://doi.org/10.1111/jcms.13362

Hayward, K. (2017). *Bordering on Brexit: Views from local communities in the central border region of Ireland/Northern Ireland*. Irish Central Border Area Network and Queen's University Belfast.

Hayward, K. (2018). *Brexit at the border: Voices of local communities in the central border region of Ireland/Northern Ireland*. Irish Central Border Area Network and Queen's University Belfast.

Hayward, K. (2021). *What do we know and what should we do about the Irish border?* Sage.

Hayward, K., & Komarova, M. (2019). *The border into Brexit: Perspectives from local communities in the central border region of Ireland/Northern Ireland*. Irish Central Border Area Network and Queen's University Belfast.

Heenan, D. (2021). Collaborating on healthcare on an all-Island basis: A scoping study. *Irish Studies in International Affairs, 32*(2), 413–447. https://doi.org/10.3318/isia.2021.32b.43

Heinz, F. F., & Ward-Warmedinger, M. (2006). *Cross-border labour mobility within an enlarged EU*. ECB Occasional Paper. 52(7).

IBEC. The KeepWell Mark – FAQs. Retrieved April 4, 2024., from https://www.ibec.ie/employer-hub/corporate-wellness/the-keepwell-mark-public-page/the-keepwell-mark-faqs

LEEF and Shared Ireland Working Group. (2024). *A study into the current conditions of the island of Ireland labour market, and challenges and opportunities for effective operation for workers and businesses across the island.*

Lissitsa, S., & Chachashvili-Bolotin, S. (2016). Life satisfaction in the internet age – Changes in the past decade. *Computers in Human Behavior, 54*, 197–206. https://doi.org/10.1016/j.chb.2015.08.001

Madden, D. (2010). *The impact of an economic boom on the level and distribution of Well-being: Ireland, 1994-2001*. UCD Centre for Economic Research, WP10/15.

McGuinness, S., Bergin, A., & Devlin, A. (2024). *A study of cross-border working on the Island of Ireland*. ESRI Working Paper, 781, ESRI. https://www.esri.ie/publications/a-study-of-cross-border-working-on-the-island-of-ireland

Medeiros, E. (2019). Cross-border transports and cross-border mobility in EU border regions. *Case Studies on Transport Policy, 7*(1), 1–12.

Murphy, M. C. (2021). Northern Ireland and Brexit: Where sovereignty and stability collide? *Journal of Contemporary European Studies, 29*(3), 405–418. https://doi.org/10.1080/14782804.2021.1891027

National Economic and Social Council (NESC). (2021). *Ireland's well-being framework: Consultation Report*.

NISRA. (2024). *Labour force survey annual summary report*, 2023.

Nonnenmacher, L., Baumann, M., le Bihan, E., Askenazy, & Chauvel, L. (2021). Cross-border mobility in European countries: Associations between cross-border worker status and health outcomes. *BMC Public Health, 21*, 588. https://doi.org/10.1186/s12889-021-10564-8

Northern Ireland Audit Office. (2018, October 26). *The UK border: How prepared is Northern Ireland for exiting the EU?* Accessed April 28, 2023, from https://www.niauditoffice.gov.uk/files/niauditoffice/media-files/Final%20Brexit%20Report.pdf

O'Connor, C., O'Connell, N., Burke, E., Dempster, M., Graham, C. D., Scally, G., Zgaga, L., Nolan, A., Nicolson, G., Mather, L., Barry, J., Crowley, P., & Darker, C. D. (2021). Bordering on crisis: A qualitative analysis of focus group, social media, and news media perspectives on

the Republic of Ireland-Northern Ireland border during the 'first wave' of the COVID-19 pandemic. *Social Science & Medicine, 282*, 114111. 10.1016/j.socscimed.2021.11411.
O'Kane, A. (2015). *Obstacles to cross-border mobility: Taxation*. CCBS website.
O'Reilly, M., O'Kane, A., Tierney, R., & Devlin, A. (2024). *A study into the current conditions of the Island of Ireland labour market, and challenges and opportunities for effective operation for workers and businesses across the Island*. Book/Report Chapter, The Centre for Cross Border Cooperation. https://www.esri.ie/publications/a-study-into-the-current-conditions-of-the-island-of-ireland-labour-market-and
O'Rourke, K. (2019). *A short history of Brexit*. Pelican Books.
OECD. (2024). *International dialogue event on cross-border governance*. Conference held in Paris, 25 November 2024.
Pollak, A. (2020). North-South cooperation on healthcare during a time of corona virus. *The Journal of Cross Border Studies in Ireland*, 63–70.
Rees, N., & O'Brennan, J. (2019). The dual crisis in Irish foreign policy: The economic crash and Brexit in a volatile European landscape. *Irish Political Studies, 34*(4), 595–614. https://doi.org/10.1080/07907184.2019.1669563
Shuttleworth, I. (2007). Reconceptualising local labour markets in the context of cross-border and transnational labour flows: The Irish example. *Political Geography, 26*(8), 968–981. https://doi.org/10.1016/j.polgeo.2007.06.004
Soares, A. (2016). Living within and outside unions: The consequences of Brexit for Northern Ireland. *Journal of Contemporary European Research, 12*(4), 835–843.
The Executive Office and NISRA, *Wellbeing in Northern Ireland*, yearly publication starting in 2020/21.
Walsh, B. M. (2011). *Well-being and economic conditions in Ireland*. University College Dublin, School of Economics, WP 201127.
Wigert, B., Harter, J., & Agrawal, S. (2023, October 9). The future of the office has arrived: It's hybrid. *Forbes*. Retrieved April 24, 2024, from https://www.gallup.com/workplace/511994/future-office-arrived-hybrid.aspx

Vanessa Boullet is a senior lecturer in Irish studies at Université de Lorraine in Nancy, France. She is a member of the research lab IDEA, and is currently part of the GIS EIRE research network. Her research focuses on the interactions between economy, society and politics in Ireland. She has developed an interest in the uneven development of the Irish economy as well as issues linked to well-being and cooperation between the north and the south of the island. She co-edited the book *The Unequal Costs of Covid-19 on Well-Being in Europe* (Springer, 2022). She also tries to develop research in Business and Modern Languages departments in France and is a member of the editorial board of the journal *Revue International des Langues Etrangères Appliquées*.

Julien Guillaumond is a senior lecturer in English studies at the Languages, Cultures and Communication Department, Université Clermont-Auvergne, France. He is a member of the Communication and Societies laboratory (EA 4647) and the GIS EIRE network. His research focuses on the political, economic, and social history of Ireland in the twentieth and twenty-first centuries. In recent years he has taken an interest in Ireland's repositioning in the world, Irish identity in its particularly economic and political dimensions, and the contemporary issues facing the Irish diaspora.